The Drama of Attack

The Drama of Attack

Didactic Plays of the American Depression

by Sam Smiley

University of Missouri Press
Columbia

ISBN 0–8262–0118–0
Library of Congress Catalog Card Number 72–176393

(C

To my parents
Ada Holland Smiley
Raymond E. Smiley

Contents

Preface

The first principle of this book is that there are two great species of drama—the mimetic and the didactic. Aristotle favored the first, Plato the second. Perhaps because Aristotle devoted an entire book to mimetic drama, whereas Plato wrote of didactic drama only incidentally to discussion of other subjects—theorists, scholars, and critics have focused their comments on the mimetic. Despite the traditional imbalance of critical attention, didactic drama, from the *Eumenides* of Aeschylus to *Viet Nam Discourse* by Peter Weiss, has always maintained a significant place on the stages of the world. Thus, I have devoted this study to the less thoroughly discussed type of drama— the thought-controlled plays, the didactic dramas of attack.

In shaping this book, I have held to three primary objectives: (1) to delineate the social and aesthetic genesis of the leftist drama on Broadway during the thirties, (2) to analyze in detail those particular didactic plays, and (3) to identify some of the major structural principles of didactic drama. My procedure was inductive; to discover some of the principles of the essential form of didactic drama, I began by examining specific groups of plays.

At once Platonic and Aristotelian, the concerns of the book may appear paradoxical, but their combination in one study is nevertheless logical. The subject plays are of the sort that Plato favored (though he probably would have disagreed with much of their philosophic content), but the critical method is essentially that which Aristotle made possible through his theoretical studies of poetics and rhetoric. I explain my method of analysis in the Introduction. Both particularly and comprehensively, this study attends to the relationships between rhetoric and poetics in the drama.

The specific plays examined herein are the forty-one leftist dramas of didactic form that appeared in major professional production in New York from 1930 through 1939. Taken together, they illustrate the variety of possible rhetorical types, and they present an image of the crucial concerns of that decade of social upheaval.

Why should these American didactic plays be more appropriate for an initial investigation of this nature than, say, the plays of the medieval church, those of eighteenth-century England, or even those of the late nineteen-sixties? Since most, if not all, didactic plays present either religious or social ideas, the first decision for this study was to focus it on plays of social concern. With that intention settled, I searched for dramas that hold ideological meaning for twentieth-century readers and found them among the plays of the thirties. Many of them deal with the major societal conflicts of the current century—individualism versus collectivism, war versus peace, capitalism versus Marxism, freedom versus slavery —and all are concerns that persist into the seventies. Still, these plays stand far enough removed from contemporary social attitudes and theatrical practices to permit the objectivity necessary for scholarly evaluation. Another choice—to treat only those plays given a major professional production in New York—narrowed the number of examples to a group small enough to treat thoroughly in a single study. My final reason for selecting these particular forty-one plays is that they are exciting, both ideologically and dramatically.

The research for and writing of this book extended over a ten-year period. I wish to thank the Eli Lilly Foundation for the Lilly Fellowship that, in 1961, provided the year of study during which I began my investigations. I also thank the Shell Oil Company for its grant, which freed me for the summer of 1966 to write the first draft of the book. The University of Evansville administered both grants. I am most grateful to that institution, to Nicholas C. Brown, and especially to former President Melvin W. Hyde.

Hubert C. Heffner provided for me the counsel and inspiration so necessary to the pursuit of scholarship, and his advice about the project was crucial to its development. Robert G. Gunderson contributed not only to the growth of this work but also to my development as a writer. I also wish to thank others who read this manuscript and offered helpful suggestions: Oscar G. Brockett, Larry D. Clark, and Gerald Rabkin. J. Jeffrey Auer, Gary Gaiser, Donald R. Glancy, Paul Grabill, Frederic Litto, Richard Moody, Richard Scammon, Barrie Stavis, Dudley Thomas, and Donald Zacharias gave me ideas, facts, and inspiration. Frances McCurdy, Ann Smiley, G. Joseph Wolfe, Audrey Wood, and Armon Yanders provided personal encouragement for completion of the project.

Four articles taken from or based upon this book have previously appeared. I extend special gratitude to the editors who chose to use the articles—Robert G. Gunderson, Margaret L. Hartley, James W. Gibson, and Wayne Brockriede. I also thank their respective associations or publishing companies for permission to use the materials again in this book. The articles are: "Rhetoric / on Stage in Living Newspapers," *Quarterly Journal of Speech*, 54 (February 1968), 29–36; "Friends of the Party: American Writers' Congresses," *Southwest Review*, 54" (Summer 1969), 290–99; "Peace on Earth: Four Anti-War Dramas of the Thirties," *Central States Speech Journal*, 21 (Spring 1970), 30–39; "Rhetorical Principles in Didactic Drama," *Quarterly Journal of Speech*, 57 (April 1971), 147–52.

Without the enduring support of my parents, my education would have been seriously limited, and I should have had no opportunity to write this study. To them I have dedicated this product of their encouragement.

I am indebted to a number of publishing companies and authors who kindly permitted the use of quotations from their books in order to illustrate my theses. I have acknowledged the sources of excerpted materials in my notes, and the formal permissions are part of the copyright notice.

S. S.
University of Missouri–Columbia
October 1971

The Drama of Attack

A writer's problem does not change. He himself changes, but his problem remains the same. It is always how to write truly and having found what is true, to project it in such a way that it becomes a part of the experience of the person who reads it.
Ernest Hemingway, "The Writer and War"

1

Instrument for Change

Aeschylus: Come, tell me the reasons why we should admire a noble poet.
Euripides: If his work offers quick wit and wise advice, and if he helps train the people of the country to be better citizens and worthier men.
Aristophanes, *The Frogs*

A contemporary dramatist faces a society of increasing complexity, expanding opportunity, and unprecedented crisis. If he is to interpret this society to his fellow men, he must engage in intense self-examination, and he must exercise intellectual autonomy. Only by actively striving for personal integrity can he prevent the operations of mammoth central governments and burgeoning communication systems from destroying both the individuality and the privacy essential to objective interpretation of his time. Use of the current extensions of human opportunities—if he is willing to assume the resultant obligations—can alter his relationship to society and can change the principles of his art. The consequences in his art may be fortunate or unfortunate. Daily encounters with the external pressures created in this period of cold war and hot conflict, of space probes and computerization, and of time-plan private ownership and profit-motive financing force the playwright to assent to or to rebel against existing circumstances. The thinking man, be he playwright or electrician, must contend with the practical and moral crises as constructor or nihilist.

A playwright, should he choose the role of constructive rebel, might help to behead the contemporary Hydra. The beast is better known today as totalitarianism; its nine heads are mediocrity, prejudice, witch-hunting by committee, the lonely crowd, over-population, collectivism, the curtains (iron, bamboo, nuclear), war, and the Bomb. As a rebellious constructor, a playwright uses his art to formulate works calculated to do more than lull the consciousness of the spectators with—at worst—sensory titillation or—at best—casual dialogue about fashionable vital issues. He may indeed consider the theatre to be what Herbert Blau called "the Public Art of Crisis."[1]

If a dramatist conceives his works as instruments of change, he has the choice of writing mimetic or didactic dramas. If he chooses the latter species, he may construct dramas on the order of those of Bertolt Brecht or Peter Weiss, plays that employ and generate ideas and feelings capable of effecting the transformation of the social context in which he writes.[2] If he chooses to write mimetic drama, he may construct plays like those of Albert Camus, which by the very act of creation uphold beauty as a virtue on which the commonly shared dignity of man is founded.[3] Neither the urgency nor the significance of his thoughts dictate whether he will compose drama as object or drama as instrument. His own genius will determine the form of his expression.

Regardless of the dramatist's choice concerning the function of his work, so long as he treats the central problems of his time artistically, he is engaged. Only if he endeavors to tranquilize his audience and prolong their feverish sleep does he avoid engagement, and even then he declares his position. Jean-Paul Sartre argued that, for a writer, engagement means to achieve absolute consciousness of his own social volition and to push his daily awareness to the point of reflective thought.[4]

In a cogent essay, Hubert C. Heffner wrote that

1. Herbert Blau, *The Impossible Theatre*, p. 16.
2. Bertolt Brecht, "A Little Organum for the Theatre," trans. Beatrice Gottlieb, *Accent*, 11:1 (Winter 1951), 24.
3. Albert Camus, *The Rebel: An Essay on Man in Revolt*, trans. Anthony Bower, pp. 272, 277.
4. Jean-Paul Sartre, *What Is Literature?*, trans. Bernard Frechtman, p. 70.

drama at its best is a highly meaningful art that reveals the nature of man as he explores the moral order of existence.[5] Pedestrian drama, like all trivial art, arouses the emotions only for the purpose of entertainment. This is not to say that drama of stature must be dull; all great drama entertains. Even the best of the didactic playwrights, George Bernard Shaw and Bertolt Brecht for examples, emphasized the necessity of the dramatist's creating delight. Drama of the highest order, however, has not only the power to entertain but also to effect changes in human beings by presenting penetrating insights about human action. Such drama permits a better grasp of the meaning of life experience. Elder Olson wrote that "the sensational forms give us the experience; the superior forms give us significant experience; and they are superior in the degree that the significance is a superior one. We judge authors," he observed, "according to their perceptions of the meaning of experience, and the attitude they induce us to take."[6]

Insight, perception, engagement, meaning, moral order—all focus attention on thought in drama. The *Oresteia* of Aeschylus demonstrates that thought operated as a necessity in drama from the first. According to Eric Bentley, a play is obviously an intellectual object involving the full exercise of human thought.[7] Every playwright who examines the world around him by means of thought while constructing his drama is engaged in moral exploration. The results of his exploration will determine his use of significant ideas to charge his work of art with meaning. By using thought as only one of several parts, he ultimately constructs a mimetic drama that reflects his vision and from which an audience can learn. He may decide, however, to use thought as the primary part in the construction of his play. If so, he does not present an object from which an audience may or

5. Hubert Heffner, *The Nature of Drama*, pp. 345–51.
6. Elder Olson, *Tragedy and the Theory of Drama*, pp. 156–57.
7. Eric Bentley, *The Life of the Drama*, pp. 102–47.

may not learn; he now offers a play that *compels* an audience to learn—a didactic drama. He has arranged the materials of his play to stir an audience emotionally, to encourage them toward realization, decision, and action.

My objective in writing this book has been to investigate what combination of principles, some poetic and some rhetorical, exists in the structure of didactic dramas. My means was a thorough causal analysis of an exemplary body of drama from an appropriate historical period. Such matter is available in the original American didactic plays given major professional productions in New York from 1930 through 1939. Not only are they available, but also the issues with which they deal remain important to the contemporary reader. This study, then, is a historical and structural examination of the American didactic plays of the nineteen-thirties.

To differentiate the didactic from the mimetic play, one must distinguish between learning *from* drama and teaching *by* drama. One may learn from any drama, but only didactic drama is created with the primary intent of teaching or persuading. The confusion in differentiating between the two kinds of drama developed, as Bernard Weinberg has demonstrated, in Italian neoclassical theory and the critical treatises of such men as Scaliger, Castelvetro, and Robortello, which presented the contemporary interpretations of the dramatic principles enunciated by Plato and Aristotle.[8]

The problem of determining whether a play is to be a device for learning or for teaching leads to study of the location and operation of thought in drama. To consider any thought in relation to a particular drama, one should first ask, what exactly is the thought under consideration? And where does that thought originate—in the mind of the beholder or in the play? One must of necessity distinguish between thought aroused *by* drama from thought *in* drama. The thought that actually exists in a play

8. Bernard Weinberg, *A History of Literary Criticism in the Italian Renaissance*, 2 vols.

should not be confused with the thought a play may potentially excite in an audience or an individual.

To examine didactic drama as drama, to make an internal investigation of structural principles, one must begin with certain basic questions. What happens to dramatic structure when a play is formulated with rhetorical purpose? To what degree are poetic principles as well as rhetorical principles dominant in the construction? What modifications occur in a drama when thought replaces plot as the controlling part? Are the Aristotelian principles of rhetoric—those concerning persuasion— useful tools for the construction or criticism of didactic drama? In attempting to find answers to such questions one may discover the principles governing the structure of didactic drama as distinct from those which operate in mimetic drama.

Although an adequate study of a mimetic drama can be made through textual analysis alone, the study of a didactic drama is not so simple. Because a didactic drama is intended to be a functional tool rather than an object of beauty, the social context in which the play was written and originally staged is of the first importance. Therefore, this book includes not only a structural analysis of the didactic dramas of the thirties but also an examination of the social milieu in which those dramas came into being.

Two fundamentally differing views of poetry, initially articulated during the rise of Greek literature, are the sources of two major lines in poetic theory that lead from Homer's century to Samuel Beckett's. Each succeeding literary period fostered agents of one or both of these views. R. S. Crane clearly identified the two, first on the basis of Aristotle's discussion of drama, which stated the principles that are peculiar to the drama as a distinctive form of art, and second on Plato's discussion, which stipulated that the truth about the drama is necessarily to be deduced from the truth about something else to which the particular drama is related either as a part or as a means.[9] The analyses of plays throughout this book are Aristotelian; they examine dramas as drama to discover internal principles.

During a scholarly conference treating the rhetoric–poetic controversy, Oscar G. Brockett adduced three basic critical approaches to poetry: as expression, as object, and as instrument.[10] The discussion in Part I of this book treats drama as instrument, but in Part II the analyses treat plays as aesthetic objects. Didactic playwrights often state their intentions in essays, prefaces, or other public statements, but a critic should be able to discover actual didactic purpose within the works themselves. The search here is to identify the instrumental principles in the dramas.

Few studies of structure in didactic drama are available. Several works treat didactic poems and novels, for examples, those about the works of Spenser, Dante, Bunyan, and Sartre. Also, there are a few good structural studies of plays by great playwrights who occasionally or frequently wrote didactically—Euripides, Shaw, and Brecht. These latter studies do not attempt, however, to identify the nature of didactic drama per se; rather, they deal with an author's individual practices. In addition, a few critics have written briefly about didactic drama in articles or books dealing with another subject. Among these is Elder Olson, who distinguished mimetic poetry and didactic poetry as two broad species.[11] R. S. Crane briefly noted that, in spite of the current vogue for didactic forms in lyric, novel, and drama, the critical "resources for dealing with the problems raised by such

9. R. S. Crane, "The Varieties of Dramatic Criticism," in *The Context and Craft of Drama: Critical Essays on the Nature of Drama and Theatre*, eds. Robert W. Corrigan and James L. Rosenberg, p. 192.

10. Oscar G. Brockett, "Poetry as Instrument," in *Papers in Rhetoric and Poetic*, ed. Donald C. Bryant, pp. 15–16.

11. Olson's chief observations on this matter are stated in *Critics and Criticism: Ancient and Modern*, ed. R. S. Crane, in two essays: "William Empson, Contemporary Criticism, and Poetic Diction," pp. 65–68, and "A Dialogue on Symbolism," pp. 588–92.

works in other than a casual and undiscriminating way are still very meager." He further suggested that the causal method of analysis be applied to such new species as are emerging.[12] Additionally, in a discussion of unity and probability in drama, Hubert C. Heffner mentioned that "certain modern didactic plays may be largely or wholly unified in terms of thought."[13] Eric Bentley has written two significant essays concerning political drama and the theatre of commitment. He examined the nature of propaganda in the theatre, and he defined didactic drama as an attempt to induce audience members to commit themselves to ideas or action.[14]

Three contemporary books deal significantly with the didactic American dramas of the 1930s: *Writers on the Left* by Daniel Aaron, *Drama Was a Weapon* by Morgan Himelstein, and *Drama and Commitment* by Gerald Rabkin. Although these works fulfill their authors' intentions, they contain little analysis of the organization of the subject plays. Aaron described the reaction of a group of American writers to communism; he dealt with author involvement and not with literary structure. Himelstein told the story of the attempt by the Communist party to use the American theatre for propaganda; he discussed the involvement of the authors and the productions of their plays. Although Rabkin wrote about many plays, he concerned himself with the commitment of the playwrights, the results of that commitment in the careers of some, and the subjects presented in their plays. These three books substantially contribute to knowledge about the political involvement of the playwrights, but they do not bear on the problems of how thought is used in a didactic play nor how other structural principles work in such plays.

---

12. R. S. Crane, Introduction to *Critics and Criticism*, pp. 18–21.
13. Heffner, *Nature of Drama*, p. 343.
14. Bentley's two most pertinent essays are in *The Theatre of Commitment: And Other Essays on Drama in Our Society*: "The Pro and Con of Political Theatre," pp. 119–59, and "The Theatre of Commitment," pp. 190–231.

In addition to these three books, many older studies and essays have been written about the American didactic plays of the thirties.[15] But none touch on the nature of the various structures used in the subject plays. They, too, discuss the involvement of the playwrights, the commercial fortunes of the plays, and the subjects and issues apparent in the plays.

*   *   *   *   *

An understanding of certain key terms and concepts is essential to my discussion of the genesis of certain plays and my analyses. First, in comparison with dialectic and rhetoric, *poetics* is a productive art of language—so termed because it requires the structuring of particular materials into organized wholes of certain beauty. The crucial difference between rhetorical compositions and poetic ones is not that of word usage so much as a difference of structures and goals. A persuasive speech may contain poetic features, or a poem may employ rhetorical devices. The significant difference lies in the basic organization: the disposition of the material, the arrangement of the events. H. D. F. Kitto identified this difference by explaining that *poetry* is the manipulation of language, but *poiesis* is the arranging of materials into a meaningful design that is mimetic. In the creation of drama, *lexis*, the poetry of words, is far less important than *mythos*, the plot or organization of the material. *Poetics* is the theory of the composition of special kinds of verbal wholes.[16] Elder Olson pointed out

15. Some of the more significant statements are: *The Awakening of the American Theatre* by Ben Blake, "Social Trends in the Modern Drama" by Michael Blankfort and Nathaniel Buchwald, *The Changing World in Plays and Theatre* by Anita Block, *American Playwrights 1918–1938: The Theatre Retreats from Reality* by Eleanor Flexner, "Social Realism and Imaginative Theatre" by John Gassner, *The American Drama Since 1918* by Joseph Wood Krutch, *The Drama of Social Significance, 1930–1940* by Joseph Mersand, *Politics in the American Drama* by Caspar H. Nannes, and *Some Social Trends in WPA Drama* by Clarence J. Whittler.

16. H. D. F. Kitto, *Poiesis: Structure and Thought,* pp. 24–26.

that to make a play a dramatic poet must first devise an action (*praxis*), next contrive a representation (a scenario), and only then compose the dialogue. Indeed, he argued, only the first two are absolutely necessary, for drama "may or may not employ language as an artistic medium."[17]

Poetics, then, may be defined as a productive art of language; involving theory, practice, and criticism; characterized by a poetic composition brought into being by a poet; in which a mimetic action operating through a representation controls the formulation of the diction; in order to create an object of beauty and human value. *Rhetoric* is a practical art of language; involving theory, practice, and criticism; characterized by a persuasive speech by a speaker; in which knowledge operating through proof controls the formulation of the action; in order to effect a given response in an audience.

The Greek word *poietes*, from which our word *poet* derives, meant maker, an effectuator who orders materials and arranges parts into a meaningful whole. In a discussion of Aristotle and his works, Kitto noted that one can be a poet, that is, a user of imaginative language for the sake of expressing one's ideas directly, but to be so termed does not mean that one is therefore automatically a *poietes*, a composer of poetic structures. *Poiesis*, the word from which *poetry* derives, implies a certain kind of creation, not just a pleasing arrangement of diction but, rather, a harmonious disposition of material.[18] To a Greek of the classical period, *rhetorike* meant the art of oratory, the practical activity of persuading others for specific ends, especially about matters of political, judicial, or social concern. Meaning in rhetoric emerges through words, but meaning in poetry inheres in the form of the composite whole as an arrangement of both quantitative and qualitative parts.

The terms *mimetic* and *didactic* are useful in distinguishing rhetorical dramas from poetic ones. In this

17. Olson, *Tragedy and the Theory of Drama*, pp. 32–33, 87–89.
18. Kitto, *Poiesis*, pp. 24–25.

study, the terms first classify a given drama by the productive use of language (poetic) or the practical use of language (rhetoric). Mimetic, of course, implies the Aristotelian concept of imitation. As Richard McKeon explained, Aristotle considered imitation to be uniquely applicable to the processes of art, not to the processes of knowledge or of nature. "Imitation functions," McKeon wrote, "as the differentia by which the arts, useful and fine, are distinguished from nature."[19] An art object is an artificial, man-made thing. It is something constructed by a human being, not something that would come into being in nature without human help or interference. For Aristotle, the object of imitation in drama is of particular things, the actions of men. Mimetic drama, then, is drama of imitation; in the strict Aristotelian sense, it is poetic drama. The word *didactic*, though not the precise opposite of *mimetic*, bears a quite different meaning. It refers to what is rhetorical rather than poetic, persuasive rather than imitative. Didactic drama is drama of instruction, a man-made functional object to be used as a tool. The term *didactic drama* also implies that a didactic play has, to some degree, the organization of a mimetic play. Both are constructed of the same qualitative parts—plot, character, thought, diction, melody, and spectacle. The purpose of this investigation is to discover criteria to distinguish between the two dramatic species.

Even these preliminary distinctions indicate that poetry is the making of an object, while rhetoric is the activity of speechmaking or persuasion. Because this study purports to be an investigation in poetics, poetic criticism rather than rhetorical criticism characterizes it. The dramas it explores are at once rhetorical and poetic. For modern didactic drama, it attempts what R. S. Crane called for as a goal in contemporary criticism: "the recognition and analysis in a scientific undogmatic spirit, of many possible forms of serious drama beside the one species of tragedy Aristotle talks about, and the develop-

19. Richard McKeon, "The Concept of Imitation in Antiquity," in *Critics and Criticism*, ed. R. S. Crane, pp. 160–61.

ment similarly, of a poetics of comedy and the intermediate forms of drama more nearly adequate to modern achievements in these forms than anything we now have."[20]

The immediate realities and threats of our time indeed require that the contemporary critic as well as the contemporary playwright take a perspicacious look at the nature and potential of drama—didactic or not—that deals directly with crucial problems. Therefore, a consideration of important ideas about the employment of thought in drama is in order.

The Greeks used *dianoia* to mean knowledge through the employment of the intellect, that is, reflective knowledge or reasoned opinion. Aristotle used the term in the *Poetics* as one of the six qualitative elements of a drama.[21] Poetry, as one of the seven fine arts, touches on matters of truth and morality in many ways. H. A. Taine remarked that if one considered some of the great creations of intelligence in any culture, one would "see that, throughout, art is a kind of philosophy made sensible, religion a poem taken for true, philosophy an art and a religion dried up, and reduced to simple ideas."[22] Because of its varied employment of thought, poetry relates to religion and to science. George Santayana epitomized these relationships: "Poetry is called religion when it intervenes in life, and religion, when it merely supervenes upon life, is seen to be nothing but poetry."[23] Émile Zola adjudged that the best drama employs the naturalistic formula, and he concluded that this formula is realized best when the drama takes on "a strictness of form emanating from its scientific nature."[24] Aristotle

20. Crane, "Varieties of Dramatic Criticism," p. 202.

21. Aristotle, *Poetics*, trans. Ingram Bywater, pp. 230–32.

22. H. A. Taine, *History of English Literature*, trans. H. Van Laun, p. 15.

23. George Santayana, *Interpretations of Poetry and Religion*, p. v.

24. Émile Zola, "Naturalism on the Stage," in *Playwrights on Playwriting: The Meaning and Making of Modern Drama from Ibsen to Ionesco*, ed. Toby Cole, p. 5.

perfected a method for studying temporal things; he recognized that man's struggle for and knowledge of the good, the true, and the beautiful is temporal, and he linked these three realms of knowledge to the "demonstrative" sciences.[25] In his words, these are the sciences of *theoria*, knowledge of truth; *praxis*, knowledge of conduct; and *poiesis*, knowledge of production. Considering these three categories, he found relationships between metaphysics (the true), ethics (the good), and poetics (the beautiful). In each category, knowledge is produced out of experience by means of *dianoia*, or thought.[26]

To consider man as a maker of things, of objects, and as one who delights in observing such man-made objects is to realize that art originates in man's very nature. In its origin, art began as an enjoyable activity, then became a practical activity for learning, and finally was an end in itself.[27] Poetry as drama came into being through a similar genesis. Harry Levin speculated that "the origins of poetry were not only didactic but also functional. Verse was developed in a preliterate period, apparently as mnemonic technique for handing on information, the deeds and the observances of the tribe."[28] Thus, even in its origins drama as the beautiful was bound to the good and the true.

The drama can be a method, however oblique, of disseminating knowledge. Playwrights and theorists alike agree that drama can and should make meaning; they disagree, however, about *how* drama makes meaning. The meanings in drama, or those to be deduced from it, proceed from thought, and the focal question about meaning in drama becomes this: In what respects is thought related to drama?

25. Aristotle, *Analytica Priora*, trans. A. J. Jenkinson, in *The Basic Works of Aristotle*, ed. Richard McKeon, p. 65.

26. Aristotle, *Analytica Posteriora*, trans. G. R. G. Mure, in *Basic Works*, pp. 184–86.

27. Aristotle, *Poetics*, pp. 226–27; see also Olson, *Tragedy and the Theory of Drama*, pp. 178–79.

28. Harry Levin, *Contexts of Criticism*, p. 19.

Drama begins in the consciousness of the playwright and ends in the consciousness of the audience; the trajectory of the communication of beauty in drama is that of thought. For this reason, much of the concern I express in this book relates to the varied ways thought appears in drama. Note the limitation of the words *in drama*. There are important differences between thought as an element or part of the construction of a plot and the thought that may exist previous to or as a consequence of a drama. The three loci of thought in association with drama are thought in the playwright, thought in the play, and thought in the audience. One might say that any play may be considered as one whole and complete speech. As such, thought may be discerned as the statement (conceived by the playwright) that the speech (the play) makes (to the audience) through the action of the whole play. That is, thought can be deduced as what a play within itself "says." But this "saying" is *within the play*, not within the playwright or within the audience. In this sense, a dramatist who makes a mimetic play cares little about the thoughts his play may arouse in spectators so long as those spectators experience the emotional powers of the play as he wrote it. But the primary concern of the didactic dramatist is with the thoughts that may be clearly conveyed to, or implanted in, an audience. Like an orator, a didactic dramatist is concerned with acting upon audiences in ways that will result in conviction and perhaps in overt action on their part.

Aristotle mentioned *dianoia* in several chapters of the *Poetics* and thereby defined the function of *thought in mimetic drama*. In such drama, thought acts chiefly as a working part in the construction of a complete action (a plot). It does so by serving as material to both character and plot. Thought appears in mimetic drama in five major guises: (1) as language, or general statement of an indifferent kind, or "the possible"; (2) as the means to amplify and diminish facts, relationships, or emotions;

(3) as the arousal or expression of emotion; (4) as deliberation and argument, or proof and disproof; and (5) as a whole argument, or the entire action as a speech.[29]

The analyses of plays in subsequent chapters test the idea that thought often appears in didactic drama in ways similar to its functions in mimetic drama. The analyses also consider the uses of thought in didactic drama that are similar to the classical principles of rhetoric. Ingram Bywater, whose translation of the *Poetics* is one of the most satisfactory, indicated that when Aristotle assumed in the *Poetics* what he had written about thought in the *Rhetoric* he was probably "thinking of his doctrine of proofs and emotions as set forth in the greater parts of Books I and II."[30] In Book I of the *Rhetoric*, the three modes of persuasion—commonly called proofs—appear as the first significant and applicable items: (1) the personal character of the *speaker, ethos*; (2) his power of stirring emotions in the *audience, pathos*; and (3) the *speech* itself as evincing truths or apparent truths by means of persuasive arguments, *logos*.[31]

The three kinds of rhetoric are also applicable. Aristotle referred to them in Chapter 3 of his *Rhetoric* as three kinds of speeches: political, forensic, and epideictic. Political, or deliberative, oratory attempts to persuade an audience to act or not to act; it is exhortation. The object of such speeches is utility for future time. Their ends are expediency and inexpediency. Their primary subjects or concerns are ways and means, whether to follow or to avoid a course of action, examination of present unhappiness and future happiness, and analysis of what is good

29. The following references are the key descriptions of thought in the *Poetics* in the edition cited: thought as a quality of character and of saying what is appropriate, Chapter 6, pp. 230–32; thought's relation to discovery, Chapter 16, pp. 244–45; thought's connection with diction and rhetoric, Chapter 19, pp. 248–49; diction's link with thought, Chapters 20 through 22, pp. 249–56; thought and diction in epic poetry, Chapter 24, p. 259.

30. *Poetics*, p. 248n2.

31. Aristotle, *Rhetoric*, trans. W. Rhys Roberts, Book I, Chapter 2, pp. 24–25.

in the given realm. Proof in these speeches is usually inductive, by means of examples. The line of argument points toward future expedient action and also to possibility and impossibility.[32] Forensic, or legal, oratory attempts to accuse or to defend for the sake of justice. The object of these speeches is to establish justice with regard to actions that occurred in the past. Their ends are justice and injustice *as result*. The major subjects or concerns of this type are wrongdoing (motives, perpetrators, and victims); pleasure; law and breaking the law; and comparative evil of actions. Proof is usually deductive by means of syllogism and enthymeme and also by maxim (a general statement about questions of conduct). The line of argument establishes past facts and also possibility and impossibility.[33] Epideictic, or ceremonial, oratory praises or censures a man or an institution by proving the reasons for granting honor or imposing condemnation. The object of such ceremonial speeches is identification of nobleness or meanness in or for the present time. Their ends are to establish honor or dishonor. Their primary subjects or concerns are virtue and vice, praise and censure. Proof in these speeches is usually by amplification and diminution. The line of argument is a measure of degree.[34]

Although Bywater mentioned only Books I and II of Aristotle's *Rhetoric* as applicable to thought in drama, Book III contains an important consideration as well. It discusses disposition, or arrangement. These considerations of rhetorical organization can be useful in analyses of didactic plays also. In Chapters 13 through 19 of Book III, Aristotle outlined the proper disposition of the material of a speech into the following parts: (1) exordium, or introduction; (2) exposition, or statement; (3) proof, or argument; and (4) peroration, or conclusion.[35]

I have established the primary principles of per-

---

32. *Rhetoric*, Book I, Chapters 3–6, pp. 31–46.
33. *Rhetoric*, Book I, Chapters 3 and 10, pp. 31–34 and 63–67.
34. *Rhetoric*, Book I, Chapters 3 and 9, pp. 31–34 and 56–63.
35. *Rhetoric*, Book III, Chapters 13–19, pp. 199–218.

suasion that Aristotle described in his *Rhetoric* as the chief criteria for dramatic analysis in this study. My major concern is to discover to what degree the theoretical means of persuasion—such as the three modes of persuasion, the three kinds of rhetoric, and the method of rhetorical disposition—are working principles in didactic plays.

A final preliminary matter concerns the genesis of American didactic drama during the Depression. The four chapters in Part I of this book deal with the causes that helped stimulate such dramas in that period. Chapter 2 discusses the material cause of the drama's origin, that is, such matters as the economic collapse, awareness of the grim quality of life on the lower levels of our society, persecution of minorities, the class and labor conflicts, the rise of fascism, and the spread of war. Chapter 3 explains the efficient cause as the commitment of the writers to multiform social concern, to political systems and parties, and to liberal theatre groups. It also presents the writers' critical points of view about their chosen materials. Chapter 4 defines the formal cause of the didactic drama as it involves the rhetorical forms—depiction, exhortation, accusation, and censure. The final cause is treated in Chapter 5, as it existed in the visions and purposes of the playwrights themselves, in their search for meaning, and in their intent to convince or convert segments of the public to their position. The four chapters together reveal the attempts of writers to identify and eradicate the causes of violent disorder in society. That their socially functional dramas resulted in noteworthy art is becoming ever more frequently recognized. Their work, viewed as the expression of a generation of playwrights, occupies a place of increasing importance in the twentieth-century attempt to restore the cultural heart of civilization.

A critic can easily reject didactic plays as poor art simply because they do not exhibit all the features of whatever mimetic works he has come to admire, or because he does not agree with the ideas propounded, or

even because he prefers not to hear any thoughts propounded in a theatre. In order to measure the achievement of a didactic play, however, a critic ought to discover the artistic principles of the play and perhaps
separate them from the play's philosophic wisdom or its
bad metaphysics. Furthermore, a critic should remember
that in external relationships with politics and theology,
beauty is perfectly compatible with nonsense and tyranny, or for that matter with wisdom and democracy.
This adaptability of beauty is fortunate because, if the
existence of nonsense and tyranny precluded the creation
of beauty, precious little art would now exist. How many
artists as they created masterpieces were working for a
church or state? How many needed religious or political
sanction to show their art works? Aldous Huxley examined these realities and observed how many masterpieces
were produced to serve as religious or political propaganda and to exalt a god, a government, or a priesthood.
But Huxley accused most kings and priests of being
despotic and all religions of being riddled with super-
stition. Genius, he wrote, has been the servant of tyranny,
and much art has been used to laud a local cult.[36] Freedom, absence of reflective thought, philosophic wisdom
—none is a *sine qua non* to the creation of high art, but
functional formulative principles are essential.

That didactic drama is significant in contemporary
theatre should be obvious to every critical observer. The
world's social problems concern great segments of the
population as perhaps never before, and playwrights as
well as other creative artists are adding the voices of their
art works to the widespread plea for peace, justice, equality, and moderation. Peter Weiss is perfecting documentary drama in both practice and theory. In Europe, Rolf
Hochhuth, Günter Grass, Friedrich Duerrenmatt, and
Max Frisch have also written didactic plays of stature.
In America, innovative playwrights are composing plays
that clamor for social and economic changes to benefit

36. Aldous Huxley, "The Art of Selling," in *Readings in Speech*,
ed. Haig A. Bosmajian (New York, 1965), p. 78.

man. Arthur Kopit, Megan Terry, Jean-Claude van Itallie, Sam Shepard, LeRoi Jones, and many others have
written plays of exhortation, accusation, or censure. It
becomes clear that only when society no longer generates
social problems will playwrights cease to create didactic
drama. Until that time, writers will continue to experi-
ment and to perfect thought-controlled dramas.

Two questions correlate this introduction with the
two parts of the book that follow. Why did American
playwrights in the thirties choose to write didactic dramas? What are the structural consequences in those
dramas?

Part I:
Genesis of the Drama of Attack

The origin of action—its efficient, not its final cause— is choice, and that of choice is desire and reasoning with a view to an end. This is why choice cannot exist either without reason and intellect or without a moral state; for good action and its opposite cannot exist without a combination of intellect and character.
Aristotle, *Nicomachean Ethics*

2

Mirror for a Society

Is there any cause in nature that makes these hard hearts?
Willam Shakespeare, *King Lear*

*The historical development of a people is to be found
mirrored in its literature; and if literature has a light to
throw on political history, history in turn performs the
same service for letters.*
Vissarion Belinski,
"On the General Signification of the Term Literature"

The decade of the American Depression appears to have
had the structure of a drama—a beginning, a middle, and
an end. During the prologue in 1929, Americans of all
classes were enjoying prosperity or the promise of it in
the near future. Masses of citizens, having become investors by purchasing Liberty bonds in 1918, now turned
to more speculative investments. Many investors, small
and large, began to use the stock market as a vehicle for
dreams of great riches. Paper fortunes flourished as credit
expanded ever more extravagantly, and the ease of purchasing stock on margin seduced even the knowledge-
able.[1] But in the midst of the nation-wide whirl of spec-
ulation came Black Thursday, October 24, 1929. The
stock market hesitated in its upward spiral, then fell. In a
setting that revealed some of the nation's star economic
performers, the country's business leaders, caught in the
debacle, the curtain opened on Depression Era, Act I.

The tragedy played from Wall Street to Puget
Sound. The Dow Jones averages for thirty industrials
dropped from a high of 381.17 on September 3, 1929, to

1. S. S. Fontaine, "Crash of the Stock Exchange Bull Market,"
The World Almanac and Book of Facts for 1930, ed. Robert Hunt
Lyman (New York, 1930), pp. 145–46.

below 198.69 by January 1, 1930.[2] On March 6, 1930, unemployed workers from varied segments of the work force demonstrated in New York, Cleveland, Los Angeles, and thirty-five other cities. In 1931 New York had eighty-two breadlines serving more than 82,000 meals a day; in 1932 hunger marchers descended in mobs on Washington, D. C. The total national income sank from $81 billion in 1929 to $49 billion in 1932, a decline of 40 per cent.[3]

The financial blow hit hundreds of thousands of adults in the stomachs, and reports of starvation among children grew. For example, during 1932 in Benton, Illinois, United Charities and the Red Cross cared for 480 families, including 1,880 children. The average expenditure per family each week ranged from $1.30 to $3.00. The grocery orders called for flour, lard, beans, salt, and sugar, but no milk—fresh, canned, or dry. Nearly 2,000 children in that community of 10,000 drank not one drop of milk during 1931.[4] Workers of all levels—skilled and professional—seized on any chance to earn money; they labored at unaccustomed, heavy physical work for meager wages in order to help feed their families, and they were grateful to have found the work.[5]

In New York hospitals during 1931, twenty people died of starvation. The number of deaths officially entered as due to starvation is misleading, however, because a starving patient was more than likely at the same time to be suffering another disease, which was recorded as the cause of death. But for the hundreds who starved, there were thousands upon thousands who endured mal-

2. Fontaine, *World Almanac, 1930*, p. 145.

3. *Nation* (April 9, 1930), 410; Gertrude Springer, "Well Advertised Breadlines," *Survey* (February 15, 1931), 531; Malcolm Cowley, "King Mob and John Law," *New Republic* (December 21, 1932), 153–55; "The National Income," *Monthly Labor Review* (March 1934), 584.

4. Mauritz Hallgren, "Bloody Williamson Is Hungry," *Nation* (April 20, 1932), 458.

5. One man worked alone, unloading a railroad car of coal each day with only a scoop shovel for a tool. He earned $5 a week.

nutrition.[6] In New York as elsewhere, the apple sellers haunted the street corners in place of the loungers of more affluent days.

Some leftist writers began to compose works of propaganda and protest, and by doing so they pointed to significant social issues of the time. Some dramatists composed agitprop (agitation-propaganda) plays in order to pose critical questions. Alfred Kreymborg, for example, wrote *America, America!*, a mass chant that asked the United States what it had done with its gold. It asked what the American financial system had done to bring poverty and misery on the people. And it asked why the children of the nation were hungry and cold.[7]

These questions struck the ears of the contemporary audience with more than musical force. Consequently, questions of social concern arose not only in the minds of the masses but also in the consciousness of creative workers in every field, with varied reactions. John Howard Lawson, for instance, traveled to the South to cover the infamous Scottsboro case for the *Daily Worker* and the *New Masses*. He was arrested almost immediately after his arrival in the town; later, he wrote about his shocking experience in *A Southern Welcome*.[8] Not all writers were directly sympathetic. Mike Gold, a member of the Communist party and a leading journalist and playwright, crowed about the economic crash: "Let me admit, I enjoyed the recent music of the victim's howls and tears. Too long has one had to submit to the airs of these cockroach capitalists. Every barber was dabbling in Wall Street. Every street-cleaner expanded his chest proudly as he maneuvered his horse-droppings into a

6. Eleanor Flexner, "No Starvation?" *Nation* (April 27, 1932), 479.

7. Alfred Kreymborg, *America, America!*, in *Proletarian Literature in the United States: An Anthology*, eds. Granville Hicks, Michael Gold, Isidor Schneider, Joseph North, Paul Peters, Alan Calmer, p. 265.

8. John Howard Lawson, *A Southern Welcome* (New York, 1934).

can. Wasn't he a partner with Morgan and Rockefeller in American prosperity?"[9]

The dramatists did not set the vehicles for their viewpoints in gear until the second season of the decade. But beginning with the American production of *Josef Suss* by Ashley Dukes—a dramatization of Lion Feuchtwanger's *Power*—on January 20, 1930, to the first performance of *Once Upon a Time* by L. J. Dugan on December 20, 1939, many plays with at least a degree of social orientation moved onto the professional stage in New York. Despite the agonies of much of the populace, however, the majority of plays showed little discernible social involvement. Of the 1,540 plays professionally produced in New York during the thirties, only 177 (11 per cent) were directly *engagé*, and less than a third of those could be called didactic.[10]

Although relatively few politically didactic plays achieved professional production and although few of those chosen enjoyed long runs, these few were wielded as weapons by the leftist artists. Not only did these dramas make a considerable impact on the contemporary American theatre but they affected patterns of American culture.

The professional theatre almost foundered in the Depression's economic storm. In the first two years of the decade, twenty-six Broadway theatres closed, and the fifty-two remaining theatres were lighted an average of 19.6 weeks a year. The Shuberts, after netting over $2 million in 1926, lost over $1 million in 1930 and later applied for receivership.[11] In 1934 more than 80 per cent of all stage employees were jobless.[12] But many theatre

9. Michael Gold, "American Jungle Notes," *New Masses* (December 1929), 8.

10. The source for these statistics is the Burns Mantle volumes from the 1929–1930 season through the 1939–1940 season. Burns Mantle, ed., *The Best Plays of 1929–30*, etc.

11. Morton Eustis, "Theatre Building and Ownership," *Theatre Arts Monthly* (September 1934), 665, 667.

12. Mordecai Gorelik, "Theatre Is a Weapon," *Theatre Arts Monthly*, 18 (June 1934), 421.

artists agreed with leftists like Ben Blake, who believed that the theatre benefited from the stringencies of the economic crisis, for they hastened "the intellectual and financial bankruptcy of Broadway" and exposed "the cancers of triviality and social insensibility" that were eating away its heart.[13]

In April of 1931 a call went out from prominent, socially concerned theatre people for plays to dramatize the social issues and for a theatre to play to the vast "oppressed" masses. Subsequently, leftist theatre developed. Small troupes who performed agitprop plays to "awaken the workers" began appearing at labor meetings, rallies, and strike demonstrations. On June 13, 1931, representatives from no less than 224 workers' cultural groups in New York City and vicinity attended a conference to form a federation of workers' theatres.[14] A year later The League of Workers Theatres was established at the first national conference of workers' theatres.[15]

Throughout the first four years of the Depression, new theatre organizations constantly arose. In 1930 agitprop troupes, such as the Workers' Laboratory Theatre and the Proletbuehne, performed militant labor chants at labor meetings and rallies. The Group Theatre was the first fully professional organization to produce socially aware plays. Organization of The League of Workers Theatres in April, 1932, marked the true beginning of the professional version of the workers' theatre movement. The Theatre Union appeared on stage during the 1933–1934 season with its production of *Peace on Earth*. Though short-lived, it was the most significant of the leftist production organizations. Its avowed purposes were (1) to produce plays that dealt with the social conflicts and economic problems that confronted the majority of people, (2) to establish a low price scale so the

13. Ben Blake, *The Awakening of the American Theatre*, pp. 13, 15.

14. Hallie Flanagan, "A Theatre Is Born," *Theatre Arts Monthly*, 15 (November 1931), 908–15.

15. Gorelik, "Theatre Is a Weapon," 424.

masses could attend the theatre, and (3) to organize a labor audience through benefit theatre parties and subscribing members. The leftist New Theatre League came into being in order to create coherence among the many groups, professional and amateur. It held conferences, sponsored publications, and operated a script bureau. Its membership included not only such New York organizations as Theatre Collective, Negro People's Theatre, Theatre Advance, Labor Stage, Forum Theatre, and Negro Theatre Guild, but also many groups from other cities, such as the Rebel Players of Los Angeles, the Blue Blouses of Chicago, and the Solidarity Players of Boston. The Theatre of Action, at first a leading amateur workers' theatre, became a professional company in 1935 with a production of *The Young Go First*, a play about the young men who worked in the government's Civilian Conservation Corps.[16]

On the stages of the workers' theatres, the radical playwrights voiced their views through a worker speaking to his own class. The small theatres echoed with slogans and advice: "Resist war, hunger, and fascism, resist anti-semitism and negro segregation, build the international solidarity of labor, defend your fellow-workers, defend the Soviet Union, the first workers' government!"[17] On Broadway, plays declaiming strong social theses began to appear frequently during the 1931–1932 season—plays like *Steel* by John Wexley, *1931–* by Claire and Paul Sifton, and *Merry-Go-Round* by Albert Maltz and George Sklar.[18] During the first third of the 1930s, then, organizational foundations that supported the later artistic accomplishments of the leftist theatre movement came into being.

During Act II of the decade, from Hitler's rise to power in 1933 to the outbreak of the Spanish Civil War in 1936, American social drama reached its zenith. Dur-

16. Blake, *Awakening*, p. 49.
17. Gorelik, "Theatre Is a Weapon," 424.
18. Burns Mantle, ed., *The Best Plays of 1931–32.*

ing the 1935–1936 season, the activist organizations produced the most didactic plays of any season in the decade. There were thirty-one such plays—21 per cent of the total productions presented that year on Broadway. By year, socially oriented plays achieved professional production on New York stages in fluctuating numbers: spring 1930, one; 1930–1931, seven; 1931–1932, fifteen; 1932–1933, ten; 1933–1934, nineteen; 1934–1935, twenty; 1935–1936, thirty-one; 1936–1937, twenty-two; 1937–1938, twenty; 1938–1939, twenty-four; fall 1939, eight.[19] Even the most popularly applauded dramatists of the period—Maxwell Anderson, S. N. Behrman, Sidney Howard, and Robert Sherwood among them—injected the adrenalin of social concern into their plays.

Marxism pervaded much of the contemporary American literature; its influence entered the theatre through proletarian plays. Characteristic of its vehicles in the various literary genres are such works as, in fiction, *The Disinherited* by Jack Conroy; in poetry, "Red, White and Blue" by Alfred Kreymborg; in drama, *Stevedore* by Paul Peters and George Sklar; and in criticism, "Wilder: Prophet of the Genteel Christ" by Michael Gold.

Although the Federal Theatre Project began production in 1936 with *The Comedy of Errors*—a title the administration of the Project later considered heavily symbolic—its later productions of socially conscious plays exploded like bombs in theatres throughout the nation.[20] Under the aegis of the Federal Theatre, didactic drama took the stage in still another guise, the Living Newspaper, an effective contemporary form that I discuss in Chapter 3 and at greater length in Chapter 7. Five Living Newspapers were produced in New York, two in Norwalk, Connecticut, one in Cleveland, and one in Chi-

19. These figures are from an examination of most of the plays and from the Burns Mantle volumes for the decade.

20. Hallie Flanagan, *Arena: The History of the Federal Theatre*, also Jane DeHart Mathews, *The Federal Theatre, 1935–1939: Plays, Relief, and Politics*.

cago. *The Highlights of 1935* was the first to appear; it ran in New York from May 12, 1936, through May 30, 1936.[21]

Throughout the decade, dramatists critically and aesthetically appraised the social and political order of the country as characterized by angry workers, the clusters of tin-can shacks called Hoovervilles, hunger marches, demoralized farmers, joyless youth, and starving children. They reacted by bringing to the stage the realities of the economic and moral breakdown America was undergoing and by expressing what they actually saw.

Never before in the history of American letters had so many writers and artists so consciously involved themselves in social and political activity and assumed specific political obligations both in their personal lives and in their works. Consequently, during the thirties many American authors committed themselves to ideas, movements, organizations, and parties that were leftist—or at least liberal—in orientation. The dramatists constructed their plays around proletarian subject matter and with didactic purpose. Chief among these writers were Arthur Arent, Leopold Atlas, Albert Bein, Michael Blankfort, Marc Blitzstein, George Brewer, Harold Clark, Paul Green, Michael Gold, I. J. Golden, Milo Hastings, Lillian Hellman, DuBose Heyward, Langston Hughes, Sidney Kingsley, Orrie Lashing, Reginald Lawrence, John Howard Lawson, Melvin Levy, Richard Maibaum, Albert Maltz, Maxwell Nurnberg, Clifford Odets, George O'Neil, Paul Peters, Elmer Rice, Daniel Rubin, Irwin Shaw, Claire and Paul Sifton, George Sklar, Barrie Stavis, John Steinbeck, Arnold Sundgaard, John Wexley, Victor Wolfson.

Some playwrights joined the Communist party because they believed, like Paul Peters, that the "social revolution will be the torch for a new flame of art, hopeful where it is now frustrated, lusty where now it is anemic, bold and gleeful where now it is bound and

21. Flanagan, *Arena*, p. 390.

surly."[22] Among them were Michael Blankfort, Marc Blitzstein, Michael Gold, John Howard Lawson, Melvin Levy, Albert Maltz, Clifford Odets, and George Sklar.[23] But most purposeful dramatists were quickly disillusioned by the rigid controls imposed by the party's commissars of culture and thereupon renounced their membership. The majority of American playwrights never became members. The events of the times, not the politics of parties, set off the forces that transformed liberals into radicals.

The searing issues of the early thirties absorbed the attention of many American dramatists and prevented some of them from writing purely for art's sake. Marc Blitzstein satirized the idea of noncommitted art with an ironic song in *The Cradle Will Rock*. The song argues comically that loving art for art's sake brings an artist to part with his heart, mind, eyes, ears, and speech. And it asserts that eventually the forces of social evil will no doubt destroy all art "for art's sake."[24]

The socially conscious playwrights, however vocal, were a minority within their profession. Most playwrights, then as now, chose to grapple for financial gain by composing commercial entertainment rather than to create art or to participate in politics. These writers defeated the Marxist dream of transforming the professional theatre from a powder puff into a weapon. A summary of Broadway's longest-running productions originating in the thirties reveals the true nature of the plays they wrote and the entertainment most theatregoers evidently preferred: (1) *Tobacco Road*, 2,611 performances during the thirties and still running on January 1, 1940, a representation of Depression conditions and potentially a social documentary, but its long run due primarily to the comic hokum introduced by va-

22. Paul Peters, "Are Artists People?" *New Masses* (January 1927), 8.

23. U.S. Congress, Senate, *Hearings Before the Committee on Un-American Activities*, 53rd Cong., 1st sess., 1935, pp. 95–115.

24. Marc Blitzstein, *The Cradle Will Rock*, in *The Best Short Plays of the Social Theatre*, ed. William Kozlenko, pp. 145–46.

rious directors and casts, thus deflecting the play from its serious purpose; (2) *Pins and Needles*, 934 performances and still running at the decade's end, the most radical of the list, a musical revue presented by the International Ladies' Garment Workers' Union; (3) *You Can't Take It with You*, 837; (4) *Three Men on a Horse*, 835; (5) *The Children's Hour*, 691, the most serious of the group, written by leftist Lillian Hellman; (6) *Dead End*, 687, another serious play, but its long run accomplished by the comic broadening of performances; (7) *Boy Meets Girl*, 669; (8) *The Women*, 657; (9) *The Green Pastures*, 640; (10) *Hellzapoppin*, 593 and still running at the decade's close.[25] Although the red tide of American drama surged to its high mark in the thirties, the list indicates the ebb to commodity theatre as economic conditions bettered. Even in its off-Broadway segment, not all the new theatre was dedicated to politics; on April 16, 1935, the Nudist Theatre Guild first opened its curtains to reveal *A Girl from Childs*.[26]

The Marxists' faith, however, was unmoved by commercial successes or amateur aberrations. They voiced fond hopes for the American theatre. One spokesman asserted that the theatre would no longer be a plaything of the rich. It would eventually become a weapon that the masses could use for making a healthy society.[27]

From international, national, local, and individual circumstances came the issues and the subjects with which the playwrights of protest dealt. Most dramatists, for example, recognized the shocking threat to freedom in the Nazis' seizure of power in Germany in 1933; for the rest of the decade antifascism was the chief international subject for dramatists as well as other writers. Joseph Freeman, the editor of the Communist paper *New Masses*, warned of fascism's destructive effect on culture

25. Burns Mantle, *The Best Plays of 1939–40*, p. 477.
26. Burns Mantle, *The Best Plays of 1934–35*, p. 483.
27. Paul Peters (presumably), Preface to the section on Drama, in *Proletarian Literature in the United States*, p. 264.

and on world peace.[28] Shortly after Hitler's rise to power, Elmer Rice wrote *Judgment Day* as a direct and vitriolic attack on nazism. Produced on September 12, 1934, it was the first anti-Nazi, or antifascist, play to appear in professional production in New York. Augmenting the ranks of American protesters against nazism were the new arrivals from the Continent, for not only did Hitler's attack on culture result in the burning of books, but also it drove German writers into exile. Many of them came to the United States, and they strove to convince American writers of the magnitude of the Nazi threat to the intellectual life of the world. Friedrich Wolf, an exiled German playwright, spoke first at the opening session of the first American Writers' Congress, April 26, 1935. He described the plight of writers in Nazi Germany and attempted thereby to stir the assembled American writers to oppose fascism, to support a united front of leftist writers, and to assist the exiled German writers.[29] Other international issues that engaged the talents of the period's playwrights were support of the Soviet Union and involvement with the Spanish Republic. Ernest Hemingway delivered the only major public speech of his career on the Spanish Civil War, and he later wrote *The Fifth Column*, a play about the same conflict, which the Group Theatre produced on March 6, 1940.[30]

Other factors, indirectly related and national in scope, were formative of the intellectual milieu of the thirties. The fiscal policies of the New Deal that devaluated the dollar caused the return of many expatriate writers; also, the Roosevelt Administration initiated the Federal Writers' Projects as a relief measure. The formation of the Congress of Industrial Organizations and its

28. Joseph Freeman, "Toward the Forties," in *The Writer in a Changing World*, ed. Henry Hart, pp. 26–27.

29. Friedrich Wolf, "In the Name of Some Heroes," in *American Writers' Congress*, ed. Henry Hart, pp. 19–21.

30. Ernest Hemingway, "The Writer and War," in *The Writer in a Changing World*, ed. Henry Hart, pp. 69–73.

inclusion of artists brought the benefits of trade unionism to the arts, and they developed economic muscle. Because of the severe economic conditions prevailing throughout the nation, writers who had been dealing with personal or conventional themes now became engrossed in social problems; writers previously dedicated to protest took a firmer grip on their cudgels. There was a distinct move in all literary works toward the broadening of subject matter. The problems of the poor and oppressed increasingly commanded the attention of writers. "Proletarian literature" appeared as a genre and grew in popularity, although—it should be noted—more copies of *Gone with the Wind* sold than all the proletarian novels combined. The national problems of housing, agriculture, injustice in the courts, unemployment, persecution of minorities, labor conditions, and prostitution, heretofore ignored, provided additional materials for socially concerned dramatists.

Because of the broadening of political interests not only among playwrights but also among all writers, the Communist party sponsored four American Writers' congresses. The subjects of these meetings typified the ferment in the minds of writers. The congresses took place in April of 1935 and in June of 1937, 1939, and 1941.

Granville Hicks, dean of leftist critics in the thirties, wrote the call for the first congress. It appeared in January, 1935, carrying the names of seventy prominent writers and including such playwrights as Mike Gold, Langston Hughes, John Howard Lawson, Paul Peters, and George Sklar. It announced "the decay of the capitalist system" and declared that many "writers recognize the necessity of personally helping to accelerate the destruction of capitalism and the establishment of a workers' government." It proposed two major problems for consideration: How to function against war and fascism, and how to solve the peculiar problems writers have in presenting "the fresh understanding of the American scene that has come from . . . enrollment in the revolutionary cause."[31] The over-all motive of the first congress was to enlist cultural allies among writers in order to aid the workers' revolution and to save culture from reactionary forces.

The second congress, planned by the leftist League of American Writers, took place two years later. The call for this congress was published in May, 1937. Twenty-two writers signed it, including additional playwrights—Marc Connelly, Archibald MacLeish, and Clifford Odets. This call invited all writers of professional standing who in general favored a united front against fascism, the new power of labor in the United States, and the social hopes and passions of the political left.

The calls for these first two writers' congresses epitomized the attitudes of many of the playwrights who wrote didactic plays during the thirties. A brief review of the reports of the two congresses shows the direction the shifting intellectual sands would take during the subsequent decade. The change in the Communist party's policy, stimulated by Hitler's rise, effectuated most of the differences. The call for the first writers' congress was prorevolutionary and stressed the class conflict, while the second was antifascist and proclaimed the united front. In the first congress, all aspects of the Soviet Union received the highest praise; Spain, in her struggle against fascism, received the deepest sympathy in the second. At the congress of 1937, politics took the spotlight from literature, and the impossibility of nurturing culture in a fascist society received more emphasis than the development of the cultural potential in a democratic society of workers. The differences between the first two congresses were marked; during the third congress, June 2–4, 1939, most writers avoided identification with communism or they openly attacked it.[32]

31. *New Masses* (January 22, 1935), 20.
32. Henry Hart, ed., *American Writers' Congress* and *The Writer in a Changing World*; Joseph Hilton Smyth, "The Third Writers' Congress," *Saturday Review of Literature* (June 10, 1939), 10; Granville Hicks, "The Failure of Left Criticism," *New Republic* (September 9, 1940), 345–46.

Although international and national issues and subjects preoccupied the playwrights at the time, without doubt local and individual problems also impelled them to write. Many playwrights, like people in all professions, were out of work or at best living under tight financial restraint. At that time, many writers probably felt like joining in the chorus of a song that was currently popular in union halls, "Boom Went the Boom." Sung to the tune of "Ta-ra-ra Boom-de-ay," the song narrates the plight of a worker who had a good job in 1929, who thought the boss was his friend, and who sneered at union organizers. But when the Depression struck, the boss cut his pay and fired him, and he learned that workers should organize.[33]

Playwrights, as well as other theatre artists, found that the jobs in the Federal Theatre Project were their major means of survival. Some eased their financial stress by living communally with other theatre people. For example, when Clifford Odets wrote his first plays, he was living in the Group Theatre's "poor house," a ten-room flat in which more than half the company resided. Odets occupied a small, cold room, and, since there was too little space for a desk, he wrote while sitting on a camp bed.[34] The young writers of the thirties utilized in their works such experiences as walking the streets in search of work, riding the rods under railroad cars, or working in stockyards. By such use they wanted not only to support the burgeoning tradition of hard-boiled radical strength in American writing but also to prove the literary authenticity of their own experiences.[35] Despite the economic crisis, playwrights of the time experienced a feeling of excitement, a spirit of crusade, a sense of movement; theirs, they knew, was a decade of disordered

33. W. O. Blee, "Boom Went the Boom," in *Songs of the Workers: To Fan the Flames of Discontent* (Chicago, 1962), p. 47.

34. Harold Clurman, *The Fervent Years: The Story of the Group Theatre and the Thirties*, pp. 103–4.

35. Alfred Kazin, "The Bitter 30's," *The Atlantic Monthly* (May 1962), 84.

society, a time of militancy. To identify themselves
with their time, they proudly, if not always necessarily,
wore the badges of radical bohemianism: roll-your-own
smokes, faded workers' clothes, a burnt-out cigarette
butt between the lips, brass knucks in the pocket.

The favorite subjects of the committed playwrights
of the thirties clearly conveyed their social outrage. They
treated subjects typical of the impulse toward "proletarian literature" or "socialist realism." In his study of the
fiction of the thirties, *The Radical Novel in the United
States*, Walter Rideout identified four categories of novels
according to the subject matter most often used: (1)
events leading up to or resulting from a strike; (2) development of class consciousness in an individual and his
consequent conversion to communism; (3) the condition
of people forced to live on the lowest levels of society;
and (4) the decline of the middle class.[36]

A sampling will illustrate the primary subjects
found in the didactic plays of the thirties: the decay of
the middle class, *American Dream* by George O'Neil,
1933; injustice in the courts and persecution of minorities, *They Shall not Die* by John Wexley, 1934; the significance of unions and strikes, *Let Freedom Ring* by
Albert Bein, 1935; the horrors of fascism, *Till the Day I
Die* by Clifford Odets, 1935; the national guilt in the
mistreatment of the black American, *Mulatto* by Langston Hughes, 1935; the plight of farmers, *Triple-A
Plowed Under* by Arthur Arent and the Editorial Staff of
the Living Newspaper, 1936; the evils of war, *Johnny
Johnson* by Paul Green, 1936; the debasement of the unemployed, *But for the Grace of God* by Leopold Atlas,
1937; the capitalist as persecutor, *The Cradle Will Rock*
by Marc Blitzstein, 1938; and the development of class
consciousness, *Life and Death of an American* by George
Sklar, 1939.

Some of the leftist playwrights wrote mimetically

---

36. Walter Rideout, *The Radical Novel in the United States,
1900–1954*, p. 171.

and others didactically. Some projected personal ideas, and others used only the theories of a political party. Some wrote as honestly as they could, and others re-shaped the truth to their purposes. Some created realistic pictures of life, while others stylized reality. As Alexander Trachtenberg, the Communist party's cultural commissar, announced when organizing the first American Writers' Congress: "This is the first time when we count noses."[37] The causes, the political parties, and the organized groups of the decade continually counted and recounted noses. But some of the playwrights, such as Elmer Rice, agreed with Hemingway—in 1935 as socially aware as any writer—who observed that after a thousand years economics would look ridiculous, while a work of art would last forever. He recognized, however, that making art is difficult and at that time plain, nonpolitical art was not fashionable.[38]

A complex of international and local, financial and ethical circumstances contributed to the social milieu in which the didactic dramatists of the thirties lived and wrote. The manner in which the playwrights were intellectually involved and in which they handled the questions posed by the Depression is the subject matter for the next chapter. The dramatists' works, along with those written in other genres, were but a small portion of the Depression's total literary product. But the art objects of the socially aware creators caught the rhythms of the time and mimed them more vividly than all the many products of commercial producers and of the then rapidly growing industries of radio and cinema. The writers of the thirties stood like embattled guerrillas; behind them was the collapsed financial structure, at either side the abysses of anarchy or tyranny, and before them the advancing armies of the world.

In Act III of the thirties, world war goose-stepped

37. Quoted in Daniel Aaron, *Writers on the Left: Episodes in American Literary Communism*, p. 283.

38. Ernest Hemingway, *Green Hills of Africa* (New York, 1954), p. 76.

ever closer to stage center. Most Americans watched the "practice" wars in Ethiopia, Spain, and on the Czech border like fear-frozen rabbits watching the approach of a fox.

A few writers composed antiwar pieces, but many more simply grafted warnings onto writings that centered on other concerns. Preoccupation with war and disenchantment with the extreme political left characterized the decade's latest movements among the socially oriented. Many writers had shed their Marxian sympathies before the mass repudiation that followed the Nazi-Soviet Non-Aggression Pact of August 24, 1939. Some writers merely yelled their I-told-you-so's and went on working. Others turned to more subjective art works. Still others traded their work shirts for ascots and sports jackets and rode around Hollywood in imported cars. A few went to jail. The weak quit writing. The militant went to war. A very few continued to agitate through literature on behalf of Marxism or Russia, but apparently no one was listening. The play of leftist theatre was over, at least for a while. The curtain closed on Depression Era, Act III. The stages of the world now reverberated with the explosions of the Second World War.

3

The Leftist Stance

This is preeminently the time to speak the truth, the whole truth, frankly and boldly. . . . Restoration calls, however, not for changes in ethics alone. This Nation asks for action, and action now.
Franklin D. Roosevelt, "First Inaugural Address"

Nobody can stand above the warring classes, for nobody can stand above the human race. . . . For art, to be "unpolitical" means only that it should ally itself with the ruling group.
Bertolt Brecht, "A Little Organum for the Theatre"

When facing the social crises of the thirties, responsible playwrights of all political views must have wondered what they could do personally to help solve society's problems. Undoubtedly, they thought seriously about how they could most effectively act to change the oppressive conditions around them. Certainly, they spoke when others were silent, and they spoke in humanistic terms. They said *man* when others said *money*, and when others said *I*, they said *every man*.

The view of the leftist playwrights was bleaker than those of their colleagues to the right and center of the political continuum, so they wrote from an intense feeling of despair; they no longer believed that the progress of humanity toward civilization was inevitable. They saw rise, fall, and stagnation as axiomatic in the limited area of economics. Some wrote from an intense feeling of loneliness; they wanted to give or receive help, but their sense of isolation frustrated their impulses. They realized that social injustices and the persecution of minorities could not be eliminated without dirtying their hands and risking bloody heads. Many of these writers indeed personally participated in strikes and demonstrations, helped form active organizations, or aided radical movements through their journalistic skills. But whatever their personal involvement, when they sat down to compose their plays, they had in their minds as materials all the tragic events and circumstances they had witnessed or heard about.

How the socially conscious playwrights employed the subject materials of the Depression era is the concern of this chapter. To be sure, conditions around and within the playwrights controlled the manner in which they constructed their plays. They, as efficient causes of the didactic drama of the thirties, were affected deeply by their commitments, their experiences, their points of view, and their theories of play construction as well as by the climate of their times.

The personal commitment of each playwright was a creative condition to much of the worth-while drama of the thirties. The word *commitment* did not then mean precisely what it does now, although the intellectual condition it now represents certainly obtained then.[1] Jean-Paul Sartre probably is responsible for the word's current meaning and widespread use, since he employed it as a key term in his influential exposition of existentialism. In *Being and Nothingness* Sartre maintained that whatever a man encounters becomes his personal responsibility. A man's "anguish" results from the condition of being "thrown into a responsibility which extends to his very abandonment" of that responsibility, or of life itself. Man, even man as artist, therefore, is inescapably involved in the action of the world. He can free himself only by a conscious act of *engagement*, of deliberate commitment.[2] Considering both the existential and the common connotations of *commitment*, Gerald Rabkin

1. Gerald Rabkin investigated the problem of political commitment among dramatists in the 1930s in his book *Drama and Commitment: Politics in the American Theatre of the Thirties.*

2. Jean-Paul Sartre, *Being and Nothingness*, trans. Hazel E. Barnes, pp. 553–56.

attempted to define the term's current meaning. It suggests "both the conscious *involvement* of the artist in the social and political issues of his age," Rabkin wrote, "and the specific political *obligations* which the artist assumes in consequence of this involvement."[3] In this study, then, *commitment* means a conscious involvement in current issues and actions through a deliberate act of dedication to a specific social attitude, to an ideological system, or to an active group. Whenever an artist makes such a conscious commitment, he also assumes certain obligations, and his work is affected.

The dramatists who wrote didactically during the Depression made three sorts of formal commitments: (1) to multiform social concern, (2) to rigidly specific political systems and parties, and (3) to leftist theatrical companies. These commitments affected their manner of working and the style in which they ultimately structured their plays.

Elmer Rice well represented those who engaged in multiform social commitment. He protested the economic woes of the Depression, the commercialism of Broadway, the ills of the social order, and the forms of censorship exercised by pressure groups and government agencies. Although he staunchly defended certain radical causes, he never found Marxism attractive, nor did he join the Communist party. Rice always lived up to his words. He resigned, for example, as the New York Regional Director of the Federal Theatre Project because of federal censorship of the first planned Living Newspaper, *Ethiopia*. At the time of his resignation, he issued a statement to the press, in which he stated his opposition to censorship; he would not be "the servant of a government which plays the shabby game of partisan politics at the expense of freedom and the principles of democracy."[4] Although *Ethiopia* never opened, Rice's protest helped

3. Rabkin, *Drama and Commitment*, p. 14.
4. Quoted in Hallie Flanagan, *Arena: The History of the Federal Theatre*, p. 66; see also *New York Times* (January 24, 1936), 20.

to reduce the degree of governmental interference in the Federal Theatre Project.[5] Rice never publicly favored any specific policy or economic program, but he encouraged a revision of the existing social order to eliminate economic and social injustice.[6] Although he reflected this attitude in his personal activities as well as in his plays, he had very little sympathy with the Communist party. His interest was "to try to inject a little intelligence into the revolutionary movement." He thought that "the dictatorship of the proletariat is nonsense."[7]

John Howard Lawson exemplified those who made commitments to specific political systems and parties. Early in the decade he dedicated himself to the creation of a revolutionary theatre.[8] Soon thereafter he joined the Communist party and became a spokesman for Marxism both as an orator and as an associate editor of *New Masses*. Lawson connected art in general and drama in particular with problems of economics and politics. He thought that an artist ought to join hands with the working class. He unhesitatingly stated his "aim to present the communist position . . . in the most specific manner."[9]

The plays that John Howard Lawson wrote during the latter half of the thirties—*Marching Song*, first produced February 17, 1937, and *Processional*, a revised version produced October 13, 1937—clearly voice the Communist message. His lack of dramatic productivity from 1934 to the end of the decade—his last produced play appeared in 1937—indicates his involvement as an activist and demonstrates the possible consequences of overly rigid commitment by a playwright. Activist play-

5. Flanagan, *Arena*, p. 67.

6. "Project for a New Theatre," *New York Times* (October 8, 1933), X, 1.

7. From a letter to James Rorty, Secretary of The League of Professional Groups for Foster and Ford, quoted in Rice's *Minority Report: An Autobiography*, p. 328.

8. John Howard Lawson, *With a Reckless Preface* (New York, 1934), p. xvii.

9. John Howard Lawson, "Straight from the Shoulder," *New Theatre* (November 1934), 11–12.

wrights evidently have difficulty maintaining their artistic output. Many others besides Lawson ceased to create when they became activists. Harold Clurman put the correct question about Lawson when he asked: Did Lawson inhibit himself creatively because of overly strict discipline, a desire for intellectual security, and self-inflicted censorship designed to force his emotions to follow the well-regulated flow of socialist ideology?[10]

Lawson turned from the disappointments of his own playwriting career to become a leading voice of the revolutionary theatrical movement. He wrote criticism, taught, lectured, wrote scripts for films, and, most importantly, wrote a formal analysis of dramatic theory in Marxian terms, *Theory and Technique of Playwriting*.[11] He believed, as evinced in his play *Marching Song*, that "the artist is forced to recognize the elementary facts of the economic struggle; he is forced to take sides."[12] By his own example Lawson indicated the side he thought an artist should take in the social struggle. So steadfast was his Marxian commitment that he even refused to renounce it at the decade's close when most other literary converts turned away from communism.[13]

The association of Clifford Odets and the Group Theatre illustrates the third type of formal commitment, that of playwrights to leftist theatrical companies. Odets first became a member of the Group as one of its lesser-known actors.[14] After the Group began its active production life, Odets' interest in playwriting grew. His friends in the organization encouraged him, and Harold Clurman was helpful to him.[15] Eventually, Odets' writing

---

10. Harold Clurman, *The Fervent Years: The Story of the Group Theatre and the Thirties*, p. 244.

11. John Howard Lawson, *Theory and Technique of Playwriting*.

12. John Howard Lawson, *New Theatre* (June 1, 1934), 6.

13. U.S. Congress, Senate, *Hearings Before the Committee on Un-American Activities*, 51st Cong., 1st sess., 1951, pp. 581–624.

14. Clurman, *Fervent Years*, pp. 36, 113.

15. For a description of the process and the friendship, see Clurman, *Fervent Years*, pp. 67–68, 94, 104, 114–20, 141–42, 145.

efforts resulted in *Awake and Sing!*, his first play professionally produced by the Group, with Clurman directing, on February 19, 1935. Five weeks later, on March 26, the Group brought Odets' *Waiting for Lefty*—first produced off-Broadway by the New Theatre League in a production involving several Group actors—and *Till the Day I Die* to the professional stage. The popularity and impact of these three plays permanently entrenched Odets as the Group Theatre's principal playwright and one of the central figures of the leftist theatre movement.[16] During the thirties, the Group was the organization that first produced Odets' plays, and *Golden Boy* was one of its two financially successful productions. Clurman stated the Group's attitude toward Odets by writing in an introduction to *Golden Boy* that the talent of Clifford Odets was greater in content than that of any other new playwright in the United States. He praised Odets as one of the rare American playwrights who could be considered a true artist.[17] Odets returned the compliment by stating that Clurman was the friendly and dedicated obstetrician who assisted with the births and beginnings of his plays. Odets also praised the Group's actors and actresses as good friends who gave inspired performances of all his plays of the thirties.[18] The commitment of Odets to the Group Theatre, although he made excursions to Hollywood during the decade, proved fortunate creatively and economically for both parties, for the national prominence of each was enhanced by their collaboration.

A notable example of commitment by playwrights to all three sorts—multiform social concern, a political system, and a leftist theatrical company—was that of two dynamic young playwrights, Albert Maltz and

16. Clurman, *Fervent Years*, p. 157; see also John McCarten, "Revolution's Number One Boy," *New Yorker* (January 22, 1938), 15.

17. Harold Clurman, Introduction to *Golden Boy*, in *Six Plays of Clifford Odets*, p. 433.

18. Clifford Odets, Preface, *Six Plays*, p. x.

George Sklar. They belonged to the Marxian-oriented Theatre Union.[19] Both men had studied drama at Yale, and both were twenty-five at the inception of the Theatre Union in 1933.[20] Maltz and Sklar, along with Harbor Allen, who wrote under the name of Paul Peters, formed the core of a writing committee that worked collectively. The committee helped each author revise his play and thus bring it to artistic and ideologic suitability according to the policies of the Theatre Union. If an author asserted too much individualism by refusing such communal assistance, his play was not produced.[21] Because the Theatre Union's demands were too stringent for established playwrights and because so few new playwrights of talent joined the leftist ranks, the organization was forced to make public appeals for writers and scripts.[22] Ultimately these three writers provided the only original plays, with the exception of one by John Howard Lawson, that the Theatre Union produced.[23]

The commitment of playwrights in the thirties resulted from shocking circumstances that aroused in them both creative and political motivations. These motivations impelled them to view certain subjects with outrage. Common concern with such subjects brought them into formal connections with movements, groups, and parties. For themselves, or in communal association, they chose to construct plays by utilizing a curative political

19. Emery Northup, "Meet the Theatre Union," *New Theatre* (February 1934), 9.

20. Burns Mantle, *Contemporary American Playwrights*, pp. 317, 324.

21. Paul Peters, "On Writing and Selecting Plays for Workers," *Daily Worker* (February 27, 1935), 5.

22. George Sklar and Albert Maltz, "The Need for a Workers' Theatre," *Daily Worker* (December 16, 1933), 7.

23. The following plays were produced by the Theatre Union: *Peace on Earth* by Sklar and Maltz, *Stevedore* by Peters and Sklar, *The Sailors of Cattaro* by Friederich Wolf translated by Keene Wallis and adapted by Michael Blankfort, *Black Pit* by Albert Maltz, *Mother* by Bertolt Brecht from Maxim Gorki's novel and adapted by Paul Peters, *Bitter Stream* by Victor Wolfson adapted from a novel by Ignazio Silone, and *Marching Song* by John Howard Lawson.

formula—the Marxian ideology—rather than a mimetic action, as the control of the artistic structures. Since they were committed to stimulating social reform, they wrote didactic plays to propound a doctrine, to create an emotional attitude toward a doctrine, or to encourage political action in accord with that doctrine.

The leftist playwrights of the thirties possessed a unique view of man and reality. Their social vision—how they saw the state of human beings in the circumstances of the time—naturally affected the manner in which they wrote and ultimately controlled the form of each of their plays. When, as committed dramatists, they treated subjects that reflected the socioeconomic chaos of the decade, they usually adjusted their method of composition to one of four particular points of view: individual protest, social protest, collective protest, or revolutionary protest. In a generalized examination of the social plays written before April, 1935, Michael Blankfort and Nathaniel Buchwald referred to such points of view and contrasted them with what they called the theatre of the *status quo*. This latter type of theatre, they said, comprised most of the modern plays written or produced in America; its distinguishing characteristics were "its lack of overt or implied treatment of social and political problems." The theatre of the *status quo* dealt with such problems occasionally but only "out of context and romantically." Blankfort and Buchwald also explained that "the characters who walk its stages lead cellophane-wrapped lives. The clashes and conflicts portrayed are usually between individual and individual, representing no more than themselves." To most leftist playwrights, the theatre of the *status quo* was the bourgeois theatre—a theatre to avoid.[24]

Committed playwrights, clearly, were not content to be "the Swiss Guard for the *status quo*." Some who were committed to multiform social concern wrote *plays*

24. Michael Blankfort and Nathaniel Buchwald, "Social Trends in the Modern Drama," *American Writers' Congress*, ed. Henry Hart, pp. 128–29.

of individual protest, which were, in many instances, mimetic rather than didactic. They presented conflicts that stimulated social awareness only indirectly, but the world created by the playwright in the play sometimes formed a suggestive microcosm of the world at large. In these plays the thin social theses took second place to the action of characters, and the messages communicated to the audiences through the dialogue were peripheral to everyday reality. Three of the most direct of these plays of individual protest, plays in which social thoughts are uppermost in their over-all structures, are *Thunder Rock* by Robert Ardrey, *Key Largo* by Maxwell Anderson, and *The Petrified Forest* by Robert Sherwood.

In *Thunder Rock*, Ardrey made a microcosm of a lighthouse on Lake Michigan. To it a man named Charleston, though still young, retires from the world because he believes it destined for destruction.[25] Living alone, Charleston creates an imaginary world peopled with the ghosts of some troubled European refugees who were shipwrecked on the site of the lighthouse ninety years earlier. Through interaction with these imagined people, who assume a degree of reality, Charleston discovers that men may be temporarily defeated, but eventually mankind will find an answer to social problems. Man's essential power is to decide how soon he will genuinely attempt to perfect humane solutions for socioeconomic dilemmas.[26] At the play's end, Charleston rejects his insulation from events. He decides to enter the world again to help mankind win the battle, at least to hasten the victory.

Maxwell Anderson placed the action of *Key Largo* in a setting removed from the socially pertinent world of the Spanish Civil War, which the action in the play echoes. The play occurs in the microcosm of a Florida Keys resort. The entire action is on the level of individuals. The most important conflict exists in King McCloud's mind—whether or not he should give his life

25. Robert Ardrey, *Thunder Rock*, p. 19.
26. Ardrey, *Thunder Rock*, p. 59.

for the sake of his humanistic ideals. The resolution transpires when he romantically sacrifices himself to destroy a gangster who represents totalitarianism. McCloud thus attempts to expiate his own inner guilt. His most radical statement is that a person dies because his destiny dictates his end; at best a man should die for what he believes.[27]

Robert Sherwood set his protagonist Alan Squier in a similar microcosm in his play *The Petrified Forest*. This time the locale is a cafe in the Arizona desert. There Squier works out his version of what to do about the world's ills. He persuades a gangster—an easy and frequently used symbol of totalitarianism in the thirties—to shoot him so that a girl can have the money from his life insurance policy. He surrenders his life for her gain because she has hope while he does not. The girl represents the energetic future, Squier represents the tired past. Squier sees in her the essential qualities of vitality, courage, and aspiration. Those are the human energies, he says, most necessary to the continuance of life on earth.[28]

A second way for committed dramatists to deal with the problems of their time was through *plays of social protest*. These writers shouted against the current economic system of exploitation. They wanted to free the individual from oppression. They believed that capitalism was perhaps inevitable in America, but that it needed changing because it created maladjustments within the middle class. Examples of this point of view are *Awake and Sing!* by Clifford Odets and *Gold Eagle Guy* by Melvin Levy.

In *Awake and Sing!* Odets presented a family brought into frustrating dislocation by the social and economic forces of the capitalistic system. In the play, militancy is the means for achieving freedom. Militancy

---

27. Maxwell Anderson, *Key Largo*, in *Eleven Verse Plays, 1929–1939* (New York, 1940), p. 118.

28. Robert Sherwood, *The Petrified Forest*, in *Sixteen Famous American Plans*, eds. Bennett A. Cerf and Van H. Cartmell (New York, 1941), p. 405.

as a metaphor appears in the imperative of the title and in the words of Jacob, the family's aged seer and radical. When Jacob dies, young Ralph awakens to the old man's call for a Marxian world vision. At the play's end, Ralph shouts that one must join with other workers. He wants everyone to spit on his hands and get to work. If workers cooperate, he claims, they can fix things so life will not be so money-oriented. The only redemption possible, according to the play, is collective action, with new blood and strong arms to free the individual from oppressive life.[29]

Melvin Levy set *Gold Eagle Guy* in nineteenth-century San Francisco in order to dramatize the original evils of the capitalistic system. That system, according to the play, produces the ruthless buccaneers of industry who control the destinies of the entire population of this and other countries. Guy Button is the central character, an "evil" one. From the status of ordinary seaman in the San Francisco of 1862, Guy claws his way up through the levels of society and becomes the epitome of rapacity by 1906 by capitalistic manipulation of a shipping business. Absolutely self-righteous, he brays that he is personally responsible for the development of the entire country. He claims that he has been the instrument of the Lord and has exercised His divine power.[30] One Marxist critic, Stanley Burnshaw, stated that this play told the unadorned truth about the corrupt business practices in the nineteenth century that culminated in America's economic crisis in the mid-thirties.[31] The play shows Guy's eventual downfall, and it indicates that all such capitalists should likewise be destroyed.

Plays of collective protest were a third means for expressing commitment. In these, playwrights raised their voices beyond merely singing the blues. They ob-

29. Clifford Odets, *Awake and Sing!* in *Six Plays*, pp. 97, 101.
30. Melvin Levy, *Gold Eagle Guy*, p. 153.
31. Stanley Burnshaw's statement to this effect in his review of the play in *New Masses* is quoted on the jacket of the 1935 edition of the play.

viously viewed the capitalistic system through a powerful Marxian microscope. Typically, in plays like *1931–* by Claire and Paul Sifton or *Precedent* by I. J. Golden, malicious capitalists trample individual members of the proletarian collective. Hope lies crippled but waiting to join purposes with the masses who seek regeneration through militancy.

In *1931–*, the Siftons depicted the decline of a central character named Adam. At first a warehouse worker, he becomes a bum, and his girl degenerates from a day laborer to a diseased prostitute. Ten interludes showing the rising anger of oppressed workers interrupt the fourteen realistic scenes. According to the authors, the play deals with one individual caught in a tidal wave of social change which is inexplicable and inescapable for the people in it.[32] The alternating scenes and interludes finally point to revolutionary action. At the end, Adam joins the workers' revolt. His key phrases concern his right to live and to work.[33]

Precedent by I. J. Golden treats the persecution of Delaney, a labor organizer, by the officials of a railroad company. The events of the play parallel the story of Tom Mooney who suffered similar circumstances in real life. Delaney is framed for a bombing, arrested, and convicted on perjured testimony. Although his death sentence is commuted, Delaney faces life imprisonment. The play questions what it calls archaic and destructive laws that make human existence less valuable than the arbitrary rules and procedures of the courts.[34] The only hope for justice, the author declared in his play, is in an activist future.

Committed dramatists wrote *plays of revolutionary protest*. They portrayed men who collectively resisted capitalism, fighting it directly and in some sense conquering it. With these propaganda pieces, they intended to incite agitation by making political revelations and by

32. Claire Sifton and Paul Sifton, Authors' Note, *1931–*, p. xi.
33. Sifton and Sifton, *1931–*, p. 144.
34. I. J. Golden, *Precedent*, p. 138.

stirring revolutionary fervor. Among these plays the Marxists prized *Peace on Earth* by George Sklar and Albert Maltz, *Stevedore* by Paul Peters and George Sklar, and *Waiting for Lefty* by Clifford Odets.[35]

In *Peace on Earth* by Sklar and Maltz, Peter Owens, a liberal professor of economics, attempts to help striking longshoremen who refuse to load munitions for the "next war." During a mass meeting a man is killed, and Owens is charged with murder. When found guilty and sentenced to be hanged, he maintains that he is innocent. But he realizes that if his crime was not murder but, rather, opposition to war and association with workers, then he is guilty. And for such "crimes" he is most willing to die. As guards lead him to execution, a sympathetic workers' demonstration shouts a crescendo.[36] This play, the Theatre Union's first production, contained many "necessary" ingredients of "acceptable" proletarian drama: capitalists as villains, workers as mass hero, police as hirelings, militant radicals as victims of suppression and murder, conversion of a significant individual, and self-sacrifice to the cause.

Stevedore by Peters and Sklar propounded a revolution. A group of black dock workers, aided by a white labor union, stands against the dock company and a mob of "white trash." Lonnie Thompson, the black protagonist, leads the way to the street barricades. He tells his comrades that they must not wait until judgment day or until they are dead. They must fight for the right to live as they wish—now![37] He invokes the revolutionary decision by asking those gathered around him to stand with him and resist. He calls on the willing to raise their hands.[38] Lonnie dies in the gunfire of the first skirmish, but the white mob is routed at the end. Not only did the play agitate successfully about injustice to the black

35. Blankfort and Buchwald, "Social Trends," pp. 128–34.
36. George Sklar and Albert Maltz, *Peace on Earth*, pp. 119–20.
37. Paul Peters and George Sklar, *Stevedore*, p. 109.
38. Peters and Sklar, *Stevedore*, p. 121.

American, but also it hammered out ideas concerning the importance of class unity between black and white workers. As a melodrama, *Stevedore* is one of the best written of the protest plays. Critic Joseph Wood Krutch, certainly not noted as a fellow traveler, called it "uncommonly effective both as melodrama and as propaganda."[39] Marxian critic Michael Gold hailed it as "one of the best, if not the best revolutionary drama that has yet appeared in this country."[40] Many critics in the thirties agreed that it made exciting theatre.

Each of the socially conscious playwrights naturally held his own theories about structure, characterization, thought, and style. Few, however, had acquired enough reputation or were inclined to expound their theories and working practices.

Paul Peters pointed out that the dramatic theory in the working-class theatre during the 1930s began with a concept akin to that of the morality plays. During the first two years of the decade, according to Peters, the leftist playwrights tried and discarded many false theories, such as the theory that, because bourgeois theatre had reached a stalemate, leftist theatre should avoid bourgeois technical equipment. As the leftist playwrights began to develop their art, they modified the agitprop and the mass chant in an attempt to make them subtler and more artistic in form. Peters claimed that the more skilled writers eventually took up those simple forms and brought them to a high literary level of achievement —Langston Hughes, Alfred Kreymborg, Alfred Saxe, and finally Clifford Odets.[41] Paul Peters, Albert Maltz, and George Sklar—all talented writers—subjected them-

39. Joseph Wood Krutch, *The American Drama Since 1918*, p. 153.

40. Michael Gold, Review of *Stevedore* in *New Masses* (May 1, 1934), 28.

41. Paul Peters (presumably), Preface to the section on Drama, in *Proletarian Literature in the United States: An Anthology*, eds. Granville Hicks, Michael Gold, Isidor Schneider, Joseph North, Paul Peters, and Alan Calmer, pp. 261–62.

selves in their writing for the Theatre Union to a theory of collective authorship and to a method of working that involved communal criticism and suggestion.[42] They hoped, by employing such methods, to create plays that were both technically sound and ideologically acceptable to the leftist political authorities.

Michael Blankfort, who wrote *Battle Hymn* with Mike Gold, believed that plays should be constructed as consciously revolutionary pieces that contribute to the audience's political understanding.[43] Mike Gold wrote about the working methods of artists who wanted to endorse the people's revolution. He asserted that art in the past came mostly from solitary artists who were baffled by social questions. The capitalistic system, he wrote, traditionally imprisons such creators so that they brood, suffer, and go mad. He argued, however, that a socially aware artist who joins the workers' movement will not face his destiny alone; such an artist will have the help and encouragement of the masses.[44]

Archibald MacLeish, although frequently attacked by Marxian critics, wrote two noteworthy plays that revealed his social awareness—*Panic,* a stage play, and *The Fall of the City,* a radio play. Writing cogently about the technical problem of creating verse for the stage, he maintained that a playwright must try to discover a form of verse to catch and carry the rhythm of the oral language of his own world. He repudiated English blank verse, which Maxwell Anderson had used, as being satisfactory for the Elizabethans but unsatisfactory for the current American stage, because the rhythm of such verse is too elevated, noble, and slow. He considered the rhythms of contemporary American speech to be rapid, excited, and vivid rather than muscular, deliberate, and proud. American speech, he observed, has vigor and

42. Peters, "On Writing and Selecting Plays," p. 5.

43. Blankfort and Buchwald, "Social Trends," p. 131.

44. Michael Gold, quoted in Introduction, *Proletarian Literature in the United States,* p. 25.

color, beauty and vitality. The solution, then, was not blank verse, but a rhythmic verse that creates an aural sound pattern, a verse that depends more on accents than on syllabic intervals.[45] John Howard Lawson, the leading leftist theorist, praised MacLeish's use of verse in *Panic*, but he pointed out that MacLeish used poetry as an element quite separate from action. Lawson considered MacLeish's poetry a dynamic substitute for action, but he judged MacLeish unable to create conflict in fully theatrical terms.[46] Lawson theorized that, at best, the diction of a play is a sort of action—action compressed and extended verbally.[47]

The Living Newspapers of the Federal Theatre Project came into being in a totally different manner than normal dramatic plays. Each Living Newspaper had a staff similar to that of a large metropolitan daily, with a chief editor, managing and city editors, copyreaders, and reporters. Arthur Arent presided as the editor-playwright of the group. They investigated the circumstances behind conditions rather than surface news. Each of the Living Newspapers was different in history and technique. All, however, depended on a large staff who dug into mountains of details, carted away tons of facts, and then refined the information into an exciting but economical dramatic presentation. The writers and directors attempted to make the productions into dramatic documents full of pantomime and facts. For form they borrowed from many sources, but they particularly depended upon devices from Aristophanes, the *commedia dell' arte*, Shakespearean soliloquy, Mei Lan Fang's pantomimes, the choruses of Greek tragedy, the camera, and the cartoon. They incorporated diverse and unusual elements—formal and factual, concrete and abstract, oral and visual, acrobatic and musical, plus the social, the

---

45. Archibald MacLeish, "A Note on the Verse," as introduction to *Panic, a Play in Verse*, pp. vii–ix.

46. Lawson, *Theory*, p. 193.

47. Lawson, *Theory*, p. 288.

psychological, and the economic.[48] Their commitment was to the reporting of facts to create public awareness.[49]

Three of the most skilled leftist playwrights were also three of the most voluble about their theories of writing—Elmer Rice, Clifford Odets, and John Howard Lawson.

Elmer Rice, writing in 1935, stressed the importance of technique; he believed that technical considerations are more nearly the essence of art than the mere framework for it. But in writing theoretically, he considered himself for the moment a playwright taking on the role of a drama critic, just one more jackdaw who struts around like a peacock. For Rice, the artistic impulse consisted of the need for self-expression and the desire to communicate. He considered craftsmanship, or technique, to be a link between a playwright and his audience. A work of art, he argued, is not a reality but merely an attempt to represent reality through symbols. Three limitations control the writing of any drama: the economic, the physical, and the psychological. Because of economic pressures from managers who need to fill their houses, plays most generally have to be written for the highest economic level of the play-going public, who have the leisure and money to attend the theatre. Plays must be tailored in such a way to make them communicable by actors, directors, and designers—most of whom have serious limitations of intelligence or personality. Plays must be written so that the action can occur in a playhouse; this factor imposes serious limitations on the playwright, who is therefore unable to represent the lushness of flora and fauna, the world of dreams, or a frank treatment of sexual themes. (Rice was writing in 1935.) Finally, an audience is a crowd with a common low intelligence and, with the fear and hostility of a herd of panic-stricken animals, instinctively huddle together

48. Hallie Flanagan, Introduction, *Federal Theatre Plays*, ed. Pierre de Rohan, pp. vii, ix–xi.

49. Arthur Arent, "Technique of the Living Newspaper," *Theatre Arts Monthly*, 22 (November 1938), 820–25.

when faced with anything that threatens the safety of the group. A dramatist is forced, Rice concluded, to create in the midst of a genuine dilemma. And, like all other artists, he wants to project reality as he perceives it. But a playwright must depend on a medium that is interpretative, conventionalized, conservative, and artificial.[50]

At age thirty-three, Clifford Odets wrote a preface to a collection of six of his then recently produced plays. He stated that he had conceived and written the plays out of a personal need.[51] He had sat down and expressed a "state of being" that was sometimes a sense of hurt or a vague mood, an ache or an excitement.[52] He wrote his plays of the thirties to be dynamically and immediately useful but still as psychologically meaningful as possible. By employing his personal insights, he wanted to create a pattern of sensory stimuli and a record of social and personal experiences.[53] Odets wrote all of his Depression plays in conjunction with the Group Theatre. Harold Clurman frequently discussed ideas and scenarios with him, and Clurman helped too with suggestions for revisions.[54] Sometimes Odets wrote his plays rapidly, as he did with *Waiting for Lefty* and *Till the Day I Die*, but at other times he labored over them at length, as with *Paradise Lost*. He often tested pieces of dialogue or scenes by reading them to members of the Group, or by having the actors read for him.[55] Occasionally, he wrote with one or more specific actors in mind, and he always tried to make his plays useful both to the Group Theatre and to mankind.[56] In every age and every place, Odets wrote, the artists who are most valuable to humanity are the

50. Elmer Rice, Introduction, *Two Plays* (New York, 1935), p. v–xviii.

51. Odets, Preface, *Six Plays*, p. x.

52. Quoted in an interview, Michael J. Mendelsohn, "Odets at Center Stage, Part 1," *Theatre Arts* (May 1963), 19.

53. Odets, Preface, *Six Plays*, p. ix.

54. Clurman, *Fervent Years*, pp. 141, 144, 155, 165.

55. Clurman, *Fervent Years*, pp. 104, 141, 144, 152, 165.

56. Mendelsohn, "Odets at Center Stage, Part 2," *Theatre Arts* (June 1963), 29.

ones who insist on the right to view existing mores and institutions most critically.[57]

In *Theory and Technique of Playwriting*, John Howard Lawson discussed the theoretical foundations of his art more intelligently and thoroughly than did any other playwright of the decade. Harold Clurman reported that Lawson wrote his book in order to correct and direct himself as much as any other writers who might be facing a creative impasse.[58] Writing in 1938, critic Anita Block claimed that during the thirties Lawson profoundly influenced those who wrote socially oriented dramas.[59]

Lawson's book resulted from his study of how various dramatists throughout history had utilized the significant thoughts of their own epoch. Clurman wrote that Lawson hoped, through an appraisal of his own ideas, by molding them into a kind of system in harmony with what he thought was the best social wisdom of the time, he could discover a manner of working that would help him out of the swamp of his personal mysticism and psychological anarchy.[60] Lawson identified the three basic principles of play construction as conflict, action, and unity. He acknowledged his debt to Hegel and Brunetière. He wrote that Hegel formulated the "law of tragic conflict," and Brunetière developed it; he himself modified it for the modern stage. Expressed simply, the "law" maintains that a tragic action requires a character with a strong conscious will to strive toward a worthy goal and along the way meet obstacles that cause serious conflict and sometimes defeat. To the concepts of Hegel and Brunetière regarding conflict and the conscious will striving toward a goal, Lawson added social necessity.[61] He insisted that the social structure surrounding a character affects his will and that which he must necessarily per-

57. Clifford Odets, Introduction, *Dead Souls* by Nikolai Gogol (New York, 1936), p. 3.
58. Clurman, *Fervent Years*, p. 158.
59. *The Changing World in Plays and Theatre* (Boston, 1939), p. 285.
60. Clurman, *Fervent Years*, p. 158.
61. Lawson, *Theory*, pp. 87–98.

form as action. A playwright draws material from the world he lives in and thereby attempts to present that world in action. Lawson concluded that a play is a series of actions that the dramatist must make organic. Such actions develop from the relationship between people and their milieu, that is, the relationship between volitional will and social necessity.[62]

The ideas of the social playwrights of the thirties have at least one characteristic in common: they wanted to express a social struggle, whether their own or that of the nation at large. They attempted to establish a societal dialectic of no and yes, of death and life, of despair and hope, of disillusionment and faith, of man and the masses, of revolt and reconstruction. The more conventional playwrights of the decade usually concentrated on one or the other of such dialectic pairs. The leftists strove for a synthesis in human concerns. In their personal lives and by means of their art products, they tried to affect the destiny of their nation. They were in search of a becoming, and their discoveries encouraged them to write didactically. The conflicts that engendered their works did not accidentally arise in their individual lives so much as they arose in the over-all chaos of the time. The fissures in the social and economic world and the troubles of their nation affected their art as well as their lives. The next chapter reveals their intentions regarding the use of specific ideas as organizing elements in their works, and it shows how they tried to formulate plays in rhetorical rather than in mimetic patterns.

Sherwood Anderson, a respected literary figure who was influential among writers in 1934, wrote a foreword to *Peace on Earth* by young George Sklar and Albert Maltz. A fascinating essay in itself, Anderson's foreword offered advice to the young leftist writers of the period. After praising *Peace on Earth*, Anderson wrote that the theatre, like any other art form, should keep trying to raise itself by its own bootstraps. He maintained that

62. Lawson, *Theory*, p. 98.

much can be accomplished if the artists remember the old lessons of discipline and work. People must create instead of merely talking about creating.[63]

63. Sherwood Anderson, Foreword, *Peace on Earth*, George Sklar and Albert Maltz, p. v.

4

Patterns for Protest

The poet's voice need not merely be the record of man,
it can be one of the props, the pillars to help him
endure and prevail.
William Faulkner, Nobel Prize Acceptance Speech

Let me observe in passing that there are more well-written
than well-constructed plays. . . . A good plot is the fruit
of the imagination; good dialogue comes from the
observing of nature.
Denis Diderot, "On Dramatic Poetry"

Each artist must reach his own decision on how art connects with life. As a craftsman, an artist observes and then reshapes the world in his terms. What in nature exists in conglomerate mass—as incidental and transient human experience—appears in art isolated and purified. Art is dynamically willed and permanently organized. In one sense, beauty in art is that which is effective as form. Working to organize his objective creations, an artist subjectively vivifies and humanizes nature in order to construct a world after his own image, or after his own imaginings.

A brief lyric poem, a simple tune, or a quick charcoal sketch may flash into an artist's consciousness in its completed form. Such units as these may be converted into art objects quickly, without much thought or much labor of reshaping. Such a brief line, short pattern of sound, or simple visual image may even act as a magnet around which a larger form takes shape. But for the total creation of a cathedral, a symphony, or a tragedy, such formulative flashes are not enough. Works of great magnitude require elaboration, subconscious nurture, and gradual creation. To no artist at any time does the sense of extended form arrive as a divine gift. The struggle for form commands every true artist as his daily joy and his daily torment. And so too did the dramatists of the Depression era labor to perfect new forms for their dramas.

The chaos, the disorganization, the misery, the overwhelming mass of detail that surrounded the dramatists of the thirties forced them—as the welter of facts ever forces artists—to formulate, to organize, and to arrange their chosen materials. Hubert C. Heffner maintained that "all art to be beautiful and effective must have form."[1] He defined dramatic form as organization, "the shape given to the materials out of which the object is made." What a dramatist formulates is "human action, consisting of what goes on within human beings, what they think and feel, what they do, and what happens to them. These actions make up what are called the incidents of the play and these, too, the dramatist organizes."[2] The framework for his organization exists in the traditional over-all forms of mimetic drama, based on the particular emotional powers of each type—tragedy, comedy, and melodrama.

Although didactic dramatists use human actions as do mimetic dramatists and are as concerned with form, they organize their dramas chiefly by means of thought. Hence to recognize the forms used by the didactic dramatists of the thirties, one must know the predominant ideas that commanded their plays. Chapter 2 indicated their subjects; Chapter 3 revealed their points of view. Here their formulative ideas and the patterns these ideas demanded are explained.

Aristotle defined formal cause as "the form or pattern, i.e. the definition of the essence . . . and the parts included in the definition."[3] The essence of the didactic dramas of the thirties lay in *ideas as form*. Granville

1. Hubert Heffner, Samuel Selden, and Hunton D. Sellman, *Modern Theatre Practice*, 4th ed., p. 56.

2. Heffner, *Modern Theatre Practice*, pp. 56–57.

3. Aristotle, *Metaphysica*, trans. W. D. Ross, in *The Basic Works of Aristotle*, ed. Richard McKeon, p. 752.

Hicks, in his influential survey of literature, connected imagination to experience and truth. He maintained that imagination is the ability to rearrange experiences into new patterns, different from but true to everyday life. For him, imagination was the power to organize simple experience into something more significant.[4] Hicks called for leftist writers who had the ability to formulate literary works according to a certain version of truth. Many playwrights responded by using either their own truths or the ideas of a particular party to organize their plays. Because of the surrounding chaos, the Marxian philosophy—or at least the socialist ideology in general—dominated even the artistic thought of the didactic playwrights of the thirties.

As evidence, the controlling ideas expressed in the playwrights' completed works can be stated in four active verbs: to depict, to exhort, to accuse, to censure. By connecting such verbs with the subjects of the individual plays and with the ideas as stated in dialogue at the climax and resolution, the key operative ideas can be identified as formal controls of the plays. The four verbs establish action as the formulative concept in the mind of each playwright.

To Depict: Lillian Hellman depicted the viciousness of capitalists in *The Little Foxes* and *Days to Come*. The latter play demonstrates the treachery and hypocrisy of the capitalist who wants a strike broken, but without the use of violence. When the leader of the strikebreakers he has hired presents his bill, he refuses payment. The strikebreakers' boss explains that he has broken all sorts of strikes for many different kinds of people, including church deacons, but this is the first time he has ever worked for a man who believes that a strike could be broken without recourse to violence. He drives home his point that strike-breaking is not likely to be a gentle, sweet-smelling affair.[5] *Brass Ankle* by DuBose Heyward and *Hymn to*

4. Granville Hicks, *The Great Tradition: An Interpretation of American Literature Since the Civil War*, 2d ed., p. 298.

5. Lillian Hellman, *Days to Come*, in *Four Plays*, p. 155.

the Rising Sun by Paul Green showed the plight of black men and women, but they offered no definite solutions. *Golden Boy* and *Rocket to the Moon* by Clifford Odets revealed the predicament of the middle class, the immorality of some individuals, and the awakening to responsibility of others. Additional ideas that other playwrights brought forward were: that slums produce criminals, *Dead End* by Sidney Kingsley; that fascism is evil and must be opposed, *The Gentle People* by Irwin Shaw; and that the workers in the medical profession are constantly faced with ethical and social decisions, *Men in White* by Sidney Kingsley. Plays such as these are quite near the critical dividing line between mimetic drama and didactic. Only a careful examination of each play and perhaps some reasoned interpretations on the part of a critic can place them in one species rather than the other. Chapter 6 examines in detail the structures of some of these plays, to point out their characteristics.

To Exhort: The controlling idea in Irwin Shaw's *Bury the Dead* proposes that common men should refuse to fight in the wars declared by their leaders. When six dead soldiers stand up in their graves to protest the evil of war, one of them observes that a grave is a peaceful place containing roots of grass and worms. But, he explains, man deserves a more profound peace than that which comes after death; man deserves peace while he is still alive.[6] *Johnny Johnson* by Paul Green and *Peace on Earth* by Sklar and Maltz also exhort against war. Both plays show honest men beset by the evils of an insane world. Paul Green's solution indicates that every man, as an individual, must decide to oppose war. Sklar and Maltz recommended that everyone join the workers' movement; only thus can war be averted. *If This Be Treason* by John Haynes Holmes and Reginald Lawrence is another antiwar play. Its organizing thesis is that, if

6. Irwin Shaw, *Bury the Dead*, in *The Best Short Plays of the Social Theatre*, ed. William Kozlenko, pp. 59–60.

the general populace of warring countries were given a choice between war and peace, they would always choose peace.[7]

The Living Newspapers were exhortative in a different pattern. Each presented on stage the various conditions of a social problem and some indications about how the problem might be solved. *Triple-A Plowed Under* explained the then current nationwide crisis in agriculture and hinted that, if workers and farmers joined forces to apply political pressure on persons in government, solutions would be found and measures taken to relieve their predicament. *One-Third of a Nation* dealt with housing problems, particularly in metropolitan slum areas, and maintained that some governmental intervention is needed. *Power* favored the Tennessee Valley Authority, whose creation and continuance were then under debate.

A more conventional play, *Life and Death of an American* by George Sklar, exhorts against a variety of the evils of "the system" and focuses on the idea that labor needs to be more assertive in establishing its rights.[8] In a gentle glow of sentiment, Victor Wolfson argued in *Excursion* that people should use courage and vision in their fight for the things they want.[9]

Waiting for Lefty, Stevedore, The Cradle Will Rock, and *Marching Song* are plays dealing with labor strikes. Their exhortative pattern is based on the beliefs that there is a continuing class war between workers and bosses, that all citizens should sympathize with the workers, and that a strike, as a prelude to revolution, is the beginning of a new society. The strike plays, because of their excitement and forceful diction, are the most intensely persuasive of all the didactic plays of the thirties.

Marching Song by John Howard Lawson is one of

7. John Haynes Holmes, Introduction, *If This Be Treason*, John Haynes Holmes and Reginald Lawrence, p. v.

8. George Sklar, *Life and Death of an American*, pp. 142–44.

9. Victor Wolfson, *Excursion* (New York, 1937), p. 183.

the few plays of the period that quite precisely matches the organizational pattern of *socialist realism* fostered by the Marxists. The formula of socialist realism requires belief that a "good" worker is inevitably converted to communism because of the oppression of "evil" capitalists, that private distress is invariably the result of "the system," that workers—because they are right—ultimately conquer the bosses, and that a strike is a "rehearsal" for revolution. All these elements and more are present in Lawson's play.

In general, all the exhortative plays concentrate on either information or protest. That they are didactic is seldom difficult to perceive. They are examined structurally in Chapter 7, as the plays of depiction are analyzed in Chapter 6.

To Accuse: The plays of accusation attack either individuals or society as "the system." Elmer Rice's play *We, the People* accuses society of being unjust. The play is a dictionary of the schisms of the time. Its controlling idea appears most clearly in the final speech, a long persuasive statement made by a major character, a man named Sloane. The play ends when, speaking directly to the theatre audience, Sloane claims that no socio-economic system that destroys the right of its citizens to live in liberty has a right to exist. He then makes a direct appeal to the audience by pointing out that they are, after all, the populace of the United States. And it is up to the citizens of this country to cleanse it and to turn it into a decent place for decent human beings.[10] *1931*— by Claire and Paul Sifton is another play that rages against "the system," especially those conditions that cause unemployment.

Three courtroom plays of the thirties are especially good examples of the drama of accusation. Elmer Rice's *Judgment Day* characterizes the fascist movement in Europe as unjust and dishonorable. It straightforwardly condemns the countries where fascism was then rising

10. Elmer Rice, *We, the People*, p. 253.

to power. In those countries, the play argues, justice is dead and liberty no longer exists.[11] The racial injustices and the economic prejudices possible under the American legal system are the effective ideas at the heart of *They Shall Not Die* by John Wexley. *Precedent* by I. J. Golden also claims that the judicial system needs modification. All the plays of accusation are thoroughly analyzed in Chapter 8.

To Censure: Some playwrights of the time organized their dramas to censure one or more of the following kinds of elements: (1) individuals who represent an economic class; (2) groups, movements, and parties; or (3) ideas and ideologies. Some plays of censure touch all three. *Black Pit* by Albert Maltz is perhaps the best, certainly the most serious, of these plays. *Black Pit* censures an individual who symbolizes all those who betray the workers' movement. The play examines the motives of a coal miner who becomes an informer for a predatory coal company. In presenting this man's fall from honor, *Black Pit* comes the nearest to being a true tragedy of any of the didactic plays of the period. The play proposes the idea that no matter what the cost—loss of job, home, family, even death—workers must be faithful to each other and to their common political cause.[12]

Clifford Odets' *Paradise Lost* and *Awake and Sing!* censure the hypocrisy and the limitations of the entire middle class. His characters are representative of the degeneracy, the impotency, the ineffectiveness, the rapacity, and the evil of the class. Some of his people, however, merit admiration, because they are capable of making personal and social discoveries that lead them to join the workers' movement in order to build a better future.

Success Story and *Gold Eagle Guy* place blame on individuals who represent capitalism. John Howard Lawson's *Success Story* offers the idea that every man has a choice between the radical path or the capitalist highway.

11. Elmer Rice, *Judgment Day*, in *Seven Plays*, pp. 367–68.
12. Albert Maltz, *Black Pit*, pp. 104–8.

Central character Sol Ginsburg chooses the latter and thereby ruins his life. Capitalistic success, the play says, is nourished by the sorrow and failure of others; further, it provides only a living death for those who succeed. *Gold Eagle Guy* by Melvin Levy pictures a sailor-become-capitalist. He becomes completely dehumanized as he exploits and cheats his associates. The real villains are his own greed and the capitalistic system that permits that greed to indulge itself. *The Pure in Heart* and *Gentlewoman* by Lawson are also plays of this type. The idea at the center of *The Pure in Heart*, the success story of an actress, is that those who succumb to the commercial system are destroyed. At the play's end, Annabel realizes that the money and the glitter of success are not as important as love. She chooses to destroy herself because the love she finds has come too late to save her inner spirit.[13] *Gentlewoman* is more deeply rooted in the issues of the Depression. The accusations in this play are directed toward capitalism itself. The lovely and sensitive heroine, Gwen, is the gentle woman of the title. She is doomed because of her connection with the decadent system rather than through any choice of her own.

Other plays of censure also attack the totalitarianism of the capitalistic philosophy or of the Nazi movement. *Panic* by Archibald MacLeish censures a capitalist business magnate. *Margin for Error*, perhaps the most comic of the didactic plays, was Clare Boothe's statement against the heartlessness and evil of the Nazi party, of German society in the late thirties, and of all the leaders of the Nazis. *Till the Day I Die* by Clifford Odets censures Nazi fascism and praises communism. It is the most violent of this group. The plays of censure are analyzed structurally in Chapter 9.

These four motivating verbs—to depict, to exhort, to accuse, and to censure—can be used to identify the active forms of didactic plays. They can also serve as

13. John Howard Lawson, *The Pure in Heart*, in *With a Reckless Preface*, pp. 98–110.

keys for the classification of didactic structures and are so used in Chapters 6, 7, 8, and 9. Didactic plays that simply depict certain conditions within individuals or in society are usually quite like mimetic plays in structure. But plays that exhort, accuse, or censure are structurally more like the three major kinds of persuasive speeches; they correspond to the three classical types of rhetoric— deliberative, forensic, and epideictic. Exhortative plays are like deliberative, or political, speeches; plays of accusation resemble forensic, or legal, oratory; and plays of censure are structurally similar to epideictic, or ceremonial, speeches.

The four types are not the only categories in which didactic dramas can be placed. They are listed here simply as being useful for making critical distinctions between the various didactic plays. Too, they are useful in revealing the structural patterns of individual plays. The three rhetorical types described by Aristotle in his *Rhetoric* are especially helpful in hinting at particular concepts of structure in obviously persuasive plays. If the didactic plays of the thirties were intended to be, or work at all as, persuasive "speeches," then rhetorical considerations are valid as tools for investigation and perhaps as criteria for judgment.

The plays of exhortation correspond to Aristotle's political rhetoric.[14] Such deliberative speeches deal with encouraging or discouraging good opinion of ideas and policies. They are directed toward inculcating useful attitudes for the future and expedient or inexpedient attitudes that control human actions. Such speeches deal with ways and means, with the advisability of a certain course of action, with an examination of conditions that produce unhappiness in the present and the potentials for happiness in the future, and with analysis of ethical behavior in particular instances. Deliberative speeches employ lines of arguments that point to future facts or to the possi-

14. Aristotle, *Rhetoric*, trans. W. Rhys Roberts, Book I, Chapters 3, 4, 5, 6.

bilities and impossibilities of future conditions. These principles are tested in Chapter 7 upon such plays as *Waiting for Lefty, Bury the Dead,* and *One-Third of a Nation.*

The plays of accusation correspond to Aristotle's forensic rhetoric.[15] Forensic, or legal, speeches usually concern accusation of persons and defense of their actions. The goal of the speech is to establish the justice or injustice of an act performed in the past and to bring about a just decision. In forensic speeches, the most important subjects tend to be crimes, legal suits, and operative laws. Whether the concern of such a speech has to do with deliberate evil or with wrongdoing that is a warped pleasure, the speaker usually takes note of motives, perpetrators, and victims. Proof is crucial in this sort of speech, and because it involves established laws it is often deductive. The lines of argument extend backward in time to past facts in order to establish probability of actions and motives or to establish possibility or impossibility of past facts. Chapter 8 utilizes forensic principles of rhetoric in its structural examination of such plays as *We, the People, They Shall Not Die,* and *Judgment Day.*

The plays of censure correspond to Aristotle's epideictic rhetoric.[16] Epideictic, or ceremonial, speeches normally contain praise or blame as their chief substance. In the twentieth century, most epideictic speeches are written to praise a man, an organization, an institution, or a way of life. They are usually speeches of celebration. In ancient times, however, speeches of blame were as frequent as those of praise, and even today some of these negative speeches are delivered—customarily in social or political demonstrations. The object of all epideictic speeches is to establish nobleness or its reverse for the present time. Such speeches deal with honor and dishonor by pointing to the virtues or vices of men, organizations,

15. Aristotle, *Rhetoric,* Book I, Chapters 3 and 10.
16. Aristotle, *Rhetoric,* Book I, Chapters 3 and 9.

or institutions. They usually employ amplification and diminution as methods for their praise or their censure, and their argument is most often one of degree. Chapter 9 applies epideictic principles to the didactic drama of the thirties, using such plays as *Black Pit*, *Success Story*, and *Margin for Error* for examples.

* * * * *

Form was the most troublesome problem of composition with which each of the didactic playwrights of the thirties wrestled. They knew what they wanted to say, but they had to discover new ways to say it. Their materials were close at hand in the social chaos of their world. They viewed the societal problems with confident political attitudes. But in order to propound the truths they wished to announce, they had to perfect new forms of drama.

To intensify their problems, formalism was, during the thirties, a political offense for any leftist artist. Formalism meant form for form's sake, form with little political content, or form with "incorrect" political content. Formalism, as nonempirical geometrical art, was to be avoided. The Marxian critics used the term *formalism* as one of reproach whenever they identified an overly conscious concern with formal beauty or with the employment of nonsocialist content.

Granville Hicks warned the Depression writers to avoid playing literary games in the manner of Henry James. He asked: "Is not James's world a world of almost complete abstractions, in which he invents the situations and the people, and only the technique is constant? Grant that he was a master of the game, and that the game, if one consents to abide by the rules, is fascinating to play; it is still a game." [17] But in their individual ways, the leftist dramatists attempted to translate the conditions created by the industrialized, economically

17. Hicks, *Great Tradition*, pp. 121–22.

dependent society into terms of social truth and formulary solutions. In Stephen Spender's words, the socially oriented writers of the time worked to gain "an inner control of a creative pattern over their external environment."[18] By organizing the mass of deplorable detail in American life, by applying certain leftist ideas as controls, and by using persuasion as an active purpose, the leftist writers indeed projected a vision of life and humanity that was unique and valuable. Their individual and collective vision, since it was socially active, is treated in the next chapter as it related to the major purposes of the playwrights. The didactic dramatists equated, as have so many artists, what is true of an individual with what is true of humanity.

As the Depression decade waned, the forms and thoughts its writers perfected began to be assimilated into the organs of dramatic art, to become accepted practice. Thus, the achievements of the socially aware dramatists in the matter of form are now a part of our dramatic tradition, even though present-day writers are sometimes unwilling to acknowledge the direction of their indebtedness. Clifford Odets attested to this churlishness when he said, "Our literary people have very bad manners. They don't have the European grace, the European sense of one thing passing on from one decade to another, one generation to another, and acknowledging it, or approaching it with some sense of gratitude or some sense of wanting to tell."[19]

The achievements of the leftist playwrights of the thirties were considerable. Their accomplishments loom large in a comparative review of the drama of the war decade that immediately followed the Depression. In the sixties, many American playwrights—among them, LeRoi Jones, Megan Terry, Donald Freed, and Jean-Claude van Itallie—wrote didactic plays directly in the tradition of

18. Stephen Spender, *The Creative Element: A Study of Vision, Despair and Orthodoxy Among Some Modern Writers*, p. 192.

19. Quoted in Michael J. Mendelsohn, "Odets at Center Stage, Part 2," *Theatre Arts* (June 1963), 30 and 78.

the committed dramas of the thirties. At the beginning of the seventies it is apparent that the innovations the Depression playwrights made in the realm of didactic drama have continued as significant influences on contemporary dramatic technique. The leftist playwrights of the Depression era assume an ever more exemplary role as contemporary writers again become aware of their potential roles, not as social philosophers, but as Furies to the public conscience. "Achievements of intellect, art, and passion," Spender declared, "are worth the sacrifice of living they involve, because they take their place in a pattern of all life."[20]

20. Spender, *Creative Element*, p. 124.

5

The Didactic Vision

The theatre is the only means of moral or artistic education a nation possesses.
Jean Giraudoux, "A Lecture on Theatre"

My property is form, it is my spiritual individuality.
The style is the man.
Karl Marx, "On Style"

Every artist creates by utilizing his own imaginative vision of human existence. For artists and for appreciators of their work, art is a principal means of creating human values. Indeed, the construction of art objects survives as one of the few methods for establishing the virtues of human life that have not yet been spoiled. The vision of a playwright, as revealed in his work, equals the organized totality of his sensations, feelings, and thoughts. An individual's vision encompasses a circular panorama of an expanse of life, with himself as the center. For an artist, such a panoramic view passes through the prism of a central idea in his mind in order to become an image in his work. The authority of any writer's vision depends upon the conviction that his central experience can, if recorded, imply a circumference of much wider life. The magnitude of a playwright's vision depends upon how widely he searches and how carefully he selects the central image for each of his dramas in order to imply a full conception of the world.

The Depression playwrights of protest encompassed in their vision the desolation in human experience, but they do not stand alone in their revelations. Other authors have written in the same spirit. *Woyzeck* by Georg Büchner is equally desolate. The awareness of spiritual aridity burns as intensely in the plays of Frank Wedekind and

August Strindberg as it does in those of John Howard Lawson or George Sklar. If the playwrights of the Depression predicted disaster, they were writing in the pattern of many of their predecessors—Euripides, for a distinguished example. But theirs was a unique vision in its combination of desolation, spiritual barrenness, and prophecy of disaster and its faith in collectivist philosophy. Although these playwrights tasted the bitterness of life in the Depression, their accomplishments grew, paradoxically perhaps, from their strangely enthusiastic and optimistic affirmation of the worth of man, of his resiliency of spirit, and of collective rebellion for the perfection of society. Sometimes, as in John Howard Lawson's plays of the thirties, their affirmation projected an orthodoxy—the dialectic of the collective. At times, as in the intellectually forthright plays of Elmer Rice, the modern individualist vision rejected the orthodoxy of any party and set up a dialectic of the solitary man. And at other times, as in the sensitive work of Clifford Odets, a writer's vision combined an orthodox philosophy with a humanist attitude, thus permitting him to develop a dialectic of the human.

To reach a full vision of life that would activate their work, the thirties' playwrights had to separate their personal values from the values of society around them, whether their tools of separation were labeled individualism, dialectical materialism, or simple humanism. In the plays of these dramatists, no less than in the plays of an Ibsen or a Brieux, there is the insight into impalpable truths that is essential to great art.

The vision of the playwrights—individually and collectively—stands as the final cause of the genesis of the didactic drama in the Depression era. Aristotle defined final cause as "the end, i.e. that for the sake of which a thing is."[1]

The playwrights of the thirties assessed the costs of

1. Aristotle, *Metaphysica*, trans. W. D. Ross, in *The Basic Works of Aristotle*, ed. Richard McKeon, p. 752.

contemporary existence in measures of human frustrations and sufferings. Their measuring instruments were not the teaspoons of the century's earlier decades, but rather the spades and scoops of the working class. Their goals were to locate and relieve the burdens borne by the masses in the oppressed social, economic, and political groups. They labored, by means of their art, to help such groups achieve understanding of their world, realize a full sense of life, alleviate their own sufferings, and fulfill their social aspirations.

The innovative dramatists of the period refused to write about life according to preconceived, traditional literary patterns. Instead, they developed new forms to reflect the aspects of life each writer knew personally. They strove to expose the contradictions between the declared ideals and the shabby realities in American life. They expressed states of mind, scenes, environments, and languages of America that had never been satisfactorily expressed. An America new to the stage appeared in the theatre—the life of sharecroppers, of persecuted blacks, of immigrants, of union organizers and labor leaders, and of "the bottom dog." With a revolutionary ladle they dipped to the economic and social depths of the American melting pot.

Those dramatists who worked to create genuinely valuable art tried to discover the underground currents of historical change moving beneath the crust of surface opinions, orthodoxies, heresies, gossip, and journalistic dirt. They tried to bring to view the simple and real needs of common men and women. True, some Depression dramatists were propagandists in the most limited sense of the word and used their abilities for partisan invective or personal vituperation. But most of the playwrights retained their personal freedom and despised the hacks of all parties. The living material out of which these writers created came to them in the rough. They saw the need to disseminate the truth about the chaotic life of the times, and they attempted to whittle to exactitude the paterns of men's instincts and compulsions, hungers and thirsts, needs and desires—all in the context of social upheaval.

The best of the playwrights, as their artistic progress during the decade reveals, agreed with John Dos Passos when he said that it mattered little "from how narrow a set of convictions" a writer starts. He will find himself if his efforts lead him to "probe deeper and deeper into men and events" and "less and less able to work with the minute prescriptions of doctrine." If a writer works genuinely with insight and intelligence, he will align himself with increasing closeness "on the side of the men, women and children right now against all the contraptions and organizations, however magnificent their aims may be, that bedevil them," and he will be "on the side, not with phrases or opinions, but really and truly, of liberty, fraternity, and humanity."[2]

The form and effectiveness of art vary, of course, with the experience of the creators. And its so-called sanctions vary, too, with the creators' experiences. The social playwrights of the thirties interpreted their experiences and the experiences of the masses of men in terms of contemporary social and political concepts. They considered these more interesting, more significant, more "normal" than the highly personal concepts of other eras. They thought of social ideas as corresponding to the general experience of man and were acutely conscious of the violent social transformations through which they were living. They hoped through their works to help direct both the processes and results of those transformations. It is easy to understand why the intellectuals who were sympathetic to the working class—themselves victims of the general socioeconomic crisis—should be more interested in unemployment, strikes, the fight against war, the rise of fascism, and the spread of revolutionary spirit than they were in the June moon, the romantic vicissitudes of growing up, or the story of boy-meets-girl in Greenwich Village. They wanted to wipe the whipped

2. John Dos Passos, "The Writer as Technician," *American Writers' Congress*, ed. Henry Hart, p. 82.

cream off the American stage and to stack on the apron bushels of potatoes and sides of beef and to pass them out to an audience who had walked to the theatre rather than to an audience who had ridden there in the latest-model Deusenberg.

While fighting oppression and working strenuously for a sane organization of society, these playwrights did not neglect the defense of freedom. They demanded the liberties of investigation, speech, and discussion while attempting to find some effective means to stimulate America's search for freedom for all and to instill humane values in its government. Their aim was not so much to convert as to convince. They struggled as vigorously as has any group of American artists to discern the relationship of art and society, of art and science, of art and economics, of art and action. If they favored revolt, it was revolt for the sake of liberating the human spirit and not —for most—to overthrow the United States government.

The playwrights themselves sometimes explained the purposes of their drama of protest in nondramatic works. Of the entire group, Elmer Rice and John Howard Lawson wrote most prolifically about their attitudes and their art. Rice expressed the view of liberal, generally committed writers when he wrote that he simply was "interested in the drama as an art form, a social force and a medium for the expression of ideas." Describing *We, the People*, Rice defined the purpose of liberal writers. He explained the play as a "panoramic presentation of the economic-social situation in America, an exposé of the forces of reaction which stand in the way of a better life for the masses of the American people and a plea for a return to the principles enunciated in the Declaration of Independence and the Constitution."[3]

Paul Green, another nonorthodox, liberal playwright, stated his vision metaphorically: "Yes, like a mighty tree, old life keeps pumping us up in sap from below to spill out as long as time shall last in rich fruit-

3. Elmer Rice, "Apologia Pro Vita Sua, Per Elmer Rice," *New York Times* (December 25, 1938), IX, 3 and 5.

fulness at the top. If some of the twigs do freeze and die, the main and leafy wonder still goes on."[4] In explaining his purposes, Green wrote that America has done and will continue to do great and noble things, and he added that, as a philosophy, democracy requires full-grown, morally responsible, and ethically mature men. He asserted that humanity marches steadily toward the goal of freedom and that our country is beginning to make its fourth adventure—the adventure into the realm of culture. He wanted his plays to be a call for man's future accomplishments.[5] The purposes of such dramatists as Elmer Rice and Paul Green—also Lillian Hellman, Irwin Shaw, and Sidney Kingsley—were certainly individualist and broadly humanitarian, no matter how didactically liberal some of their plays might have been during the Depression.

No less honest or admirable, if far less inclined toward individualism, were the convictions of the didactic playwrights who stood further to the left during that time of crisis—men such as Clifford Odets, Albert Maltz, George Sklar, Paul Peters, and John Howard Lawson. Odets stated his belief in the functional nature of art on several occasions. He declared that "the truth followed to its logical conclusion is inevitably revolutionary."[6] During the thirties he tried to write plays that were immediately functional because he was existing at a time when all works of art should fire bullets.[7] The avowed purpose of Maltz, Sklar, and Peters, in their joint undertakings, was well summarized in the announcement made in 1933 when the Theatre Union, for which they were the chief writers, established itself as a producing organization. Their manifesto stated that they wanted to produce plays that would deal "boldly with the deep-going social conflicts, the economic, emotional and cultural problems that confront the majority of the people." Their plays would

4. Paul Green, *The Hawthorn Tree*, p. 70.
5. Green, *Hawthorn Tree*, pp. 70, 75, 77, 79–80.
6. *New York World Telegram* (March 19, 1935), 16.
7. Clifford Odets, Preface, *Six Plays of Clifford Odets*, p. ix.

"speak directly to this majority, whose lives usually are caricatured or ignored on the stage"; they would not "fall into the accepted social patterns." Theirs was to be "a new kind of professional theatre, based on the interests and hopes of the great mass of working people."[8]

Albert Maltz gave his version of the slogan "Art is a weapon" to be not that "art is a weapon like a leaflet, serving immediate political ends," but rather a weapon insofar as it reflects or attacks social values.[9] Paul Peters announced his purpose to write a good revolutionary play that presented class struggle, clear action, and a militant solution.[10] He would help create a workers' theatre by writing plays that voiced the hopes of the working class, plays that functioned directly as weapons.[11] John Howard Lawson, in many ways the most militant of all the playwrights, stated in 1934 that he planned "to serve the revolutionary working class" both in his writing and in his practical, political activity.[12] In 1936 he wrote that the primary objective of drama is communication and that a play issues from the essence of a writer's will and consciousness. According to Lawson, a playwright attempts to persuade an audience to share his emotion about the meaning of his play's action. The identification of an audience with the play is not only the acceptance of the action's reality, but also of its message.[13]

Such were the avowed purposes of the playwrights of the extreme left. To be sure, there were other dramatists who stood between the individualist stance of Rice and the collective position of Lawson. But all wrote di-

8. Quoted in Anita Block, *The Changing World in Plays and Theatre*, p. 275.

9. *New Masses* (February 12, 1946), 19–20.

10. Paul Peters, "On Writing and Selecting Plays for Workers," *Daily Worker* (February 27, 1935), 5.

11. Paul Peters (presumably), Preface to the section on Drama, *Proletarian Literature in the United States*, eds. Granville Hicks, Michael Gold, Isidor Schneider, Joseph North, Paul Peters, and Alan Calmer, pp. 263–64.

12. *New Masses* (April 17, 1934), 29.

13. John Howard Lawson, *Theory and Technique of Playwriting*, p. 299.

dactically when they became aware of the potentials of art as a tool for persuasion. They envisioned a drama that would treat the social questions of the decade, dramatize the conflicts between social groups, and side with common people against repressive forces.[14]

*　　*　　*　　*　　*

A description of the milieu in which the didactic plays of the thirties were written would be incomplete without an important consideration—the audience. Since this study focuses upon didactic plays as art objects and purports to investigate their structural principles, the conventional gauges of a play's success or failure are inappropriate. For the plays of any age, length of run in a commercial theatre or the amount of money earned—in a word, popularity—cannot be related to their artistic merit or structural perfection. An economic analysis of the didactic plays of the thirties is therefore interesting but not essential here. Nevertheless, since the plays were indeed meant to persuade and since they were aimed at certain theatregoers, some notice of the extent and composition of their audiences will reveal the success of their writers' purposes. To know what audiences the playwrights addressed and to know what effect they hoped their plays would produce will also help to define those purposes.

The didactic playwrights usually analyzed the audiences toward which they directed their plays. Most of them wanted to reach ordinary working people who did not habitually attend the commercial theatre in New York. The writers and the producing organizations, therefore, tried to reduce ticket prices so that masses of common people could and would go to the theatre, there to absorb the plays' messages.

Harold Clurman's program note for the Group Theatre's second production, *1931–*, expressed the attitudes of many liberal producers and playwrights. In it he ex-

14. Ben Blake, *The Awakening of the American Theatre*, p. 27.

plained that every theatre organization should try to create its own unique audience. If a theatre succeeds in doing so, it will have an audience that genuinely identifies itself with a theatre. Then, both artists and audiences can sense that they are truly related to each other. Only together can people create theatre as a true art. To create such an atmosphere was the Group's major objective.[15]

Hallie Flanagan, director of the Federal Theatre Project, realized that the general American public had never been able to afford going to the professional theatre and that during the Depression "a great many other people who had previously regarded theatre as recreation and education were forced to give it up."[16] She believed that, since the Federal Theatre Project was tax supported, it should be a people's theatre. With such encouragement, the Federal Theatre became the home of many leftist writers and didactic plays during the thirties. It offered free productions for under-privileged groups, and in rare cases low admissions of 10¢, 25¢, and 50¢, and never more than $1.00.[17]

The theatre organizations of the far left strove to establish a proletarian audience composed of "longshoremen, clerks, coal miners, doctors, cooks, poets, laundresses, professional reviewers, steel puddlers, lawyers, starving idle people."[18] The Theatre Union announced at their opening that they had "established a low price scale so that the masses of people who have been barred by high prices can attend the theatre."[19] The didactic playwrights wrote with the intents of their production organizations well in mind—Clifford Odets with the Group Theatre, Arthur Arent with the Federal Theatre Project, and George Sklar with Theatre Union. Most of these

15. Harold Clurman, *The Fervent Years: The Story of the Group Theatre and the Thirties*, p. 72.

16. Hallie Flanagan, *Arena: The History of the Federal Theatre*, p. 13.

17. Flanagan, *Arena*, pp. 35 and 236.

18. *New Theatre* (January 1934), 2.

19. Blake, *Awakening*, p. 35.

socially conscious playwrights recognized, as did John Howard Lawson, that, for their plays to succeed, they must consider the social composition of the audience. Most of the leftist plays were written with the realization of the class character of the conventional Broadway audience, rejection of their standards, and a hope to establish a theatre of the people.[20]

The reaction of audiences to the plays was at times —especially on opening nights—excited and overwhelmingly favorable. John Gassner reported that the audience at the opening of *Stevedore* was "whipped into a frenzy" that "brought the house down."[21] Harold Clurman noted that with the Group Theatre's production of *1931–* came a genuine fervor in the nightly reception accorded the play, especially by the people of the lower economic strata who packed the balcony.[22] And stories abound in print—even by word of mouth over thirty-five years later—about the excited reaction of audiences to Odets' *Waiting for Lefty*. Clurman's report of the opening night of *Waiting for Lefty* is enthusiastically lyric. He claimed that the audience and actors became one, as one line after another stimulated applause, whistles, and shouts of encouragement. For him and his friends, *Waiting for Lefty* represented "the birth cry of the thirties"; they shouted "strike for greater dignity, strike for a bolder humanity, strike for the full stature of man." That night the audience stormed the stage at the end of the performance, and during many subsequent performances the audiences became nearly delirious in their awakened awareness and confidence.[23]

As a group, however, the didactic dramas of the thirties failed to create either a sizable audience of workers or a large audience of any kind. Apparently, most middle-class and upper-class theatre patrons did not like

20. Lawson, *Theory*, p. 302.

21. John Gassner, "American Social Theatre in the Thirties," in *Theatre and Drama in the Making*, eds. John Gassner and Ralph G. Allen, Vol. II, p. 993.

22. Clurman, *Fervent Years*, p. 71.

23. Clurman, *Fervent Years*, p. 148.

social dramas, and the lower economic class either would not be persuaded to go to a theatre at all, or else they preferred the escapist entertainment of the then rapidly growing motion picture industry. In a carefully documented book, Morgan Himelstein concluded that during the thirties the Communists failed to turn drama into a good or effective weapon because "they were unable to control either the playwrights or the audience."[24]

Few of the didactic plays ran very long, and most did not pay off their production expenses. The following list presents in numerical terms the success or failure—measured in performances—of some of the leading didactic plays:

Play	Season	Performances[25]
Precedent	1930–31	184
1931–	1931–32	12
We, the People	1932–33	49
Gentlewoman	1933–34	12
Peace on Earth	1933–34	144
Stevedore	1933–34	71
They Shall Not Die	1933–34	62
Black Pit	1934–35	85
Awake and Sing!	1934–35	209
Judgment Day	1934–35	93
Waiting for Lefty	1934–35 and 1935–36	168
Paradise Lost	1935–36	73
Marching Song	1936–37	61
Power	1936–37	99
Johnny Johnson	1936–37	68
One-Third of a Nation	1937–38 and 1938–39	237
Life and Death of an American	1938–39	29
Margin for Error	1939–40	264

24. Morgan Y. Himelstein, *Drama Was a Weapon: The Left-Wing Theatre in New York*, pp. 230–32.

25. These statistics were taken from Burns Mantle's volumes of the best plays of each season from 1929–1930 through 1939–1940.

Such "bourgeois" plays as *You Can't Take It with You*, *Boy Meets Girl*, and *Abie's Irish Rose* far outran the total performances of the entire group of didactic, nonmusical plays. It is true that *Pins and Needles*, a "red" review; *Tobacco Road*, an adaptation from a social novel; and *Dead End* were long-running socially oriented productions. But these long runs were the results of an exaggerated emphasis on their theatrical, comic, and sensational aspects rather than their social content. A few of the didactic plays had repeat performances after their first professional runs, but not many. *Waiting for Lefty* was probably played more times by more groups during the thirties than any of the other leftist plays, and it reappears occasionally in the seventies. It has had a long and tempestuous career, arousing bureaucratic indignation on the political right and cheers of approval on the political left.

The social theatre of the thirties no doubt reached many new segments of audience, especially with the advent of the Federal Theatre Project, the organization that presented its productions with the lowest ticket prices and the best publicity. Characterizing the new audience for the Project's plays, a member of that audience wrote in *Federal Theatre Magazine*: "We're a hundred thousand kids who never saw a play before. We're students in colleges, housewives in the Bronx, lumberjacks in Oregon, sharecroppers in Georgia."[26] However fervid the audience reaction to the didactic plays, they were not financially successful, for the enthusiasm was sporadic and limited. The extent of the leftist theatre movement was actually small when compared to the total theatrical output of the decade. But at the same time, the social theatre was the most stirring and noteworthy germ in the entire body of the Fabulous Invalid.

*　　*　　*　　*　　*

26. Quoted in Harold Clurman, "Groups, Projects, Collectives . . . ," *Theatre Arts* (September 1960), 18.

A description of the didactic drama of the Depression era, as offered in Part I of this book, sets the stage for a thorough understanding of the analyses of individual plays in Part II. The preceding genesis discloses the basic motivations that brought this specific set of didactic dramas into being. "The nature of a thing is a beginning," Aristotle wrote, "and so is the element of a thing, and thought and will, and essence, and the final cause—for the good and the beautiful are the beginning both of knowledge and of the movement of many things."[27]

The material cause of the didactic drama comprised such Depression subjects as the economic collapse, the life of the bottom dog, the persecution of minorities, the class and labor conflicts, the rise of fascism, and the spread of war. The efficient cause was the commitment of the playwrights to multiform social concern, to political systems and parties, and to theatre groups as well as the writers' intellectual points of view about materials. The formal cause of the didactic drama in general relates to the type of rhetorical form selected for it, whether depiction, exhortation, accusation, or censure. The final cause for the dramas of the Depression existed in the visions and purposes of the playwrights, in their search for meaning, and in their intent to convince if not convert. They attempted to identify and destroy the causes of the violent disorder in society. That, in their pursuit of a persuasive end, they also created noteworthy art is coming more and more to be recognized. Their work, however, should not be glamorized nor praised out of proportion to its real accomplishments. The plays stand more as road markers in the progress of the social drama of ideas rather than as models of a universal pattern for the writing of such plays. The revolutionary energy these playwrights generated in their works was in many ways their greatest achievement. That fervor, combined with their optimistic search for the human values that for the communal good connect man to man, tends to lift their work

27. Aristotle, *Metaphysica*, p. 752.

to a place of significance in the twentieth-century attempt to stimulate the cultural heart of civilization.

Numerous critics smugly write off the committed drama of the thirties with little more than the label *didactic* and a deprecating smile. Should they dismiss Euripides, Dante, Spenser, Milton, Shaw, and Brecht in a like manner, simply because they let their rhetorical purposes show? Although most of the didactic dramatists of the thirties would not pretend to close comparison with such masters, for my purposes here the question is apt. Since a surprising proportion of drama from Greece's Golden Age to the present has been more rhetorical than poetic, and since at least in part of the world much of mid-twentieth-century drama is didactic, contemporary critics are obligated to examine the nature of poetic didacticism. Too few critics or directors of plays can identify the intrinsic differences between a didactic and a mimetic play. Viewing the drama of the thirties from the precipice on which we stand today, it appears that to wait for Lefty is at least as exciting as to wait for Godot and that to work for peace on earth is at least as worth while as to celebrate cascades of hair.

Thought in society, especially that which is capable of impelling social change, is constantly altering. Thus, the preachers of new thought must speak out. Of course, society does not exist solely to argue and exchange ideas. But ideas—their gradual development, embellishment, and popularization—are vitally important because they must always precede change in everyday existence. A situation creates a societal need; the need is recognized; solutions are conceived; and finally a change is effected to satisfy or extenuate the need. Hence, after a period of stasis comes a period of recognition and struggle, and out of that period arises the one during which the ideas and solutions must be actualized. From stasis to thought to action, this is the recurring pattern. If the twenties were stasis, if the thirties were recognition and struggle, and if the forties were action, where do we stand today in the repetitive evolutionary pattern?

Whether or not, in our reading or producing, we listen to the strident voices of the thirties, we can certainly learn from them that important interrelationships function between the subjective and objective worlds. We can learn from them also that the individual must affirm the human purposes of existence. Man evidently needs to reaffirm for each generation that the world is singular and plural, degrading and beautiful, uncertain and predictable, warlike and peaceful, and physically and spiritually both a torment and a pleasure.

Part II:
Analysis of the Drama of Attack

*With his principles a man seeks either to dominate,
or justify, or honor, or reproach, or conceal his habits:
two men with the same principles probably seek
fundamentally different ends therewith.*
Friedrich Nietzsche, *Beyond Good and Evil*

6

Manifestoes in Melodrama

A work of art need not contain any statement of a political
or of a social or of a philosophical conviction,
but it nearly always implies one.
Ezra Pound, *Patria Mia*

The dramatists of the Depression interpreted their mission as a struggle against a conspiracy to destroy the significance of being human. Their works are essentially
attempts to make art triumph over social misfortunes.
Further, most of them behave as comments on the words
in their plays—a reversal of the way actions of characters
comment on the words they speak. But like all dedicated
artists, the best of these playwrights invested their
greatest energies in specific works. The nature of those
works best illustrates the writers' aesthetic theories and
practices.

Many of the didactic plays of the Depression resemble conventional mimetic plays. The dianoetic or
thought-controlled plays analyzed in this chapter skirt
the border between the mimetic and didactic species. In
general, their authors intended them *to depict*. They
meant for the plays to present a picture or an image of
life from which the ideas might be deduced by the intelligent playgoer. These plays reveal their didacticism
when the complex of thought each contains is identified
in relation to the other materials. Although thought is
the ultimate control in these plays, each employs many
organizational principles that to some degree help the
work to imitate an action. Thought acts both as control
and sometimes as material to plot and character.

More specifically, all the thirteen dianoetic plays
mentioned in this chapter closely resemble mimetic melodramas. Because they use many features of that form,

including a strong story, they might well be identified as dramatic fables. A moral can be stated to epitomize each. And for a thorough understanding of their structure, the traditional principles of mimetic melodrama are useful.

Melodrama utilizes a serious action, one that usually arises because an "evil" character threatens a "good" character. The situation is, however, temporary, and the "good" character is happy at the end of the play. The ending is, in fact, one of the key means to identify a melodrama. The best ending for a melodrama is a double one: the unsympathetic characters are punished and the sympathetic ones rewarded. The emotional powers in melodrama are fear (for the good characters) and hate (for the bad characters). The story requires that events be arranged in a suspenseful sequence, with movement from harmony to upset to conflict to victory. The characters of melodrama are usually static because their basic moral choices are set before the action begins, and they do not change. Also, good and evil are most likely to appear as unalterable codes of behavior.

When the term *melodrama* refers, as it does in this study, to one of the major dramatic forms, it does not imply that all melodramas are like the nineteenth-century versions of the form. Nor are commercial mystery plays, as Broadway knows them today, the definitive examples of melodrama. Such highly artistic plays as *The Homecoming* by Harold Pinter and *Look Back in Anger* by John Osborne are closer to the structural form of melodrama than any other form.

For those playwrights who wished during the thirties to communicate a complex of thought, the form of melodrama was especially useful. It was easy for them to depict the "good" people in their plays as having the "right" thoughts about man and society and the "evil" people as having "wrong" thoughts. Other principles of the form, too, served them well as they utilized melodrama for didactic purposes.

The Gentle People by Irwin Shaw best represents the dianoetic melodramas discussed in this chapter because of its structural perfection. Jonah, the central character, summarizes the play's controlling thought. He explains to his friend Philip, "If you want peace and gentleness, you got to take violence out of the hands of the people like Goff and you got to take it in your own hands and use it like a club. Then maybe on the other side of the violence there will be peace and gentleness."[1] The action, or secondary control, of the play is: protect yourself from unjust exploitation and oppression.

The story depicts two gentle old men, Jonah and Philip, who own a battered outboard motorboat in which they escape the realities of life four evenings a week; they fish while enjoying their freedom. They have saved $190 toward their dream of buying a boat adequate for a permanent escape to the tropics. Goff, a minor racketeer, extorts protection money of $5 a week from them; he also captures the attention of Stella, Jonah's restless daughter. From her, Goff learns of the $190. When he demands the money and when Stella says she and Goff plan a trip to the tropics, Jonah protests to the police. A corrupt judge sides with Goff against the old men. They then realize they must protect themselves. At Jonah's suggestion, they trick Goff into their boat, divert his attention, hit him on the head, and heave him overboard. A detective nearly discovers their action, but they evade investigation. Jonah gets back his now-subdued daughter and his money. At the end, the two old men have resumed their fishing and their dreaming of escape.

The Gentle People is an apt example of a didactic drama that incorporates many features of finely wrought melodrama. The action is at least temporarily serious. Goff, an antipathetic villain, threatens Jonah and Philip, highly sympathetic persons, to a degree that arouses fear and hate in the play as emotional powers. Both emotions are quenched, of course, when the old men kill Goff and get away with it. Thus, the proper ending for melodrama evolves. The heroes get rewards of money and happiness,

1. Irwin Shaw, *The Gentle People*, p. 61.

and the villain is punished with violent death. Also, the play clearly depicts good and evil in the characters, and the basic nature of each never changes during the play. Jonah is peace-loving, kind, and aware of his personal position in life. Philip is even more gentle. In their plan against Goff they are serving justice, for the totally evil Goff acts only to satisfy his greed. The minor characters align themselves with one side or the other, most of them on the side of good.

Never for a moment would an audience doubt with whom to sympathize. The villain, Goff, initiates most of the action of the play. All goes fairly well in the lives of the two old men until Goff threatens and mistreats them. They try various ways to avoid his oppression, first, by placating him, but Goff only demands more and then more money. The old men's suffering increases until they turn to the representatives of the law, but they fail them, too. They discover that nobody will help them. Finally, in a seriocomic scene in a Turkish bath, they realize that they must take matters into their own hands. This is the point of reversal in the plot. After that moment, the heroes are volitional; whereas before then they were the object of pursuit, they now become the agents of pursuit.

Several other structural principles are active in the organization of *The Gentle People*. A chain of causally related events—a progression from the possible through the probable to the necessary—provides unity and cred-ibility in the plot. An example of the possible—the be-ginning of a logical sequence—is Goff's threatening the two old men during Act I, scenes 1 and 3. The actions in these two scenes make clear that, although Jonah tem-porarily capitulates, he will resist Goff. In scene 3, Jonah tells Goff that Goff will not live long enough to get old (p. 29). This line points to the possibilities of future action; significantly, the speech occurs only seven short speeches from the end of Act I. The probable—the sec-ond stage of a play's logical sequence—is exemplified in Act II, scene 2. When Goff raises his demands, it is prob-able than Jonah will try some new device to foil him, perhaps the law. He does just that. It is also probable, because of Goff's lack of concern, that when Jonah calls the police he will receive no help. That also proves true in the night court scene when the judge sides with Goff. In Act III, scene 2, the necessary—the final stage of the logical sequence—occurs at the climax of the story. Jonah and Philip have succeeded in luring Goff out in their boat. In the middle of the bay Jonah kills the motor as planned and gets Goff to assist him in starting it. But when Jonah gives the prearranged signal for Philip to hit Goff, Philip cannot do it. Almost immediately, Goff realizes his peril, and he starts to take a gun from his pocket. At that moment it becomes urgently necessary for the old men to kill Goff. Jonah jumps him from behind, Philip hits him on the head with a piece of pipe, and together they throw him overboard. This establishment of the necessity of killing Goff helps, also, to diminish the amorality of the old men. They must kill Goff in self-defense; they simply could not do it until it became truly necessary.

Despite the unity of the plot, several accidents move the action forward. Surprise also occurs often during the play, and the degree of suspense in the story is high, as good melodrama requires. The suspense accumulates from the first threat to the climactic fight and through the subsequent investigation.

Thought is an important material in each of the characterizations. Thought finds expression as desire, for instance, when Philip wishes for peace (p. 15), when Stella hopes for excitement (pp. 23, 53), and when Goff tells what he wants out of life (p. 72). The Turkish bath sequence of Act II, scene 5, offers an example of thought as deliberation. The two old men deliberate expediently about what to do and then about how to do it, and ethically about whether or not they should kill Goff. Many decisions also reveal thought in the play. Three of the most important decisions are made when Jonah and Philip decide to give in to Goff (I, 1), when they choose to appeal to the police (II, 2), and when they decide to kill Goff (II, 5). Thought is also apparent in what the characters obviously represent: the old men, peace lovers; Goff, aggressors; Stella, the dissatisfied; Eli, Stella's beau, the conventional; the Judge, corrupt government; Magruder, the cop, good government; and Lammanawitz, a bankrupt businessman, the victims of financial exploitation.

The thought of the play, as a single speech, pits the force of the violent against the staying power of the gentle. The gentle people win because they realize that sometimes one must fight for life and that one must on occasion be violent in order to retain peace. Because the gentle people have the courage to fight, they are victorious.

Irwin Shaw utilized thought in *The Gentle People* both as material to character and plot and as their control. The characters act on the basis of thought, and because of their actions the plot takes its final form. The result is a thought-to-character-to-plot arrangement. As is demonstrated in subsequent chapters, this relationship does not appear as clearly nor as importantly in the more overtly didactic plays. Shaw labeled his play variously as "a Brooklyn fable" or a "fairy tale with a moral."[2] He achieved his didactic goal with the play, but he depended on many mimetic structural principles. *The Gentle People* serves as one of the best examples of a social dianoetic play that comes close to being mimetic in organization.

Thunder Rock by Robert Ardrey, like *The Gentle People*, is a modern parable, and it too contains many mimetic features. As World War II approached in 1939, both of these plays offered advice to the nation about the hopelessness of isolationism.

Just as Jonah and Philip could not ignore the world, so protagonist David Charleston cannot withdraw in isolation to the stone tower of the lighthouse on Thunder Rock. Charleston took the job of lighthouse keeper because he had seen so much of evil, because he was afraid of losing the fight against evil in the world, and because he no longer believed in the capability of mankind to

2. Quoted in Edmond M. Gagey, *Revolution in American Drama*, p. 134.

solve its problems. He isolated himself because he thought the world was headed for destruction.

Ardrey's play is unusual because its action is a fantasy that dramatizes the reflective process of the leading character. In an imaginative as well as a structural sense, the action of the play *is* thought. *Thunder Rock* is a dianoetic melodrama with unique organization and powers. The action of the play is: to decide whether to withdraw from the problems of the world or to join mankind in helping to solve them "a little sooner." Stated briefly, the story depicts the reflective struggle of a man who has withdrawn from life in order to avoid the truth of history. But he cannot escape historical truth nor his own abiding faith in humanity. Therefore, at the end, he returns to active life.

In Act I a pilot friend brings supplies to the Thunder Rock lighthouse in Lake Michigan, and he challenges Charleston to go to China to fight the Japanese. Charleston refuses. He explains that he has invented an imaginary group of six characters, who live with him. He has based his inventions upon the log of a ship that was wrecked near the lighthouse in 1849. The pilot tells Charleston to sit on his rock, pick his nose, talk to his ghosts; the pilot is going to take action in China against the evil of the world.

All of Act II and almost three quarters of Act III are fantasy. Curiously, one scene takes place at the beginning of Act II and is immediately repeated: the first time through, the fictional characters enact the scene as Charleston's imagination directs them; the second time through, the imaginary characters and their actions become real because Charleston's mind permits them to act according to historical truth. Charleston can dismiss or change fiction, but he cannot change truth. Each of the characters, with the exception of the old ship's captain, is a European immigrant who was running away from a problem. Charleston undertakes to show them that they were wrong to run away. Act II moves to a climax when the characters realize they are dead and exist only as extensions of Charleston's imagination. In anger, Charleston tries to dismiss them, but they will not go; they have gained a measure of reality. He can no more dismiss them than he can tear pages from history books and thereby change history itself.

In Act III the fantasy characters force Charleston to realize that he cannot remain in his ivory tower, nor can he return to the world as an uninvolved spectator. Insisting that they are segments of his intelligence speaking to him, they explain that he must and will have faith in the future. They assure him that there is a time in each man's life when happiness grows dim and the fight seems hopeless; then a person needs the help of all the dead of history to remind him, in a unified voice, that the significant battles of life can be won.[3] Charleston then decides to leave the lighthouse and return to society in order to help mankind win its battles, whether victory requires one day or a thousand years.

The plot moves through three conflicts, and Charleston faces three choices. In Act I the pilot offers him the chance to fight in China; they argue; and Charleston refuses. In Act II Charleston causes a conflict when he chooses to create the historical characters truly rather than as entertaining fictions. When he lets them come truthfully to life, they oppose his judgment of their lives, and they refuse to be dismissed. Between Acts II and III Charleston stays up all night to wrestle with his conflict. He decides, finally, to return to the world as a disinterested spectator. In Act III the characters from the past will not permit his qualified return to life. They compel him to decide to re-enter the world as an active participant for the future good of mankind.

Thunder Rock contains a complex of thought more gentle by far than that in *The Gentle People*. It also depends less upon the emotional powers of fear and hate. Nonetheless, it employs many formulative principles of melodrama. But the two opposing forces inhabit the

3. Robert Ardrey, *Thunder Rock*, pp. 60–61.

single character of Charleston, rather than two separate sets of characters. Charleston possesses the hateful desire to withdraw, and he also possesses an admirable concern about humanity. The hero is one part of his inner self, and the villain is another. Fear and hate do not rise to a high degree of intensity in this play, but they do exist. The play sustains the fascination of surprise and suspense as the various fantastic elements occur in the action. Interest grows with scenes of mounting intensity and nonviolent conflict. By the end of the play, it is clear that Charleston's return to active life is not the result of decision but rather a function of his fundamental nature; his return is inevitable. Charleston does not decide; he simply realizes what he must do if he is going to live in peace and in truth with himself and with historical fact. He finds the reward of happiness at the end because he is returning to life to do the "right" thing. At the conclusion, when the ghostly characters finally agree to disappear and when Charleston becomes acceptably human again, the play provides relief of tension.

Thought acts as the focal element throughout the play. For example, Charleston says that ideals are damnable things because they are like seeds; when you bury them, they crop up again (p. 18). He also points out why he quit the *Daily News* as a reporter upon his return from the Spanish Civil War: He suddenly realized that he could no longer be objective, that he had no future as a reporter. He then took the job on Thunder Rock to remove himself from the social chaos of the world (p. 20). Also, Charleston comments on social conditions: nations mortgage their resources for one decadent reason—expansion. And expansion means conquest, war, and the horrors of war. When a nation steps toward expansion, then civilization disappears, along with democracy, the freedoms, dignity, and truth. Such principles are quickly forgotten in war, and usually they never return (pp. 20–21).

Thought in *Thunder Rock* operates both as the organizing factor and as material to plot and character. It does not employ principles of melodrama as fully as *The Gentle People*, and to the same degree the play is more didactic. It is a gentle fable with a melodramatic action developed for the sake of a thesis: No man may isolate himself; he must share fully in the battles against evil in the world.

In any context *The Little Foxes* by Lillian Hellman and *Golden Boy* by Clifford Odets are unusual and effective dramas. But the fact that they both are based on didactic organizations is easily overlooked. Each of these two plays has as its principal structural element a complex of thought. Both also exhibit some features of melodrama, but far fewer than the plays of Irwin Shaw and Robert Ardrey. *The Little Foxes* and *Golden Boy*, unlike the two plays discussed above, spot a central character in a negative light. Regina is an out-and-out villain and Joe Bonaparte slowly degenerates into a semivillain. Also, both of these plays have strange endings. These two factors—the central character and the ending—are strong hints about the didactic natures of the plays.

Whereas *The Gentle People* is a parable, a melodrama built around a hero, *The Little Foxes* is an object lesson in evil, a didactic melodrama centered on a villain. Because in a conventional melodrama the villain initiates most of the action, the villain is usually more interesting than the hero. Hellman utilized this principle most fully in depicting Regina and the Hubbard clan. The Hubbards —Regina, Ben, Oscar, and Leo—represent the rising industrial capitalists in the South around 1900. They display the rapacious nature of those responsible for the beginning of contemporary capitalism. With this play Hellman attempted to alert the audience to the significance of ambition and greed in the capitalistic system, and she tried to stimulate her audience to ask what can be done to control such evils.

The Hubbards are ruthless and far more corrupt than the few fading aristocrats in their milieu, represented in the play by Oscar's wife Birdie. Ben, the head of the clan, has persuaded a Chicago industrialist to help the family to open a cotton mill. The industrialist is to furnish 49 per cent of the investment, and the Hubbards are each to put up a third—$75,000—of the remaining 51 per cent. Regina sends Alexandra, her daughter and one of the few "good" characters in the play, to bring home Horace, Regina's estranged and ill husband. She must get her share of the investment capital from Horace, who is the local banker. He refuses her the money. But Ben and Oscar urge Leo, Oscar's son who works in Horace's bank, to steal $80,000 in negotiable bonds from a box in the bank. Regina quarrels with Horace, and he reveals that he knows about Leo's theft. He tells Regina that he plans to change his will so the stolen bonds will be her only inheritance. In pure malice Regina reminds Horace of their unhappy relationship and thus causes him to suffer a heart attack. When he asks for his medicine, which will save his life, she turns her back and lets him die. Subsequently, Regina blackmails Ben and Oscar into giving her three-fourths of their 51 per cent share in the mill. Ben capitulates, but he avenges his loss by wondering, in Regina's presence, about the circumstances of Horace's death. Alexandra quarrels with her mother and determines to leave home. Regina faces a lonely and perhaps dangerous future, but she emerges the winner of the material prizes.

The Little Foxes is a unique didactic melodrama because of its unconventional ending. However temporary the victory may be, in the play the villain wins. It is, thus, an inverted melodrama and social problem play. It succeeds in arousing some fear for the well-being of Horace, Alexandra, and Birdie, and a high degree of hate for all the Hubbards, both individually and as a group.

The action progresses through a sequence of threats, from Oscar's warning to Birdie about talking too freely, to Regina's threats that force Horace to give her the money she wants.[4] The action is unrelentingly serious throughout the play, and it is initiated and executed by

4. Lillian Hellman, The Little Foxes, in Four Plays, pp. 169, 213, 231.

the antipathetic characters. Because the evil characters are focal, the action of this play is to acquire material wealth whatever the cost. In other words, a woman schemes to fulfill her material desires, and in the process of winning what she wants, she destroys all the sources of friendship and love around her, blackmailing her brothers, driving off her daughter, and killing her husband.

The Little Foxes resembles a typical melodrama because of its plot of discovery, but it is unlike a conventional play because it has no reversal and no double ending. There are also other differences. It offers no relief of fear by aversion or escape, nor does it provide rewards for the good people or punishment for the bad. The powers of melodrama are not fulfilled in this play. Why? Structurally, the play does not end, although the curtain closes; the formal construction remains incomplete. This is not to say, however, that the play is unfinished as an organized whole.

The characterizations and the thoughts behind the action of the drama help to round out the play structurally, and yet permit its suspended ending. The characters have made their fundamental moral choices before the play begins; they do not become good or bad by means of desires, deliberation, or decisions that are elicited by the action of the play. They are inherently good or bad. The characterizations are dramatically unique, however, in that the evil agents become increasingly evil and move to triumph over the good. They are static in category but not in degree.

The antipathetic characters, especially Regina, embody all the seven deadly sins of the morality play—pride, covetousness, wrath, envy, gluttony, sloth, and lechery. Regina is fascinating, however, like a poisonous snake coiled to strike. She reveals her thoughts in all she says and all she does. Her desire for money involves thought: "There'll be millions, Birdie, millions. You know what I've always said when people told me we were rich? I said I think you should either be a nigger or a millionaire. In between, like us, what for?" (P. 178.) She deliberates aloud in Act I when she convinces Ben that she should have a larger share of the family's wealth than Oscar (pp. 182–85). Thought as a part of Regina's characterization appears strongly in the sequence leading to her murder of Horace; it emerges in what she says, in what apparently lies in her mind as subtext behind the words, and in her refusal to give him his medicine.

Ben Hubbard works with less passion than Regina, but with more care and more threats. Oscar is not as strong as Ben and Regina, but he is no less vicious. His philosophy of life is that every man's first duty is to himself. Leo is the weakest and most dissolute of the Hubbards, and he is the most openly evil.

The sympathetic characters are representations of wider significance than merely personages in the play. Birdie represents the pathetic and decadent aristocracy, incapable of action. The black servants are the exploited workers who are too fearful to resist their dominators. Horace represents those in the capitalistic class who are impotent and can eventually be destroyed. And Alexandra represents—especially because of her final denial of her mother—the one element of hope for any possibility of good in the future. The plot and the characters reflect the leftist feelings of the thirties in their contempt for capitalism, but the Marxian formula does not control the play. There are no significant workers, no threats against capitalism, and no indications of rebellion to bring about a new synthesis.

Thought in the play often takes the form of memory, such as Birdie's longing for the happiness of her youth (pp. 220–27). Thought as planning occurs in each scene when the Hubbards are gathered. Strangely, there are few moments of ethical deliberation or decision in the play; most deliberation and the significant decisions stem from expedient thought. It is usually difficult to epitomize a play as one speech; there is always the danger of oversimplification. But such a condensation of the thought, if carefully done, is revealing. This play expresses the truism that the advance of capitalistic exploitation is made possible by people who are greedy, rapacious, and selfish. Uncontrolled capitalism will continue to destroy the weak and the meek. Love is no deterrent, for it is lacking in the exploiters. What can be done to stop the injustices of capitalism?

That question is posed by the nonending of the play. The absence of an ending is one of the reasons for the triumph of the villain in this play. The unconventional ending also stands as proof that the play is not well made except in a superficial sense. Hellman disavowed the label "well-made" as applied to her plays. For her, a well-made play is a drama that has contrived effects and a story with incidents more tightly related than those in life. Such a play is too closely plotted to be convincing.[5] By this definition, or by the formula of conventional melodrama, *The Little Foxes* is certainly not well made. Skill and coherence are evident in its structure, but its ending obviates the use of the term. This play contains a beginning and middle, but no end. With the exception of Horace, no resolution completes the story of any of the characters.

There is no sense of eased tension at the finish. The play leaves the audience unsatisfied, but not frustrated. Some good *can* result. Alexandra points to its means. After she hears Ben tell Regina that he will go on fighting, Alexandra says: "Addie said there were people who ate the earth and other people who stood around and watched them do it. And just now Uncle Ben said the same thing. . . . Well, tell him for me, Mama, I'm not going to stand around and watch you do it. Tell him I'll be fighting as hard as he'll be fighting . . . some place where people don't just stand around and watch" (p. 247). Although in the play evil defeats good, Alexandra says that there is hope for the triumph of good if one is willing to fight the people and the system now in control.

In a discussion of nineteenth-century melodrama, Oscar G. Brockett wrote that "perhaps the most impor-

5. Introduction, *Four Plays*, p. x.

tant feature of melodrama is its observance of strict moral justice . . . and the reversal at the end of the play is extreme."[6] The morally just ending is nowhere in evidence in *The Little Foxes*. How, then, is justice to be brought about? The answer is left entirely to the audience. They must complete the play by administering justice in the reality of their own lives. The didactic ending of *The Little Foxes* requires far more thought from an audience than the ending of a conventional melodrama. Although the play contains a strong and complex line of action, it is organized as a purely persuasive piece. The major factors contributing to its persuasive power are the absence of a normal ending and the lack of a central hero or heroine who is on the side of "right." The play points to the question of how to combat the evils of capitalism.

Clifford Odets also concerned himself with the significance of endings to plays. To examine the ending of any of his plays is to see that he uses them to make his meanings explicit. But his endings are much different from that of *The Little Foxes*. The ending of *The Little Foxes* remains open in the play as well as in the minds of the audience. Odets closed his endings and made them specific and "immediately useful." Chapters 7 and 9 contain analyses of his most fully rhetorical plays. Here, discussion of his two plays of the thirties that use features of melodrama most typically, *Golden Boy* and *Rocket to the Moon*, is suitable. Of the two, *Golden Boy* stands as the more noteworthy construction.

The golden boy of the title, Joe Bonaparte, has decided to try professional boxing as a means to gain material success. Joe convinces fight manager Tom Moody to let him enter the ring, and Joe renounces the career of violinist, which he and his father had planned since he was a boy. At first Joe tries to reconcile his material and his artistic ambitions, but he soon becomes brutalized in the boxing world. Although he falls in love with Lorna,

6. Oscar G. Brockett, *The Theatre: An Introduction*, p. 236.

Moody's mistress who has also sold herself for material gain, and although Joe wins quick success as a fighter, he finds no happiness. He realizes that he has sold himself to the materialistic world of gamblers and gangsters, but he challenges all comers and continues to win his fights. In the fight that can establish him as the top contender for the championship in his class, he kills the other boxer. Subsequently, he realizes the totality of his own dehumanization. At the end, he deliberately destroys his Deusenberg, Lorna, and himself in an auto accident.

Odets constructed *Golden Boy* as a dianoetic melodrama. Here is the familiar rags-to-riches story with a difference; it ends with a catastrophe that points a moral. Several characteristics shared by tragedy and melodrama are incorporated in the play. The action is serious throughout, although one character, Joe's brother-in-law Siggie, typical in the melodramatic formula, provides comic relief. Fear arises as concern for the protagonist; Joe's basic nature is valuable. He is a sympathetic character even though he makes wrong decisions. The other characters, too, have more human dimensions than those in the other three melodramas examined. Joe, Moody, Lorna, Joe's father—all show many differentiating traits. They are convincingly lifelike. Even personages with small but deftly characterized roles in the story emerge as not exclusively good or purely evil—Tokio the trainer; Frank, Joe's brother who is a strike leader; and even Fuseli the gangster.

Joe's story is one of driving ambition and perverted values. The materialistic side of Joe is one of the "villains" in the play. The other villain comes more clearly into focus as the play progresses; it is "the system," the real villain. The system makes it impossible for an individual to achieve inner fulfillment and some measure of public success simultaneously. The dichotomy between materialism and human values remains too strict for *Golden Boy* to be a tragedy, and the action is too closely under the control of thought for it to be a mimetic melodrama. Structurally, it is a serious, persuasive play.

With *Golden Boy*, Odets clearly meant to convey specific thoughts. The character of Joe's brother Frank demonstrates such intent. He functions in the play as contrast to Joe. Frank fights too, as a strike leader for the CIO. In the final scene Frank, who has been hurt in a strike, makes clear the alternative to the path Joe took in life. Frank declares that he is not fooled by the kinds of things that fool Joe. Although Frank does not have automobiles and expensive clothes, he gets something that Joe does not—the satisfaction of acting as he thinks, of finding his place in life, and of being at harmony with masses of workers.[7]

Also, the Marxian influence in *Golden Boy* is readily apparent. The play offers music (or constructive pursuits) as thesis, and boxing (or destructive force) as antithesis. The dialectical synthesis can be achieved in life only when one fulfills his own natural potential and turns his destructive power against the real enemy, the system.

To compare the endings of *Golden Boy* and *The Little Foxes* is to understand better the structural nature of each. In *Golden Boy* the action concludes with an approximation of the reversal and double ending of the conventional melodrama. Joe steadily climbs the ladder of success until, in Act III, scene 2, he discovers he has killed the other boxer. The reversal swings Joe in the opposite direction immediately after the discovery when he realizes that he committed the murder with his fists. He wonders what his father, the person who represents his conscience, will say about the fact that Joe murdered a man, and he realizes that in killing the other boxer he has murdered himself (p. 315). *The Little Foxes*, by contrast, evinces no reversal of fortune for the central character, Regina. Also, the conventional double ending of melodrama is strangely employed in Odets' play. The "villains"—the materialistic facet of Joe's personality and the system—are cheated of the fulfillment of Joe's

7. Clifford Odets, *Golden Boy*, in *Six Plays of Clifford Odets*, p. 318.

growing position in the world of financial success. Joe and the "good" characters receive two rewards, the realization of "true" values and the renewal of faith. Any such realization or renewal must happen outside the action of *The Little Foxes*; in it, there is no punishment or reward of any kind. Moral justice is meted out *within* the structure of *Golden Boy*; if it is to be applied at all, it must occur outside of *The Little Foxes*.

Golden Boy, one of the most successful of the didactic plays of the thirties, employs ideas clearly but not in an overtly propagandistic manner. Its story is strong and its characterizations are full. The persuasive intent of its structure is skillfully integrated with all the other materials. That the play is still studied and occasionally produced attests to Odets' artistry in making a didactic play palatable to the general theatre audience.

The four didactic plays already examined in this chapter represent the most pertinent examples of what might be called dianoetic melodrama. They demonstrate not only the degree to which melodrama can be employed rhetorically but also the creative accomplishments of the leftist playwrights in the thirties. Several other plays are also organized similarly to the four analyzed above.

Lillian Hellman wrote *Days to Come* and *The Children's Hour* as didactic plays that resemble melodramas and contain social criticism. *Days to Come* is a didactic strike play, but it focuses on capitalists rather than on workers. A decadent family of industrialists, the Rodmans, when faced with a strike in their brush factory, hire professional strikebreakers. When violence and murder result, the strike falls apart, and so do the Rodmans. They face the punishment of a despicable existence for the remainder of their lives. This play, like Hellman's others, depicts the distasteful results of capitalism.

The Children's Hour reveals less social orientation than the author's other Depression plays, although it too is formulated as a dianoetic melodrama. Its story concerns an evil child who destroys two women, one of whom had tendencies toward lesbianism. But the play says more than that some people are evil; only because the soil of society is ready to accept the seeds of gossip and hate can the evil child's gossip succeed.

Rocket to the Moon is Clifford Odets' other marginally didactic play written during the Depression years. Resembling a psychological melodrama, the play offers a picture of a decadent middle-class dentist, his wife, his secretary, and his acquaintances. They live in a "nervous time" filled with stresses, and the balanced normal life so necessary for love is not immediately attainable.[8]

Two of Sidney Kingsley's plays also depend upon the principles of melodrama and present another variant of the type of play under discussion. *Men in White* pictures daily life in a hospital. George Ferguson, a young intern, faces the decision between an easy life as the husband of a rich girl and a "subsidized" general practitioner, and a life of hard work as a hospital staff doctor and research scientist. The thought of the play points to the materialistic ills of society. It declares that there are values in life that are more precious than material success. Kingsley's other didactic play is *Dead End*. It depends on contrasts for its most striking effects. A good man from the slums, Gimpty, differs sharply from an evil man from the slums, Baby-Face Martin. Gimpty devotes his life to helping others, but Martin wishes only to help himself. Elements of melodrama appear, too, when Gimpty discovers that his mission in life is to help young slum children. Police kill Baby-Face Martin. The didactic ending communicates a message about moral justice. Each of Kingsley's plays has an episodic structure, a large number of characters, naturalistic touches of style, detailed sensationalism, a partial use of melodramatic form, and a thought complex as a control of their structure.

But for the Grace of God by Leopold Atlas and *Little Ol' Boy* by Albert Bein are also dianoetic melodramas that depict a slum environment as villain. Ghetto life

---

8. Clifford Odets, *Rocket to the Moon*, in *Six Plays*, p. 404.

according to these plays, is a natural and despicable product of the capitalistic system. Both plays focus on the ethical development of a boy, and both contain the structure of socially loaded melodramas. In the Atlas play, Josey Adamec learns his standards of morality in the gang life of the streets and learns to hate in the sweatshops that exploit children. At the end, he kills a boss to get money to help a dying brother, and although he is arrested, others place the blame on his environment. *Little Ol' Boy* pictures how associations in reform school pervert young boys of potential worth. The distinction of this play lies less in its organization and plot than in the depth and variety of the characterizations and the verisimilitude of the dialogue.

One other set of plays among these dianoetic melodramas depicts the condition of black people in the South. The most energetic long plays about the exploitation of blacks are examined in Chapters 7 and 8. *Brass Ankle* by DuBose Heyward is the only one of the long plays dealing with the problems of blacks that approximate the form of a mimetic melodrama. It has some similarities to *The Little Foxes*. The chief antipathetic character, a murderous white bigot, receives only limited punishment at the end, and society at large, which promotes racial persecution, is not punished at all. The play lacks full character motivations, arouses fear and hate, and ends exactly at the moment of climax.

More carefully written is Paul Green's short play *Hymn to the Rising Sun*. By depicting the cruelty of white people toward black people and the stoic acceptance of fate by the victims, Paul Green wrote the most lyric dianoetic melodrama of the entire period. His play not only offers an indictment of the Southern penal system but also shows man's eternal power to resist. The play dramatizes that power, especially when the black prisoners find that songs and a lyric view of life are possible in spite of the horrors of their situation. In the ending of this play no one punishes the evil whites, nor do the blacks find much reward or alleviation of their misery except in their stoic acceptance and their day-to-day lyricism. The characters are good or bad, sympathetic or antipathetic. The threats are extreme and are usually carried out. Although this play is didactic, Paul Green did not let the impulse to protest overwhelm the structure; the play is far from being crude propaganda.

Each of the nine plays discussed above possesses its own unique structure. And most of them are attempts by leftist dramatists to deal with new and socially pertinent subject matter. Although their artistic levels of accomplishment vary as much as did their financial success in New York, each has a good measure of originality as a didactic drama.

*   *   *   *   *

Though each of the thirteen plays mentioned in this chapter has elements of melodrama, not one can rightly be called a mimetic melodrama. Each has a complex of thought that affects its structure and thereby employs the principles of melodrama in an altered state or omits them. Hence, the term *dianoetic* can appropriately be applied to them. They hover quite near the dividing line between the mimetic and the didactic, and they are therefore difficult to analyze correctly. Many Depression plays, although definitely mimetic, demonstrate their authors' awareness of the social turmoil and utilize some social thoughts. But these thirteen are certainly didactic because they evince the fullness of their authors' social consciousness and because they express those thoughts with persuasive intensity. The melodramatic elements among the thirteen vary from play to play, but each diverges in a rhetorical manner from the theoretical form of melodrama. They are dianoetic, too, insofar as they are more thesis-oriented and thought-controlled than normal melodramas. Also, they relate closely to the exhortative plays of Chapter 7.

The four plays examined in detail—*The Gentle People, Thunder Rock, The Little Foxes,* and *Golden Boy*—

stand as the highest achievements of the group in their organization, communication of social awareness, and intensive employment of thought. Although not one is totally a Marxian play, each shows the influence of the Marxian pattern of thought then so prevalent. These plays present a meaningful picture of the past and a predictable pattern, of some sort, for the future. They do not project the Marxian revolt of the economically oppressed, but they clearly indicate the necessity for change —social, economic, political—and for each person to find a system of values within himself. They urge upon the audience the need for individuals to change before society can be changed.

These dianoetic melodramas use subject materials to depict (1) individual involvement in the prevention of oppression, (2) capitalistic exploitation, (3) the hollowness of material success, and (4) evil conditions that make possible man's inhumanity to man. Many specific speeches occur in the plays as obvious expressions of their central thoughts, as keys to the characterizations, and as means for advancing the illustrative stories.

A complex of thought controls the form of each play, and yet each uses a specific action as a vitalizing element in its story. To state the typical actions abstractly, the plays enact first, the triumph of the good and the punishment of evil; second, the triumph of evil; third, the conversion or awakening of the hero; or fourth, the unrelieved oppression of the good by the evil. Moral choice is rare in these plays. Only *The Gentle People*, *Thunder Rock*, and *Golden Boy* present it in any guise. Even in those plays, such choices are not central in the action. Most of the plays have a plot of discovery—again, with the exceptions of *The Gentle People*, *Thunder Rock*, and *Golden Boy*—rather than a plot of reversal. To sustain interest, most depend heavily upon surprise and suspense. Excepting *Dead End*, the plays contain simple plots. *The Gentle People* has the most conventional organization; it most nearly approximates the form of mimetic melodrama. The rest diverge more from the typical features of the form. This in no way implies, however, that *The Gentle People* is a less skillfully written drama. It is, rather, the most adroitly structured and coherently written of the thirteen. The most atypical structural feature to be found in the group is that some of the plays—notably *The Little Foxes*—stop, but they do not end; their resolutions are left for the audience to achieve outside the theatre.

The manner, or style, utilized in these plays is primarily realistic, although naturalism, fantasy, and romantic whimsey also occur in them. The plays call for elaborate, though not unstageable, spectacle. They variously demand such unusual settings as a boat beside a pier, a lighthouse, a living room, the locker room and gym of the fight game, the special rooms of a hospital, the bank of the East River, a dentist's office, and the prison camp of a road gang. What is more, the different actions demand such settings as active environments, not merely as picturesque backgrounds. The operation must occur in *Men in White*; the two old men must fish in *The Gentle People*; and the horrors of the prison camp must occur on stage in *Hymn to the Rising Sun*.

The primary purpose of the author of each of these plays was to make a drama worthy of stage production, but his concurrent goal was to awaken the social consciousness of the audience through the communication of ideas. Hence, all the plays can be called allegories or fables. Most of them to some extent contain the emotional powers appropriate to melodrama, fear and hate, but even more intensely they stimulate outrage. They are serious plays because they present actions that are important not only to the well-being of the sympathetic characters, but also to the well-being of the audience. These considerations of final cause help demonstrate why they are didactic. Tragedies are written to provoke insight, comedies to identify the anormalities of man, and melodramas to show instances of reward and punishment. But the thirteen plays of this chapter depict evil in society and restore faith in the intrinsic goodness of the common man. They tend to stimulate specific social thoughts about contemporary society and therefore are truly dianoetic melodramas.

Neither literature nor the art of drama can, unaided, solve social and political problems; only the actions of men can do that. Plays such as the thirteen treated in this chapter entertain by making life more vivid and exciting, but they also instill in people a better understanding of life and a desire to oppose the evils in society. Such didactic dramas promote social awareness through their persuasive pictures of contemporary life.

7

Revolutionary Statements

I ask of absurd creation what I required from thought—revolt, freedom, and diversity.
Albert Camus, *The Myth of Sisyphus*

What is truth in poetry? Should it be implicit or explicit? Must drama be an object for contemplation, or can it furnish a blueprint for action? By writing more or less closed metaphysical or open propagandistic works, each playwright evinces his answers.

For the didactic playwright, the objective of poetry is instruction and conversion. His choice among the species of poetic art reflects the faith of each writer that he can impose a practical abstraction upon his experience. For the didactic writer, his personal doctrine is truth, and in didactic plays that selected truth is the organizing idea. In determining the principles of a didactic play, there can be little separation of principle from idea because the idea is the chief principle. Further, the form of the play comes close to being the content. But some separation of form and content, structure and thought, principle and idea is possible for critical purposes.

To examine didactic poetry on its own terms would be to determine the truth or falsity of its statements or its effectiveness as persuasion. But to consider didactic poetry as what it is—an object—makes possible the examination of its structure and working principles.

The twelve plays treated in this chapter are exhortative; their instruction is more direct than that of the dianoetic melodramas. Exhortative plays fall naturally into three groups, with a chief connecting feature: the attempt to transform man from a state of violence to a state of freedom. The first set of exhortative plays argues against war; the second utilizes a strike as central incident; the third attempts to dramatize national social problems.

Antiwar plays comprise the first of the three groups under discussion: *Peace on Earth* by George Sklar and Albert Maltz, *Bury the Dead* by Irwin Shaw, *Johnny Johnson* by Paul Green, and *If This Be Treason* by John Haynes Holmes and Reginald Lawrence.

Peace on Earth, produced in November, 1933, preceded the other plays on stage by two to three years. It is the most dynamically persuasive, although each of the others contains virtues of imagination and craftsmanship that it lacks. It also contains most of the materials, types of proof, and devices that the others do, although in somewhat less polished form. Reading *Peace on Earth* or any of the other three antiwar plays can be a startling experience. Many of the comments and predictions advanced by these plays apply to World War II, the Korean conflict, and the Vietnam war. These plays, perhaps with some omission of Marxian jargon, could be produced with immediate application now.

Peace on Earth reveals its persuasive purpose from the first scene onward; the play is persuasive first and artistic second. It exhorts, preaches, damns, praises, inculcates, and polemicizes. It simplifies and clarifies the facts and issues of world-wide and national situations in order to produce understanding. It attempts to enlist support for its ideas, especially for the solutions it proposes, by arousing emotions of sympathy and hate. It directs these emotions against war and urges action as a specific response to the experience of witnessing the play. *Peace on Earth* presses its audience to speak out against war, to oppose war preparations, and to foster the unity of thinking men and workingmen against warmongers. It preaches the solidarity of workers, hatred of bosses, and sympathy with the bottom dog. These intentions comprise the play's final cause.

The key idea in *Peace on Earth* is: Join the active protest of the vanguard of the working class against war! This idea operates implicitly in the entire play and finds

116

expression in many individual speeches. During the play's first few minutes, an agitator explains what action can be taken. A willing person can carry around petitions, join antiwar demonstrations, deliver speeches, and act as a picket; there is plenty of action to be taken.[1] Later, an attorney argues that Owens, the focal character, went beyond mere protest. He struggled actively by throwing in his lot with workers who were striking to stop a shipment of war materials. He joined a strike that has since become symbolic of the humane struggle against war (p. 108). This argument summarizes the story of the play; it is story as idea.

Peter Owens, a professor of psychology, joins a free-speech demonstration and is arrested. After his release, he goes with his friend Mac to a meeting of strikers who have refused to load munitions onto a ship. During a subsequent protest march, Mac is killed. Later that night Owens attends a faculty party where he accuses John Andrews—industrialist, university board chairman, and owner of the munitions factory—of killing Mac, of fomenting the strike, and of pushing the country into war. Then, during a ceremony at which Andrews is awarded an honorary degree, Owens and the striking workers enter. A fight ensues, and an alumnus is killed. Owens is arrested for the shooting. At the beginning of Act III Owens awaits his execution for the murder. While he waits, he envisions the machinations to promote war. The authors chose to dramatize Owens' thoughts in a montage that includes businessmen, priests, and politicians. Also, Owens recalls the major events and speeches from his trial. At the play's end, he walks to his execution while the striking workers demonstrate in protest against his death and against war.

Thought controls the play. The expressed thought in the speeches comprises the same types as in a mimetic play—amplification, diminution, expression of emotion, argument, and deliberation. But in the didactic play,

1. George Sklar and Albert Maltz, *Peace on Earth*, p. 11.

such speeches do not have the same relationship to character and action as they have in a mimetic play. Here thought is not merely material to the characters and to the action; here it is also the organizational control. At the faculty party Owens confronts Andrews the industrialist. In their argument, thought occurs as amplification, as diminution, as argument, as deliberation, and as decision (pp. 60–61). Thought also operates in speeches given by antipathetic characters, which render the thoughts of the opposition in such a way that it appears ludicrous. For example, financiers pompously explain why the country should go to war, and a minister condemns the enemy for killing; he then declares that Jesus would join the side of the right (p. 117).

Chance, accident, and circumstance control much of the action. For instance, Mac is shot accidentally in the first fight; someone shoots the alumnus by accident; and it is on circumstantial evidence that Owens is condemned. Total manipulation of the action by the authors is obvious as well in the fact that Owens' prosecution and trial occur between Acts II and III—a device by which the authors avoided the trial scene. Trials concentrate on the past, and they wrote their play as a recommendation for the future.

The play has the organization of a well-made oration. In Act I, scene 1, Mac introduces the idea that Owens and the others should actively oppose the war by joining the strikers (introduction). The idea grows in the next scenes when free speech is prohibited and when an able student is dismissed from the university at the request of the chairman of the board of trustees (statement). The argument of the action involves the following facts: a strikebreaker has killed a worker; the boxes labeled soap actually contain gun cotton; Mac is killed; the militia arrives to put down the strike; Owens is falsely arrested, accused, and sentenced to death (proof). The ending consists of Owens' final major speech, a few moments before he walks to his execution (conclusion).

The style of any play is necessarily a mixture, because no play exactly conforms to any single definition of realism, romanticism, expressionism, or whatever. The general style of *Peace on Earth* is realism, but it differs considerably from the conventional realistic play. The scenes that use small numbers of characters tend to be unusually flat in speech, simple in characterization, and obvious in unit purpose; those with larger numbers of characters have a strong choric element. The final act departs totally from realism; between its opening and closing exhortative speeches, Act III is a fantasy montage. In this play, realism gives way to expressionism, and dramatic presentation becomes theatrical demonstration.

The play's spectacle also shifts from the dramatic to the theatrical, from particular to general. The first scene is set in a specific living room; the final scene flows everywhere that Owens' imagination can reach. Act I consists of five scenes and four sets; Act II, three scenes and three sets; Act III, one multiple scene and one space-stage setting for the montage.

Not only is the play organized as a speech, but many of the characters' speeches and actions illustrate its exhortative nature. The central idea, protest against war, points to future action and expediently promotes the welfare of man. The play asserts that it is inexpedient for mankind to continue its present course through one conflict after another. The subject is the appeal to undertake the course of action most likely to further the antiwar movement. The major proofs offered by the play are: the story of Owens, the attitudes of the striking workers, and the characterizations of the supporting personages.

The materials of the play correspond to the three modes of rhetorical proof. Sklar and Maltz controlled the characterizations in a manner similar to the way a public speaker strives to project a favorable image of his own personality. The sympathetic characters manifest the virtues of intelligence, dedication to humane ideals, sense of brotherhood, outrage at injustice, and desire for peace. The antipathetic characters show traits of greed, ignorance, selfishness, prejudice, and the desire for violence. The logical proof is set forth in major speeches, both positive and negative.

The diction also forms a part of the play's persuasive material. The terms *appropriate* diction and *possible* diction apply differently to a didactic play than to a mimetic play. In a mimetic play, appropriate diction is the more important because it supports the characterizations and the story; possible diction is only incidental. In a didactic play, however, possible diction is the more important. The appropriate speeches in a didactic play are speeches suitable to the characters or the story, but the possible speeches present the central thought. The latter are the organization and the message of the play. The use of significant *possible* diction is apparent throughout *Peace on Earth*. The thought-oriented speeches in this play establish the three chief requisites for language in all didactic pieces: connection with the central thought, clarity, and interesting credibility.

Owens, the most fully developed character in the play, enacts the process that is proposed to the audience. This process characterizes him and forms what there is of a story line. He begins by simply expressing an interest in the rights of man according to the Constitution. As his awareness of the "true" conditions that limit liberty and favor war increases, so does his commitment to and active participation in the antiwar movement as effectuated by the striking workers. By the middle of the play, his realization is full, his decision made, and his commitment complete. Ultimately, he sacrifices all—job, family, even life—for the sake of the ideal. His suffering heightens in both intensity and fact until the end of the play, although his discoveries are complete by the middle of the play. There is no reversal of the sort often found in a mimetic play. His awareness, commitment, and suffering constantly grow. Whereas in a mimetic play the climactic moment and the potential moment of reversal would be his moment of decision, in this play the climactic moment is the final one when he is led off to die for the central ideal propounded by the play.

Bury the Dead by Irwin Shaw presents a loose and fantastic story, but as an exhortative work structured to project an idea it advances economically, coherently, and effectively. The organizing thought is: Before it is too late, each person, no matter what his status, must renounce war. The resultant story presents six soldiers who have died in a war. They stand up in their graves and refuse to lie down again until war is no longer a reality or even a possibility. No persuasion or argument from the generals, their own women, or organized religion can put them down. At the end, they march off, followed by living soldiers, to spread the thought of peace and to enlist the common people in their ranks. This play contains many of the characteristics of *Peace on Earth*, but more imagination operates in it, and it is less realistic.

All the scenes in *Bury the Dead*, although rather short, show a high degree of selectivity for the sake of the central idea. Most of the words and actions argue for the major thought. The function of the play is to persuade by arousing outrage based upon fear and hate. The control of the form is the thought. Each character of importance expresses agreement or disagreement about whether the war should end. The spectacle and the time sequence throughout make the play resemble the montage fantasy of Act III of *Peace on Earth*.

The features of the exhortative speech are identifiable in *Bury the Dead*, just as they are in *Peace on Earth*. Most of the speeches are overtly exhortative and make little pretense of characterizing the personages. The materials of proof are less applicable to characterization than to the central thought; the audience is forced into a certain frame of mind by means of the key speeches and the imaginative situation. The play stimulates the audience to imagine the potentialities of the symbolic rising of the common soldier. The choice of vocabulary and the grammatical structures are skillful, imaginative, and connected to the central thought. For example, Driscoll, the leader of the six soldiers, says that the thought of rising against war would not let him rest. He identifies himself as the first to stand up in their dark grave because the antiwar sentiment is strong enough to give new life to the dead.[2] Many of the speeches in the play are impassioned pleas full of anger and urgent protest. But the logic in *Bury the Dead*, insofar as it is a poetic structure, does not match its emotive power. Nevertheless, it is one of the most effectively persuasive antiwar plays of its length in the literature.

Johnny Johnson by Paul Green exhibits the most dramatic imagination and variety of presentation of any of these antiwar plays.[3] It too rests upon an idea: Men should not indulge their bestiality but should strive for a better world by individually working to end war now. The vision of man's opposition to war presented in this play is more individualistic than in *Bury the Dead* or *Peace on Earth*. The rejection of war as a means to solve international differences, *Johnny Johnson* seems to say, resides in each individual. Hence, Johnny labors against the overwhelming odds of all the prowar forces society can muster, and although at the end he walks alone into the future, he has not lost. Only the material and communal things in life are gone from him; he retains his integrity and spirit.

Although the story assumes much more importance in Green's play than in the others of this group, it remains under the control of a central idea. The play expressionistically presents the story of Johnny Johnson, pleasant and indefatigable pacifist. Johnny, a tombstone sculptor, opposes the incipient war (World War I), until he learns that it is to end all wars. He then joins the Army and is sent to the trenches, where he begins his personal campaign to end the war. He has come close to accomplishing his purpose when he is committed to an institution for the mentally ill. He remains there for many

2. Irwin Shaw, *Bury the Dead*, in *The Best Short Plays of the Social Theatre*, ed. William Kozlenko, p. 71.

3. Paul Green, *Johnny Johnson*, in *Five Plays of the South*, pp. 1–104.

years. Finally released, he discovers all his desires in life are lost and another war is imminent.

The argument of this play exists more in the character of Johnny than in either the diction or the story. Johnny is sympathetic, amusing, courageous, and uncompromising. He opposes war by never firing his rifle while at the front, squirting laughing gas into a pack of generals, establishing a congress for peace in the asylum, and opposing the Boy Scouts with their "junior war uniforms." The play is as episodically constructed as the other two antiwar plays—a construction that presents certain loosely related scenes as the most rhetorically effective in propounding their central ideas.

If This Be Treason by John Haynes Holmes and Reginald Lawrence has the most conventional dramaturgy of the four antiwar plays.[4] It might even be called a dianoetic melodrama. Its distinguishing feature, indicating its heightened didacticism, is that more of its actions and speeches bear upon the central thought than those of the other plays and that its thought is more singular. If the common people, the play says, are in a time of crisis truly given a choice between war and peace, they will always choose peace, and there will be no war. The play advances the idea that people accept war only because they never have an opportunity to choose any other course of action. If governments would give the people an honest chance to serve the interests of peace, peace and not war would always result. When provoked to fight, governments must refuse; leaders of nations bear the obligation to make peace instead of war.

The story shows pacifist John Gordon, on the day of his inauguration as President of the United States, learning that Japan has attacked Manila. He immediately orders all Army and Navy units, many of which are already rapidly setting the war machine into gear, to stop war plans. In Act II most of Gordon's cabinet, the coun-

4. John Haynes Holmes and Reginald Lawrence, *If This Be Treason.*

try's business leaders, and all of Congress fiercely oppose him. He decides to travel alone to Japan to arbitrate for peace, even though the two nations are by then involved in an undeclared war. In Act III he meets the Japanese premier and other leaders. Although they refuse at first to listen to his overtures, the cause of peace is saved by a popular leader of the Japanese common people, who has been released from prison by a protesting crowd. Together, the two men avert a holocaust.

In this play the authors successfully maintained a realistic style in dialogue, characterization, and story. It is no mean accomplishment to depict a President credibly, let alone a pacifist one. The key to the didacticism in this play is that President Gordon has made his ethical decision before the play begins. The entire drama deals only with expedient deliberations, decisions, and actions; this circumstance, combined with the primacy of thought, pushes the play into the realm of the didactic. Finally, it is noteworthy that in 1935 the play predicted the war between the United States and Japan that began in 1941.

Among these four antiwar plays, *Peace on Earth* presents its thought with the least aesthetic interference; this is not to say it is unimaginative or ineffective as persuasion. It also most overtly suggests revolt—of workers and intellectuals. *Bury the Dead* is the most theatrical, and it is directed toward the common man. *Johnny Johnson* is the most varied in technique and perhaps richest in over-all imagination; it is aimed toward reaching each man individually, no matter who or what he is. *If This Be Treason*, the most realistic, is pertinent to everyone in general as "the people," and to governmental leaders in particular.

Each of these four plays dramatically propounds the evils of war, and in the manner of a poetic exhortation each urges its audience to adopt the antiwar sentiments it depicts. With surprising accuracy, these plays of the early and middle thirties predicted World War II, and they have a shocking pertinence today.

Five plays that deal with strikes make up the second

group of the exhortative type: *Marching Song* by John Howard Lawson, *Stevedore* by Paul Peters and George Sklar, *Waiting for Lefty* by Clifford Odets, *Life and Death of an American* by George Sklar, and *The Cradle Will Rock* by Marc Blitzstein.

Lawson's *Marching Song* represents not only the exhortative strike play but also the genre of "proletarian literature," so central a concern among leftist writers during the thirties. Proletarian literature in fiction, lyric poetry, and drama dealt with the woes of the bottom dog, with the troubles of the worker. Many writers followed a formula that was similar to that which the Marxians applied to politics and social organization. Lawson reproduced it in *Marching Song*.

In the Marxian pattern, a worker of genuine worth is placed in a group milieu, usually a factory setting, and an industrial crisis. The worker has the choice to aid the proletarian collective cause or ignore it. He suffers under the conflictory pressures, temporarily tries to go it alone, but is finally converted to the collective effort. The mass is the represented hero, the capitalistic system the villain, and the class war the conflict. Of all the American didactic plays, *Marching Song* most closely follows this pattern of socialist realism.

Lawson was able to do more, however, than merely follow the formula in a doctrinaire manner. He adapted the theory of dramatic conflict to Marxian purposes. He gave the worker as well as other characters a conscious will, and the formula itself presents the goal toward which the conscious will struggles. The obstacles come naturally from the class conflict. He also utilized the concept of volition to propel many of the characterizations. *Marching Song* is not a great mimetic tragedy, comedy, or melodrama; it was not meant to be. It attains considerable stature, however, as a didactic play and as an example of the leftist formula.

The functional purpose of the play is to persuade an audience, to enlighten them, and to incite them to action. It attempts to arouse a consciousness of the class conflict and of the economic basis of societal ills, and to move the members of the audience to join the proletarian cause. The powers of this drama are fear for the sympathetic workers and their families and outrage against the antipathetic bosses, their minions, and their hired gunmen. The central, organizing thought appears in the story, in key speeches, and in the characterizations. Because the country is a battlefield of the warring classes, the play says, the workers must wake up, join forces in brotherhood, and use the industrial power of the nation, which is in their hands, to resolve society's ills.[5]

The line of action in *Marching Song* details a conflict of wills between a group of exploited workers and a gang of vicious strikebreakers. The single setting is the interior of an abandoned factory, and the action spans the time from the morning of one day to the night of the following. In Act I Pete Russell and his family have just been evicted from their home; the bank foreclosed their mortgage because Pete was blacklisted during a recent strike at the Brimmer automobile factory. Other workers sympathize with Pete and his wife, but Pete is so desperate he contemplates hanging himself. Bill Anderson, a union organizer, instructs Pete and the others to renew the strike at the Brimmer plant. The Inspector and his deputies arrive to hunt Anderson and also to force Pete to remove his furniture from the sidewalk in front of his home. Act II begins with more instruction from Anderson. Pete rejects the idea of a strike, but his sister Rose and most of the other workers want to act. The workers hide Anderson in the furnace of the factory. When Binks and Toad, hired killers, arrive to search for Anderson, Pete refuses to help them. In Act III, scene 1, the killers force a young transient to reveal Anderson's hiding place, but Anderson temporarily escapes. Pete is beaten and his baby killed. The strike is growing in size and intensity. Pete joins the collective. In scene 2, the killer-strikebreakers sadistically torture and beat Anderson to

5. John Howard Lawson, *Marching Song*, pp. 58, 145, 148–49.

death on stage. The strike grows as the crowd fills the streets. The killers rush out to attack the crowd with machine guns and gas bombs. The crowd enters the factory to escape the gas. While they are there, all the lights go out; the strike is spreading to the electrical workers. When a black speaker incites the crowd to more action, they all rise, symbolically, to his cry, "Power is people!"

The thought of the play is expressed in speeches at the climaxes of the four scenes (pp. 70–71, 110–11, 148, 158). For example, at the end of Act I Anderson urges the crowd to collective action. He says that they ought to feel a personal connection with Pete's case. Such issues are collective concerns, not individual ones. And he goes on to remind the crowd that they are not alone; there are millions of others simultaneously protesting. The united mass of workers comprises a belt that wraps seven times around the world (p. 70).

Thought also operates in speeches as expression of emotion, as deliberation, as amplification, as argument, and in the didactic manner as exhortation. When the characters suffer, they express thoughts; when they make discoveries, they do the same. Thought also emerges in distasteful speeches from antipathetic characters.

The style of *Marching Song* is realistic. The people speak with a common vocabulary and use slang expressions. The scenes are causally related and lifelike in their progression. The spectacle called for is realistic as well, although symbolism is implied. The ruined dynamo in the abandoned factory is obviously a figure of the failure of capitalism. The lighting indicated in the stage directions is suggestive; for example, during a scene of violence, lightning flashes sporadically. At the close of the play, the electric lights suddenly go out, communicating the idea of solidarity among workers and indicating the spread of the strike to the rest of the town and to all the workers of the world.

The play also exhibits the features of a deliberative speech. Anderson, Lucky, and Rose exhort the other characters ethically and expediently. The object of the actions of all the workers is utility for the future. The ends for which all strive are expedient; they wish to extend the size of the workers' collective and to stimulate the class war. The choice of their course of action is the chief involvement of the focal character, Pete Russell. Proof of the strength of the workers and of the evil of the capitalists comes through examples, characters, and incidents. And the line of argument of the entire play is toward the future, not only in the town and the specific milieu of the play but also in the nation and the world.

Marching Song's plot is one of suffering. There are some discoveries on the part of the workers who awaken, but there is no true reversal. A rising line of action and tension maintains interest to the last moment. The beginning of the story in the play is the eviction of the Russells. The middle is the development of that story as illustrative of the spreading strike. An ending to the play, in the manner of a mimetic drama, does not take place. This play, like others of the didactic type, has an open conclusion, a persuasive one. The workers must go out in solidarity and carry on the class war, and the open ending exhorts the audience to do the same. It is up to everyone to act for social reform. The ending does not bring punishment of the villains, like that of conventional melodrama; hence, the outrage is not stopped in the play. It remains. The only reward for the sympathetic characters is the brotherhood of their fellows and their newly acquired vision into the future. The lack of punishment or reward, in what is in many other ways a melodrama, has the effect of urging the continuance of sympathy and outrage; the play is an attempt to make everyone aware of the need for solidarity among workers and for continuing the battle against capitalists.

In *Marching Song* the strike is a class war in microcosm. The play offers class conflict as the only solution to intolerable economic and working conditions. The strike also works as a symbol of the world-wide, permanent, and necessary workers' revolution against the capitalistic system—according to the play's argument. The

play clearly presents the motives and sacrifices necessary immediately for the strike to succeed and ultimately
for the workers' revolution. *Marching Song* well accomplishes what it sets out to do through the use of selected
elements of dramaturgy for the sake of persuasion.

Stevedore by Paul Peters and George Sklar also belongs among the strike plays, but in this work the focal
group, rather than engaging in an ordinary strike, fights
the class war.[6] Of all the exhortative dramas discussed in
this chapter, this play and *If This Be Treason* accomplish
their goals of persuasion with materials, in a manner, and
with a structure most nearly like a mimetic play. Like a
conventional melodrama, *Stevedore* arouses fear and hate,
but with a difference. The fear and hate arise for the sake
of a realization. The realization must be the understanding of the central thought, which controls the selection
and ordering of the quasi-mimetic incidents and characters. Narrowly expressed, the thought in *Stevedore* is
that black workers must stick together and fight for their
rights—peace, a fair wage, just treatment, and life as
free men. More broadly interpreted, the thought is that
all segments of the working class, to accomplish their
common rights and objectives, must join forces in the
class conflict.

The action of *Stevedore* takes place in New Orleans.
After a white woman is beaten by her lover, she claims a
Negro attacked her. This sets off an explosion of violence
by police and white gangs, and it stirs the black people
to increased resentment and unrest. A group of black
stevedores plan to join an interracial union and engage
in an anticipated strike. The police accuse Lonnie, one of
the black stevedores and a union organizer, of attacking
and raping the white woman. After his arrest, he escapes.
He hides at first with the stevedores and then at the
restaurant where they all eat and loaf. Lem Morris, a
white union leader, helps them at nearly every turn of
events. When a gang of white hoodlums enters the res-

6. Paul Peters and George Sklar, *Stevedore*.

taurant, a fight ensues, and one of the black stevedores is killed. At his funeral, Lonnie and Lem organize the black people. In the final scene, the blacks man a street barricade, and when the white gang shoots Lonnie, another leader arises. With the help of the white workers, the black men rout the gang by killing its leader and fighting off the others. The play ends with all the workers standing around Lonnie's body in a moment of grief and dedication before renewing the fight.

The Marxian pattern of socialist realism, like in *Marching Song*, controls *Stevedore*. An enlightened leader instructs a group of worthy, exploited workers. They decide to commit themselves to building solidarity and waging the class war. Each of the causes looms larger than any single life. The ending of the play points to the future. It is really a beginning. As in the other didactic plays that resemble melodramas, the good characters are not rewarded, except with a temporary routing of the white gang, and the evil characters are not punished, except by the loss of the gang leader. The real fight is yet to come. The close of the play is not a dramatic ending, for it is to lead to further consequences. Thoughts find less frequent expression in speeches in this play; they occur in the conventional guises. Rather than weakening the thought or making it less apparent, the fewer overtly didactic speeches stand out more strongly than in many other persuasive plays.

The style of *Stevedore* is realism as employed for didactic purposes. The entire play proceeds quite like an exhortative speech; it deals with expediency for the future. The materials, too, work as proofs. The sympathetic workers contrast with the antipathetic hoodlums, bosses, and police. The incidents are devised to put the audience into the desired frame of mind. The proof offered by the action, the characters, and the speeches makes up the argument of the play.

The form of *Waiting for Lefty* by Clifford Odets also relates to Marxian theory. The play argues for the acceptance of Marxian precepts both theoretically and actively. The arousal of outrage in the play grows to the full power of militancy. The play's goal is persuasion. It urges agreement with the committee's recommendation to strike; all downtrodden workers should rouse themselves to action and strike as a class against the intolerable conditions in the country. Clearly, the taxi-drivers' union is intended as a microcosm of the nation, and its actions should stimulate nationwide response.

The stage action of *Waiting for Lefty* occurs in seven episodes. It opens with a harangue by the corrupt Harry Fatt, secretary of the taxi-drivers' union. Fatt argues that the cab drivers ought not agree with their elected committee, all but one of whom are seated on stage, and he tries to persuade the members not to vote for a strike. The membership of the union is the theatre audience. Following Fatt's speech, each member of the workers' committee rises to exhort the audience to strike. Joe leads off. Instead of the speech of each man occurring as such, it is presented as a miniature one-act play and forms a vivid item of proof in the argument for the strike.

The central thought, toward which the whole builds and for which the structure exists, comes clear in many exhortative speeches. Three in particular communicate it well. In the first scene, Joe starts the idea by saying that the group must come to a decision.[7] Soon thereafter, in the first retrospective episode, Joe's wife says to him (and to all workers) that the bosses are making suckers out of laboring men every day. And the companies are persecuting workers' wives and children, too, by paying starvation wages (p. 10). Finally, in the next to the last long speech in the play, Agate and the strike committee shout for the workers to fight with them for right. It is the class war; the working class should unite to fight, so the old life will disappear and freedom will truly ring (p. 30). The words of the play reflect the spirit of the call to action that concludes *The Communist Manifesto.*

Waiting for Lefty—in thought, structure, character,

---

7. Clifford Odets, *Waiting for Lefty*, in *Six Plays of Clifford Odets*, p. 7.

and diction—offers the most incendiary emotive appeal of all the exhortative plays. Many critics have pointed out its relationship to the agitprop plays of the early thirties. But such similarity is important only when the point is made that the techniques of direct appeal through audience involvement in dialogue and through mass chant are the agitprop devices Odets found useful in his structurally sophisticated play.

The use of spectacle in *Waiting for Lefty* is the least illusory of the didactic plays under examination. Even during the partially mimetic flashback scenes, the strike committee remains visible in the perimeter of the playing area, and Fatt occasionally blows tobacco smoke into the scene. The presence of this force in the play helps to prevent overly close audience identification with the action. Just as the individual episodes are dramatizations of individuals' speeches, so the entire play is a dramatization of Odets' exhortative speech. To implement its motive to shape satisfying life conditions for workers, the play recommends to the American proletariat an expedient course of Marxian action.

The whole of the play works as an effective persuasive speech of exhortation, and each of the seven scenes is both a small speech of the same type and also a piece of evidence in the larger speech. Some of the Marxian principles that help to vitalize the play appear in the over-all organization. A group of workers of worth are examining the causes and results of the intolerable economic and social conditions under which they live. They discover that these conditions are the fault of the capitalistic nature of society, which causes exploitation and prejudice, war and violence, and even psychological despair and the destruction of love. They awaken as a group during the meeting (the play) just as their elected leaders had awakened as a result of personal incidents.

Life and Death of an American by George Sklar might be called a full-length agitprop play.[8] Much more

8. George Sklar, *Life and Death of an American.*

than *Waiting for Lefty* it resembles the agitprop mass chants, especially because of its extensive and continual use of "chanters." These personages speak sometimes as an uncharacterized group, sometimes as collective narrator, and sometimes with temporarily assumed characterizations. The play is not only longer than the agitprops, but it is also more imaginative and skillful in dramaturgy and persuasive appeal. The play might well have been titled *Life and Death of the American Working Stiff*. It demonstrates how, generation after generation, the factory worker is mashed into the same mold and crushed by capitalistic exploitation.

The over-all exhortation of this play is more argumentatively and aesthetically direct throughout than in many other didactic plays; it is delivered more oratorically and narratively than dramatically. The major organizing principle is the use of certain circumstances to demonstrate how the worker is prevented from getting an education, is pushed into war, held down economically, and encouraged to reproduce another generation of his kind. All these things *happen* to the worker; he *chooses* almost nothing other than his mate. In the play he chooses one more action—the strike, which precipitates the climax of his life and offers his sole hope for salvation. The plot, then, supporting the central idea, is one of suffering.

The Cradle Will Rock by Marc Blitzstein was one of the last plays to be initiated by the Federal Theatre Project. Since the federal government forbade the opening of the play because of its "dangerous" nature,[9] producer John Houseman and director Orson Welles presented it under private sponsorship. The play is dedicated to Bert Brecht and uses Brechtian devices obviously. It also utilizes effects drawn from earlier socially didactic plays. But *The Cradle Will Rock* is the most original of the didactic plays in its execution. It employs many devices of poetic diction and some accompanying music. The mu-

9. Hallie Flanagan, *Arena: The History of the Federal Theatre*, p. 202.

sical element works as material to the entire conception in auditory spectacle and in the rhythm and melody of the speeches. Here poetic diction and music blend in a manner unique to the didactic play and different from the conventional musical comedy. Also, the play is unusual among the didactic plays because of its satire.

The purpose of *The Cradle Will Rock* is to arouse favor for the workers' movement by ridiculing the capitalist and his money-oriented pimps. It attempts to persuade the audience to disavow allegiance to the captains of industry. It tries to bring about the realization that a storm is coming with the rise of the workers—a storm that will destroy capitalism by destroying the capitalists and their minions. It attempts to expose, to threaten, and to predict by satirizing, deriding, and scorning certain segments and relationships of society. It arouses outrage and sympathy as do the other didactic plays, but it does so by means of scorn and laughter. Of all the didactic plays of the period, it most closely approximates the form of comedy.

Few didactic plays of the thirties employed humor, so the list is brief: *The Gentle People, Thunder Rock, Dead End, Johnny Johnson, Excursion,* and *Margin for Error.* Humorous lines, of course, appear in other plays. But these are the only ones in which humorous scenes or sequences occur.

The central thought of *The Cradle Will Rock* amounts to this: As the people discover what, and who, is responsible for society's ills, they must and will rise to overthrow the chief capitalists and their middle-class servants.[10]

The ten scenes and eight locations of this short play frame its episodic action, and the story helps indicate its structure. Each scene works as a discovery, revealing the relationship of one or more of the characters to the capitalistic Mr. Mister. Little suffering of the kind seen in the plays of capitalistic oppression occurs in this play,

10. Marc Blitzstein, *The Cradle Will Rock,* in *The Best Short Plays of the Social Theatre,* pp. 166–67.

which focuses on the villains in the class war rather than on the heroes. Much of the script requires musicalized oration instead of acting. The characters are the nearest to caricature of all the didactic plays of the period; even their stereotypical names are satiric. The villains of the play are the same as those of all the didactic plays in the Depression: the industrialist, policeman, preacher, and businessman. The villainous institutions, too, are familiar: large corporations, the Army, the church, the police force, and the government.

The rhythmic and comic elements in *The Cradle Will Rock* also induce the audience to the desired emotional attitudes. Such elements are illustrated in the speech of the football coach, Professor Trixie, when he demonstrates how he will recruit young men for the cause of capitalism. Naked from the waist up, he barks rhythmic slogans about signing up for the military course, with three cheers for two years, etc. He chants about training, security, the uniform, sex appeal, and virility (p. 154).

The diction of the play is clear, but it does not resemble ordinary speech; yet, it is appropriate to the form and manner of the whole. It is well adapted to the presumed emotions of the hearers, the characters of the speakers, and the nature of the subject. The music of the diction is the most formally organized of that in any of the period's didactic dramas. Other polemic plays utilized some formalization other than simple songs, for example, *Hymn to the Rising Sun*, *Johnny Johnson*, *Bury the Dead*, *Waiting for Lefty*, *Life and Death of an American*, the Living Newspapers, and *Panic*.

A final observation concerning the structure of this play is that it presents a rising line of intensity of a lyric type rather than the traditional line of a story—conflict, crisis, and climax. In a number of ways, then, *The Cradle Will Rock* is a most original and compelling drama, quite different from all the other didactic plays of the period.

Although many of the leftist plays of the thirties contain Marxist–Communist sentiments, the five strike plays most clearly utilize Marxian ideas as formulative principles. In these plays, the theories of Marx operate as accepted patterns of occurrence.

The most frequently employed Marxian ideas in the strike plays are: (1) The world is undergoing an endless adjustment and change from capitalism to socialism, but socialism cannot be supreme until socialized productive relations and the rise of a nonpropertied proletariat have supervened. Hence, support for the rise of the proletariat and the denial of personal property rights are basic actions for each strike play. (2) By simplifying the dialectical method employed by the writers, it can be said that the reigning capitalistic *bourgeoisie* represents the thesis, the rise of the proletariat the antithesis, and the synthesis is the concern of the audience (presumably the rising proletariat of the future) after they leave the theatre. History moves under the stress of class struggles engendered by economic development, and the social history of man will culminate in the triumph of the industrial proletariat. The strike plays depict this conflict and point to the solution by presenting the facts and appealing to the audience. (3) Unity of action in the dislocated society can result only from harmonious cooperation with the predictable historical course of events and from a recognition of the material forces at work. The action of each strike play moves the workers closer to socialism and the great people's revolution. As much or more than principles of drama, these Marxian ideas control the structures of the five strike plays.

Drama never operated more didactically than in the Living Newspapers produced by the Federal Theatre Project. Immediately after its official beginning on August 27, 1935, one unit of the Project—created by Hallie Flanagan, Elmer Rice, Arthur Arent, and others—aimed "to dramatize the news."[11] The first Living Newspaper, *Ethiopia*, never reached the stage because it was censored by authorities in Washington. This power to censor caused Elmer Rice to resign as head of the New York re-

11. Flanagan, *Arena*, p. 29; Arthur Arent, "Technique of the Living Newspaper," *Theatre Arts Monthly* (November 1938), 820.

gion of the Project, but it gave Project writers fresh impetus for composing another Living Newspaper. Before the federal government canceled the entire Project on June 30, 1939, five Living Newspapers reached the stage in New York: *Triple-A Plowed Under*, March 14–May 2, 1936; *Highlights of 1935*, May 12–May 30, 1936; *Injunction Granted*, July 24–October 20, 1936; *Power*, February 23–July 10, 1937; and *One-Third of a Nation*, January 17–October 22, 1938.[12]

Flanagan and Arent claimed originality in their works, but admitted to borrowing devices from Aristophanes, *commedia dell' arte*, mime theatre, and other sources.[13] The authors proudly labeled their drama as informative and propagandistic. Here, for one of the few times in the history of drama, dramatists considered informational content and rhetorical device to be the chief virtues of their works.[14] Willson Whitman, writing in 1937, called these plays propaganda pure and simple. She declared that anyone who believed that propaganda must be dull would have difficulty understanding the impact of these plays.[15] In May of 1938, critic Mary McCarthy wrote that *Power* was the best of the Living Newspapers, partly because of its "clean, geometric didacticism."[16]

Hallie Flanagan began the process leading to the creation of the Living Newspapers even before the Federal Theatre Project became a reality. She suggested "a plan of dramatizing contemporary events in a series of living newspapers which would have a rapid, cinematic form and an emphasis on many people doing small bits rather than roles demanding a few stars."[17] The key intent was to dramatize news in order to enlighten the audience about causes and to persuade people to adopt certain attitudes about solutions.

12. Flanagan, *Arena*, p. 390.
13. Flanagan, *Arena*, p. 70; Arent, "The Living Newspaper," 820.
14. Arent, "The Living Newspaper," 820–21.
15. Willson Whitman, *Bread and Circuses: A Study of Federal Theatre*, p. 84.
16. *Mary McCarthy's Theatre Chronicles 1937–1962*, p. 36.
17. Flanagan, *Arena*, p. 20.

The specific materials of the five major Living Newspapers came from such sources as newspaper articles, the *World Almanac*, and the *Congressional Record*. *Triple-A Plowed Under* took as subjects the farm situation and the death of the Agricultural Adjustment Administration. *Highlights of 1935*, the least successful structurally and financially, concentrated on no single subject but reviewed noteworthy events of that year, such as the trial of Bruno Hauptmann, kidnapper of the Lindbergh baby. *Injunction Granted* told the history of the struggle of labor in the courts. *Power* gave information about the control of electric power throughout the country. And *One-Third of a Nation* presented information about the wretched housing conditions for the poor in New York.

The organization of the writing staff resembled a large city daily, including an editor-in-chief and various subsidiary editors.[18] The writers emphasized content rather than style, and they tried to find new and unusual techniques and devices for lending dramatic impact to the "flat" facts. They rigidly clung to the use of the direct quotation, and they inserted "creative" characters and scenes only when they felt they were necessary for more vivid dramatization of the facts. The writers utilized a method they described as a combination of "the newspaper and the theatre and to hell with the traditions of both."[19]

The formal cause of the Living Newspapers during their composition and in the resulting plays was first the selected problem. In each of the three best Newspapers, one can epitomize the problems as questions: How can the farm situation be improved, and what can the government initiate to replace the AAA? What federal controls should be exercised in the area of electrical utilities? What factors are responsible for the degrading housing in which the poor of the nation reside, and what can be

18. Hallie Flanagan, Introduction, *Federal Theatre Plays: Triple-A Plowed Under, Power, Spirochete*, ed. Pierre de Rohan, p. vii.
19. Whitman, *Bread and Circuses*, p. 84.

done to change them? Every word and action in each play relates to the central problem as information, analysis, demonstration, or solution. In addition to the central function of the problem as formal cause of the plays, the structural theories of the head of the editorial staff, Arthur Arent, affected the genesis of the form the plays took. According to his account, the writers tried to dramatize a problem rather than an event, a character, or a story. They consciously utilized the pattern of cause and effect and wrote episodes rather than formless montages. Arent directed his staff to construct each scene to have "three primary functions: 1, to say what has to be said; 2, to build to the scene's own natural climax; and 3, to build to the climax of the act curtain and the resolution of the play." Arent and his staff tried to dramatize abstractions; he called this factor the essence of the Living Newspapers.[20]

Of the three major Living Newspapers, *Power* possesses the most refined form and best exemplifies this unique type of drama. Its over-all purpose is to inform and persuade. This volatile document communicates by summary and symbol the socioeconomic origins behind case histories. The play presents an historical survey, an economic analysis, and a political recommendation. The structure of *Power* rests upon the central problem it examines: How is the public interest best served in the generation and distribution of electric power and the establishment of a cost yardstick?[21]

Thought and information appear most frequently (1) in announcements by the Loudspeaker and others; (2) in question–answer sequences; (3) in montages of quoted speeches; (4) in conflicts between fictional characters; (5) in single argumentative speeches from such figures as Senator George W. Norris and Samuel J. Insull; and (6) in mass chants. Speeches, such as the one delivered in Congress by Senator Norris during the summer of 1935, stand quoted and footnoted in the script (p. 37).

20. Arent, "The Living Newspaper," 820–24.
21. Arthur Arent, *Power*, in *Federal Theatre Plays*, pp. 68, 87.

These Living Newspapers must be the only plays the scripts of which contain extensive footnotes.

No conventional story carries the play. Selected incidents, having only distant antecedents and consequences, occur to express thoughts necessary to the didactic pattern. The scenes reflect the chronology of actual developments, but, more importantly, they stride ever higher toward a climax of performance intensity. *Power* uses rhetorical disposition. It introduces the subject of electric power (exordium), shows its importance and the circumstances of profiteering through its control (exposition), demonstrates how and why the government should be permitted at least partial participation and control (proof), and finally concludes that such governmental control is both unarguably constitutional and highly desirable (peroration).

No fully individualized characters take stage. The Loudspeaker delivers more lines than any other personage in the play. In the author's words, the Loudspeaker does not function in *Power* merely as an "annotator or a dateline"; it takes on "individuality and coloration." It speaks lines, editorializes, becomes "a definite character, but never the same one for very long."[22] At the end, it explains that the Supreme Court will soon decide the constitutionality of the Tennessee Valley Authority.

The manner in which the Living Newspapers teach frequently involves the conversion of the abstract into the concrete. An instance of this occurs in scene 7 of *Power*. A fictional character explains the nature of a holding company by illustrating business connections with colored blocks (pp. 30–31). Other uses of spectacle are projections, motion pictures, charts, maps, graphs, and the like. More of the script calls for narration or oration than for acting.

The entire play employs principles of the deliberative speech, with its exhortation of the audience, empha-

22. Arent, "The Living Newspaper," 824.

sis on the utility of power, and ideas about power for the future good of the populace. The subject concerns ways and means of getting the best deal on power for the consumer, and the play shows what is financially fair in the control of electricity. The proof stems from specific facts, statistics, and examples.

The materials of this play are these same facts woven into a climactic pattern that proposes a solution to the specific problem. Character receives little emphasis, either for dramatic or dialectic purposes. The Consumer and other illustrative fictional characters appear sympathetically but not fully. Almost the entire weight of proof rests on devices meant to establish certain attitudes in the audience. The diction is simple and clear; the only embellishments occur in the quoted speeches. The level of the diction and the simplicity of the concrete illustrations indicate that the play aims at a general audience, assumed to be ignorant about electrical power or economics. The emotion that results from reading or witnessing the play comes not so much from the words as from the juxtaposition of information, the climactic arrangement of the material, and the novelty of the communicative devices. The play efficiently accomplishes its purposes of presenting a problem and inculcating attitudes about its solution.

Triple-A Plowed Under, the first Living Newspaper produced, shows less structural refinement than *Power*. The general purposes identifiable in the script are the same: to inform and to inculcate. More specifically, it directs the audience's awareness to the connection between the plight of the farmers and the quandary of the ordinary city consumer. At the time of production, the AAA had just been destroyed; many farmers were consequently destitute. In the final scene the Loudspeaker makes the key appeal. It points out that the Soil Conservation Act is at that time being written and that the audience should immediately make the Administration and the Congress aware of their attitudes about the legislation. There follows an enumeration of such needed measures as benefit payments, retroactive payments, and diversion of funds from war appropriations and large industry to farm relief on an expanded scale.[23] Such components form the controlling thought of the play: What has caused the predicament of the farmers—decline of profitable markets and of living standards, and how can their predicament be relieved?

As in *Power*, *Triple-A Plowed Under* follows the rhetorical structure of an exhortative speech. Of its twenty-six scenes, fewer contain conflict between characters, and there is less anthropomorphism than in *Power*. One device that is used in *Triple-A Plowed Under* and *One-Third of a Nation* but not in *Power* is a series of news flashes of events that occurred during the day of each performance (p. 56)—an effective means for introducing immediacy into the action. *Triple-A Plowed Under* quotes well-known people more frequently than *Power*. The play contains sympathetically presented speeches by such men as Chester Davis, chief of AAA; Earl Browder, head of the American Communist party; and Al Smith, the Democratic party's leader. Obviously, *ethos* functions strongly in this play. Nevertheless, the main proof is the factual information given a theatrical presentation. This play ends on a positive note; *Power* ends with a question. The ending of *Triple-A Plowed Under* resembles the best of the agitprop chants in its use of a large chorus of farmers and workers chanting to the audience of their need for help.

One-Third of a Nation is the most famous of the Living Newspapers, probably because photographs of its setting—a tenement with numerous rooms open to audience view—were widely reproduced, and it ran far more performances (237) than the others. Its title comes from President Franklin Roosevelt's Second Inaugural Address: "I see one-third of a nation ill-housed, ill-clad,

23. Arthur Arent and the Editorial Staff of the Living Newspaper, *Triple-A Plowed Under*, in *Federal Theatre Plays*, pp. 52–53.

ill-nourished."[24] With the usual informational and persuasive purpose, it attempts to arouse the audience. What caused the slum housing conditions suffered by a third of our population, and what can be done about them? The play inculcates a generalized attitude of protest. It points out that everybody knows about the bad conditions, but no one has ever done anything about them.[25] And the way in which citizens can do something is to protest.

The problem of housing involves people more directly every day. Hence, this play contains more personages than the other plays, and each of these persons exhibits more traits of character. Attractions are more often anthropomorphized; even the tenement house speaks to the audience (pp. 66–68). Still, the thought and information appear, for the greater part, in the same rhetorical guises as in the other editions. The play operates as an exhortative speech. A stunning piece of spectacle, however, arouses extra interest at the beginning and end, and this device lends the play coherence and reiterates the problem. The play opens and closes with a realistic fire in the tenement house that forms the stage set. Also, the authors used more imaginative materials and created more fictional scenes. These scenes overpower the abstract ones and render the play less effective as persuasion, though not necessarily more interesting theatrically.

The proffered solution to the housing problem is less satisfactory than the solutions suggested in the other two plays. This play asks the audience to protest generally. The other two stimulate spectators to support specific governmental programs. Four features in the play, however, help explain its success. First, it contains greater emphasis upon device and spectacle. Second, although the problem was nationwide, the play deals only with

24. Franklin D. Roosevelt, "Second Inaugural Address," in *The Public Papers and Addresses of Franklin D. Roosevelt*, ed. Samuel I. Rosenman, 1937 vol., p. 5.

25. Arthur Arent, *One-Third of a Nation*, in *Federal Theatre Plays: Prologue to Glory, One-Third of a Nation, Haiti*, ed. Pierre de Rohan, p. 118.

manifestations in New York City; it better satisfies the rhetorical requirement of audience adaptation than the plays that deal at long distance with the farm problem or the fight about dams in Tennessee. Third, the heightened characterizations foster greater audience identification. Fourth, this play owns a vestige of story. The Everyman of the Living Newspapers did not show himself in *Triple-A Plowed Under*; he appeared in *Power* as the Consumer, but only in a few scenes and not fully individualized. In *One-Third of a Nation*, the Little Man not only participates quantitatively in a third of the action, but also creates, with the Loudspeaker, the thin story. This individualization increases interest for the whole, but the thought still fully controls even this trace of story. Although *One-Third of a Nation* does not approach its persuasive goal as closely as does *Power*, it reaches further aesthetically.

The final cause in the Living Newspapers can be summarized simply. They inculcate selected information to induce attitudes. Using principles of a speech of exhortation, or deliberation, they provoke some degree of protest and indicate some line of action. Like other Depression plays of exhortation—*Bury the Dead, Marching Song, Waiting for Lefty*, and *Stevedore*—the Living Newspapers arouse the emotions of sympathy and outrage, but they depend more directly upon the natural human desire for knowledge.

As for formal cause, the statement of a problem and a recommended solution control the structure of each Living Newspaper. Their supplementary organizational patterns are cause and effect, question and answer, and specific instance to general climax. The plays analyze problems with an economic and historical orientation. The arrangement of materials in the Newspapers is more like that in oratory than in more conventional drama. They use few elements of story.

The efficient cause involves their manner of communication. Their strictly presentational style admits only bits of illusory realism. The features of the deliberative speech prevail in each more strongly than do the features of any type of dramatic organization or any other kind of speech. The plays might be identified metaphorically as deliberative speeches delivered in the congress of common men. Specifically, they employ actual deliberative speeches from the United States Congress. The devices of communication help to formulate the presentational style. Not only the immediate nature of problems studied but also the variety and juxtaposition of devices arouse audience interest.

Their material cause relates to rhetorical proofs. The three sorts of agents that give impetus to sympathetic *ethos* are personifications, fictional personages, and real-life characters. The selection of materials always pertains to audience adaptation; the questions asked by many characters are those which presumably arise in spectators' minds during the production. Also, the plays orally and visually present statistics and other factual items. The diction as proof works effectively in the quoted speeches; the language displays attributes of clarity and appropriateness. These plays use "appropriate" diction of a rhetorical rather than a dramatic sort. The authors attempted to adapt the language to the presumed emotions of the audience, the character of the speaker (in the theatre situation), and the nature of each selected subject. The Living Newspapers, especially *Power*, are the clearest and most rhetorical of all the major didactic plays written in the 1930s.

Each of the three groups of exhortative plays—antiwar dramas, strike plays, and Living Newspapers—works effectively in selection, organization, and presentation designed to persuade. All these plays stimulate some feeling of outrage, and one cannot read them attentively without seriously contemplating the problems they treat. As George Bernard Shaw wrote, when we adjust our societal structure "to solve social questions as fast as they become really pressing, they will no longer force their way into the theatre."[26] Many of the pressing social problems these exhortative plays examined and attempted to solve still exist. While these exhortative plays did not accomplish their purpose to solve certain problems, they did achieve some measure of universality, for they grappled with problems that face man in every age.

26. George Bernard Shaw, "The Problem Play," in *The Cry for Justice: An Anthology of the Literature of Social Protest,* ed. Upton Sinclair, rev. ed., p. 488.

8

Pleas for Justice

The man who refuses to defend his convictions
for fear he may defend them in the wrong company,
has no convictions.
Archibald MacLeish, "Spain and American Writers"

The thirties were a time of extreme cultural flux. The myths of America were changing. In any revolutionary period—and the thirties contained both the seeds and the shoots of revolution—people drop their allegiance to one myth or symbol and shift another to its place. Some of these myths are newly discovered. The symbol of bourgeois nationalism no longer sufficed for many Depression writers—certainly not for the leftist playwrights. Many of them espoused the symbol of the worker and the myth, be it true or false, of the class war. This new symbolism characterizes the dramas that pleaded for justice.

The playwrights evidently decided that the most effective way to exhort the audience was to show the class struggle and then conclude with an implicit or explicit appeal to action. Some discovered that to examine the justice or injustice of the then current system was to accuse those in positions of responsibility. This examination of justice and injustice, which involved accusation and defense, led directly to courtroom plays. Three trial plays of the thirties—*They Shall Not Die* by John Wexley, *Precedent* by I. J. Golden, and *Judgment Day* by Elmer Rice—were fully didactic.

As with the exhortative plays treated in Chapter 7, the general goal of the plays of accusation is persuasion. But they are less concerned with the future action of the audience than with the recognition by the audience of injustice in the past. This purpose is, in a sense, similar to the purposes of the forensic speech that Aristotle discussed in his *Rhetoric*.

John Wexley's *They Shall Not Die* examines the arrest, trial, and conviction of nine black youths who allegedly raped two white girls.[1] The action occurs in a small community in a Southern state, and it illustrates the injustice and prejudice that warp the relationships between black people and white people in American society. Although Wexley stated that the characters, locales, and names of organizations in the play are fictitious, the situation is similar to the infamous Scottsboro trial of the early thirties. The fact that the actions of this play and of the other two trial plays in this group are closely related to actual situations and trials determines their classification as didactic. Because Wexley's play presents the events and characters of a real trial in such a way as to make known that the trial and its surrounding circumstances were unjust, the play becomes in detail and in over-all effect a forensic speech.

The forensic, or legal, nature of the inner segments of *They Shall Not Die* come clear in the trial itself and in the scenes of arrest, questioning, and indictment. The forensic nature of the entire play emerges because the play itself is a piece of evidence to the jury—the audience; in the courtroom—the theatre; and in the court—the entire nation. The play, then, forensically judges the Scottsboro case, and it excites indignation and outrage toward all such trials. Once the audience becomes aware of such travesties of justice in the past, the play seems to say, then the members will more easily and correctly judge them in the future, and they more likely will insist that the judicial system of the nation, or world, be purged of prejudice and injustice.

The central thought of *They Shall Not Die* is to plead that our nation's courts should observe the law, which grants equal rights to all races and peoples (p. 147).

1. John Wexley, *They Shall Not Die*, p. 6.

The play also concerns itself with the fight for the basic rights of all human beings (p. 145). Although it contains many features of a melodrama and although it advances somewhat like a mimetic play, it is identifiably didactic. It represents a commentary on the Scottsboro case, and it exposes the injustices of the situation rather than merely arousing aesthetic powers by means of the action. It takes the form of a speech of accusation. And it does not end, as do most mimetic plays, but rather, it stops with an open ending and an appeal that the nine black citizens should not die and that such injustice be eliminated from all courts in the land.

In the county jail of Cookesville—presumably in Georgia, Scottsboro is in Alabama—a telephone call reports that "a half dozen white kid hoboes" were thrown off a freight train by nine blacks; two white girls were also on the train. Soon deputies bring in the girls, both of whom are prostitutes. When the nine blacks are brought in, they are obviously mere boys, aged thirteen to nineteen. A county prosecutor and a sheriff conspire to make an example of the boys as blacks acting aggressively toward white women. They cajole the girls into accusing the boys of rape. Although the officers know the boys are innocent, they immediately establish a "legal" case for the boys' execution. In Act II the nine black boys are in the death cell, and they decide to let the National Labor Defense group take up their cause. The first scene of Act III depicts the engagement of Rubin, a famous New York criminal lawyer, by the NLD group. The final scene is a new trial that brings all the powers of the state to bear on the case. The state's attorney general now heads the prosecution, which makes its appeal to the jury on prejudice and name-calling. Rubin proves the innocence of the youths by the testimony of three eyewitnesses. Even though the just verdict is clear, at the end the audience can hear the all-white-male jury of Southerners laughing derisively in the jury room. Rubin then cries that he is only getting started. He promises that if he does nothing else with his life, he will try to expose the lynch justice practiced in that state. And finally he promises that the boys will not die (p. 152).

Some elements of thought occur differently in this play than in the didactic plays examined previously. They appear as both the form and the content of the scenes in which either the prosecution or the defense plan strategy or make a preliminary examination of witnesses or victims. The villains, as evil-hearted as ever appeared in a melodrama, reveal their racial prejudices when they conspire to persecute the boys. Thought in another guise appears in the trial speeches when the attorneys question witnesses.

Obvious persuasive thought also occurs in the final forensic summary speeches by the members of both the prosecution and defense. Speaking first for the prosecution, County Solicitor Slade makes direct appeals to racial and religious prejudices, to bigotry, and to regionalism. He warns the jury that if the black boys are freed, the white fathers of the area will fear for the safety of their daughters as they go to sleep each night. He advises the jury to announce that in the South justice cannot be purchased with what he calls Jewish money from New York City (pp. 143–45). Cheney, former attorney general of Tennessee, begins for the defense by explaining his own background and heritage of pride in the South. Then he says that if his father were there in the court he, too, would fight for the basic rights of all human beings, regardless of color or creed. He tells the jury that they are not considering a question of black and white but of justice and injustice (pp. 145–46). Rubin follows with the key thought of the play, which emphasizes the equality of all persons under the law (p. 147). Dade completes the forensic speeches by appealing to the jury's prejudices that relate to sectionalism, race, politics, and tradition. In the worst racist tradition Dade concludes that if the jury lets any of the boys go free, then all black people will run amuck and that white wives, sisters, and daughters will be threatened in life and honor (pp. 149–51).

Wexley rendered this play in a realistic and illusory manner. At the instruction of a stage direction, the characters never address the audience. But such direct address would be likely, however, since in presentation most trial plays permit the actor who plays a lawyer to encompass the audience as he delivers courtroom speeches. The play is necessarily episodic, because it presents most of the boys' stories leading up to and including the trial.

The most unusual features of this trial play are rhetorical in nature and relate them to forensic oratory. Each of the forensic principles works in *They Shall Not Die* in two ways: (1) in the play as a story of the prosecution and defense of the nine black boys, and (2) with the play itself taken as a speech that exposes the parody of justice that is occurring in this trial, which is representative of other such trials.

The six basic principles of a forensic speech are applied in *They Shall Not Die*. First, accusation and defense operate in the play as the activity of the characters when they prepare and execute their cases. Many of the individual speeches—of both sides—are accusations, and the play as a whole accuses all those who use the judicial system as a tool for implementing racial, economic, or social hatreds. The second principle bears on justice as the object of persuasion. Justice is the central issue in the trial of the innocent black boys. The play as a whole seeks to inculcate the idea that justice is for all, regardless of social, economic, religious, political, or racial characteristics. The interest of the characters, as they are involved in proof and disproof, is in time past—the third feature of any forensic speech. As with all trials, the activity is present action for the sake of future result, but the concentration of thought is upon time past. Fourth, the end toward which the legal system moves is justice or injustice. Fifth, the characters and the action are concerned with wrongdoing—perpetrators, motives, and victims. Sixth, as in a regular trial, the proof is deductive in the play, and it contains syllogistic enthymemes and maxims or general statements about practical conduct.

The story in *They Shall Not Die* is much like that of a melodrama. There is the initiating incident of the arrest of the boys, the threat from the legal forces of the state, the struggle between the prosecution and defense, the crisis scene in court, and the climax—the raucous laughter issuing from the jury room, which indicates the verdict. Like in a number of the didactic plays that resemble conventional melodramas, the ending is rhetorical rather than dramatic. The argument of the play is not completed, and the story remains unended. The curtain closes, but the play does not end. Rubin and the National Labor Defense group declare their intention to carry on the case forever, if necessary; the play implicitly appeals to the audience to help them.

It is important to note that at the time of the original production of the play the Scottsboro case had not been settled. The true incident on the freight train happened on March 25, 1931, the play opened February 21, 1934, and the final action on the real Scottsboro case occurred in 1938. The State of Alabama dropped charges against four of the boys, and it gave four of them prison terms for assaulting a sheriff. The ninth boy was sentenced to death, but the penalty was commuted to life imprisonment in 1938. These facts help illuminate the purpose of the play and the structure of its ending.

In *Precedent* I. J. Golden utilized principles of the forensic speech much as John Wexley did in *They Shall Not Die*. The similarities in structure between the two plays reveal how two authors handling two different sets of materials used the trial situation in much the same way to achieve specific persuasive effects. From these two examples, the fact is apparent that trial plays lend themselves well to didactic purposes.

Golden wrote *Precedent*, too, about actual people and events. A different thought about justice, however, controls the play's form. *Precedent* accuses the judicial system of containing vicious and archaic laws, which make the life of a man less valuable than ridiculous rules and procedures written in legal statutes.[2] The play is a slightly fictionalized account of an actual event—the framing, trial, and imprisonment of Tom Mooney, a labor organizer. One important feature of the stories of *Precedent* and *They Shall Not Die* is their early point of attack. Both plays begin early enough in the total narrative to show the scenes in which the victims are framed. Both make clear, long before the stage trials and verdicts, that the accused are innocent.

Precedent presents the story of labor union organizer Tom Delaney. A railway company, against whom he works, frames him for a bombing. Subsequently, a judge finds him guilty and sentences him to death. A newspaper editor discovers the truth of the case and is able to get the sentence changed to life imprisonment. The governor decides to uphold outmoded legal precedents, otherwise Delaney would get his freedom. During an epilogue fifteen years later, Delaney's friends assure him that they are still working for his release.

In *Precedent* as in *They Shall Not Die*, a second or appeal trial forms the play's major crisis scene. During the trial the most important speeches of argument and persuasion are the concluding forensic speeches of the prosecution and defense. Again, the victim of injustice is good and innocent, and he is not allowed to speak in his own behalf. The focus of the trial in the play and of the trial as a speech is justice. In *Precedent*, however, the subject is not the influence of prejudice on the legal system but rather the archaic and unjust precedents that control so many legal decisions. These precedents permit, so the play implies, the powers of capitalism to persecute individuals who oppose them.

The play accuses not only a specific precedent, but it also accuses the entire legal system of being the tool of capitalistic interests. Some reform is imperative, the play

2. I. J. Golden, *Precedent*, p. 138.

maintains, in a legal system that makes possible the miscarriage of justice by means of corruption, perjured testimony, and packed jury (p. 134).

Precedent, too, is related to an actual, unfinished situation in life. This fact plus the play's didactic intent account for its open ending. Although in the epilogue Delaney has little hope, his friends nevertheless swear to continue fighting for justice. The play implies that the audience should also carry on the fight. The operative emotional powers are sympathy and outrage—sympathy for the persecuted innocents and outrage against the system and social conditions that permit injustice.

Judgment Day by Elmer Rice differs from the other two trial plays in several respects other than merely the employment of different materials. *They Shall Not Die* treats the matter of prejudice and white supremacy in the courts; *Precedent* the intrinsic faults of the judicial system; and *Judgment Day* indicts the rise of nazism in Germany. *Judgment Day* is a fictionalized account of the events and the trial connected with the burning of the German Reichstag in February, 1933, and it accuses fascism, then rising in Europe, of tyranny, wholesale slaughter, and endangering the peace of the world.[3] The organizing thought in the play is charging the fictional dictator Grigori Vesnic (and his corresponding real-life figure, Adolf Hitler) with the crimes of fascism.

The story deals with the trial of two men and one woman. The state charges them with an attempt to assassinate the dictator, Vesnic. The defendants are innocent, but they are indicted because they are members of an opposition party. They are the first victims of the fascist leader's plans to destroy all vestiges of resistance among the opposition. The trial proceeds with the testimony of bought witnesses. Three of the five judges of the "High Court of Justice" are corrupt, and they support the dictator. One judge opposes them and supports truth and justice. The Chief Judge is uncertain and can-

3. Elmer Rice, *Judgment Day*, in *Seven Plays*, p. 369.

not decide where his loyalties lie. In the final scene, Vesnic, the fascist leader, enters the court to testify and to force the issue. Rebels suddenly force their way into the court and confront Vesnic. The courtroom becomes a battleground. The play ends when the judge who refused to condone the injustice shoots Vesnic.

Judgment Day achieves its goal of arousing sentiment against the totalitarian control of government by offering emotional proof with words, characters, and story elements. By using the example of distortion and corruption of a legal system in an undesignated European country, the play exposes the evils of fascism. Although in *Judgment Day* the representatives of "the people" seem to be on trial, the play actually tries fascism itself. This direction of the play is indicated not only by the appearance of Vesnic in court but also in a speech by Khitov, the *raisonneur* of the play, in which, near the end of the trial, he declares that no one present has been duped for a moment. He tells the judges that the proceedings are not a trial of the defendants but, rather, an exposure of Vesnic and his dictatorship (p. 369).

The form of the play follows the procedure of a trial, and it utilizes many features of the conventional courtroom melodrama, which Elmer Rice was so adept at composing. But two emotionally effective differences push it toward didacticism. First, Rice contrived the court rules, procedures, and controlling characters so that they would best permit the illustration of the thought. Second, the ending is not logically necessary as a causal result of the rest of the play. For example, the court believes the defendants to be guilty until proven innocent; the antithetical points of view of two judges permit an ideological argument during the deliberations; and the appearance of the country's dictator is unusual and, to a mimetic melodrama, unnecessary. Rice evidently established these elements to permit the key speeches to be delivered in an emotionally charged atmosphere that is sympathetic to the accused. The trial arouses outrage through the piling up of obviously false evidence and the refusal of the judges to acknowledge the innocence of the defendants. The ending results from the shooting of Vesnic. Although this forms a completed ending, the incident's lack of logical necessity or even very strong probability indicates that the shooting simply stops the play with a theatrically startling circumstance. The shooting is a wish fulfillment for the sympathetic characters and an indication to the audience about the kind of action that must be taken against such dictators rather than a credible conclusion for the action of the play. Since accidental circumstances precipitate the shooting, logic is obviously not operating. The ending is contrived to show the audience the only antidote to fascism.

All these observations do not mean, however, that *Judgment Day* is poorly written. The dialogue is clear, credible, and interesting, and there is good suspense throughout the story. It is theatrically and didactically effective as a drama. The play was, indeed, so effective that in the mid-thirties Hitler protested against production of the play, and to appease him, several European countries banned it. Thus, *Judgment Day* was proven on the best evidence to have been successful as propaganda.

These three trial plays demonstrate how well basic legal formalities can be utilized as organizing factors for a didactic play. *Judgment Day*, as a whole and in many of its individual speeches, corresponds to forensic speech as a persuasive type. In Chapter 13 of the *Rhetoric*, Aristotle explained that just and unjust actions can be classified in relation to laws—those of a particular state or those of nature, and in relation to the persons affected—an entire community or individual members of society. These three plays illustrate such legal conditions as unjust laws (*Precedent*), just but perverted laws (*They Shall Not Die*), and unjust circumvention of law (*Judgment Day*). The persons most seriously affected in each case are the innocent individuals in the play and the entire community, represented by the audiences. In all three plays, specific laws of a state are made to appear less important than basic laws of humanity. Trial procedure, then, is another effective structural pattern available to a didactic playwright.

The other didactic plays of the thirties that persuade in the manner of a forensic speech use neither the form nor the principles of the legal speech as fully as the trial plays. The other plays are *We, the People* by Elmer Rice, *1931–* by Claire and Paul Sifton, and *Mulatto* by Langston Hughes. Each of these plays accuses the entire social system or some facet of it, but none of them is so precisely concerned with justice as the plays discussed in the previous section. None of these three adheres so closely to the procedures previous to and during a trial.

We, the People by Elmer Rice best typifies these other plays. It catalogues the social and economic disruptions of the time. No other play of all the didactic dramas of the thirties blends so many issues. With a variety of thoughts, with several story lines, and with numerous groups represented in specific characters, *We, the People* culminates in a militant and direct call for social justice. Although it protests the evils of capitalism as stridently as do the Marxian strike plays, it differs from them in that its appeal for justice is not doctrinaire. It does not call for a socialistic revolution. And, although one of the climactic scenes is a trial, it does not focus upon legal justice. The trial in this play is merely one incident among many in a larger story.

We, the People points to the reasons for and results of unemployment, poverty, racial discrimination, social persecution, and war. The play teaches that, in the present socioeconomic condition of the country, justice and freedoms are denied to the masses for the profit of the few. The play inculcates knowledge by means of arousing sympathy and outrage. It encourages protest rather than revolutionary action.

The play accuses the capitalistic system and its leaders, and it opposes economic exploitation, militarism, war, political corruption, and social injustice. It argues that protest is not futile. The play's final speech expresses the central thought: Freedom, justice, and equality of opportunity are the unalienable rights of life, liberty, and the pursuit of happiness; it appears that this country has put lynch law in the place of justice, class rule in place of democracy, and tyranny in the place of liberty. The speech further contends that Americans themselves must cleanse the nation, make it orderly, and restore it as a decent place in which decent people may live.[4]

Measured by the structural principles of the best mimetic plays, *We, the People* would appear diverse, episodic, and lacking in depth of characterization. Because of the play's didactic purpose and controlling idea, however, it emerges as a carefully organized, sweepingly large, and excitingly persuasive drama. It dramatizes the destruction, as a result of the economic and social disorder, of one family that lives in the city and of another that lives on a farm; the machinations of the rich provide an ironic contrast throughout. The characters engage in little dramatic action; most of the changes are the results of outside circumstances pressing in upon them. Theirs are lives of reaction rather than volition.

The play could be labeled a drama of suffering because the sympathetic characters are simply victims. Discovery plays a minor part in the plot, and in this play it is a function of the audience rather than of the characters. In fact, this shift of discovery from the players to the spectators is one of the significant features of most didactic plays.

Unity and probability exist in *We, the People* differently than in a mimetic play and differently, too, than in other plays of accusation, the trial plays especially. The basic intent in each scene is to expose certain conditions. As the action progresses, these conditions increase the suffering of the characters; the play's order is emotionally climactic. The motivation of the characters and the incidents of the first nineteen scenes lead inevitably to the appeal scene that ends the play. In addition to utilizing

4. Elmer Rice, *We, the People*, pp. 252–53.

thought in the form of exhortative and deliberative speeches at the end, the play repeats thoughts in key speeches by sympathetic characters. Rice also unified the play in three other ways. He related most of the rich characters through family, business, or political interests; they know each other well. He connected the poor people by writing at least one character from each story line into another story line. Sympathetic characters from all the various lines join in the final scene to appeal for justice and to protest against social disorder.

The causal relationship of incidents and character reactions is not so important in *We, the People* as the expression of thought aroused by circumstances. The logic is rhetorical rather than causal in the usual dramatic manner. Many incidents occur without an antecedent or a consequence. For example, the incident in scene 1 is not a real *beginning* because it has no consequences in any of the following scenes. In effect, the entire play corresponds to the *middle* of a conventional mimetic play. The *ending* of this play, as in so many other didactic plays, is not an end, in the sense that it is an incident with antecedents but no consequences. Indeed, the rally that comprises the last scene does not end the story of any of the characters, but all the story lines converge in the final scene to make vivid the rhetorical speeches directed at the audience.

The action of *We, the People* is serious, and in many other respects the play resembles a melodrama. It arouses sympathy for the poor people, who face various threats, and the ending stimulates fear for their welfare. The threats are mainly economic: no money, no food, no job, no decent place to live. The antipathetic characters are hateful. Sympathy and hate combine to create a sense of outrage for the sake of persuasion. The form of melodrama is unfulfilled; the play lacks reward for the good characters or punishment for the evil ones. Also, the characters change little, or not at all. During the play they make no moral choices; their commitments and major decisions predate the play. The action serves to reveal them more openly. They cling ever more firmly to their preconceived convictions, which do not change.

Most of the conflict in the play is slight, low-keyed, emotion-laden argument between individuals. The scenes of major conflict become, by contrast, more compelling: scene 10, the meeting of the student newspaper editorial board; scene 14, the meeting of the demonstrating workers in front of the factory; scene 15, the firing of a liberal professor by his university's president; and scene 18, the workers' protest rally. It is strange that in this play, which purports to show the struggle of the poor against economic and social conditions, only twice is there conflict between the poor and the rich—scenes 14 and 18. In both scenes, the poor meet only the hirelings of the rich, and the fight occurs accidentally rather than through the choice of any major character. The only scenes of intellectual conflict are 10—the student meeting, and 15—the dismissal of the professor. The dialogue of the play narrates most of the struggles; few occur on stage. Even the over-all protest of the play proceeds with words more than action. The final appeal—to put the country in order—urges a general attitude on the audience rather than asks them for specific action.

The rhetorical appeal *We, the People* makes to the audience in the final scene is, however, most direct aesthetically. The only device for achieving a more direct appeal would be to have the actors shed their roles and speak as themselves. Were it not for the final scene, the play would be far less successful as a didactic drama, and it would also need to be much longer to tie up the various stories in a dramatic conclusion. As it stands, the conclusion of *We, the People* is perhaps the most persuasive of all the final scenes among all the decade's didactic plays. The play closes with the accusation that millions of people have to exist in hunger and darkness so a select few can have a thousand times more material goods than they need. The play suggests that the solution lies in protest, in union with the millions of poor and oppressed everywhere, until mankind shakes off the chains of poverty and wins for itself the right to live in freedom and happiness (pp. 249–50).

Claire and Paul Sifton's play, *1931–*, presented by the Group Theatre as its second production, might be called an unemployment drama. *1931–* resembles *We, the People* in its episodic arrangement and its picture of the intensifying oppression of sympathetic characters, but it differs in its basic thought, structure, and appeal. The controlling idea is that, in order for life to be bearable, every man must be able to exercise his right to work and his right to achieve some happiness.[5] The play presents a solution to the unemployment problem with its resultant poverty—the solidarity of the working class in revolution. In addition to fourteen story scenes, this play employs ten interludes, which contrapuntally deepen the meaning and broaden the significance of the action.

The story is of Adam, a worker in a warehouse, being fired and then struggling to find work. He nearly starves in his search for a job, and the occasional employment he finds only demeans him. He tries a sidewalk robbery but is too honest to follow it through. Finally, he prays to God for a chance to work. The ten interludes occur between the fourteen story scenes, and all of them are set at a factory gate. They progressively show unemployed workers banding together and confronting a boss, the police, and the state militia. When the crowd begins to fight in interlude 10, the militia gasses the workers. In the play's final scene, the story characters join in rebellion the crowd that acted in the interludes. The Finale opens on an empty stage. In the wings, the masses sing a song resembling the "Internationale." Suddenly a silent mass of marching workers fills the stage; Adam, the central character, is among them. They steadily march across the stage in the face of gunfire.

The "Authors' Note" in the published version of the play is unusually revealing in its discussion of the con-

5. Claire Sifton and Paul Sifton, *1931–*, p. 144.

trolling ideas and the structure. The Siftons wanted to present an individual's experiences when he is caught in a movement of unemployed workers that is a struggle against circumstances they can neither understand nor change. The authors tried to establish a contrapuntal design, balancing the story scenes with the interludes to indicate the emotional motivations toward revolution. They saw the story as a line of individual action and the interludes as a concomitant line of group action. They wanted the individual to be drawn toward the group because of unhappiness, frustration, and despair, and they intended that the rhythm of the play should gain speed and impetus until its climax in revolution.[6] The play is certainly a fulfillment of the Siftons' intentions.

Adam is volitional in his struggle against his situation, but the situation is so strongly in control he never is able to make a decision. When misfortune hits him, he struggles, but he can never choose the cause or the effect. By contrast, the mass of unemployed in the interludes is volitional and decides to take action in several of the scenes. Thus, the play argues that only in mass solidarity and active resistance can the individual oppose the system. One man alone cannot, according to 1931–, successfully fight the system. The crowd action in the interludes is the most unusual means for amplification of thought in all the didactic plays of the Depression; it is amplification through the activity of characters rather than through their speeches.

The villain of the play is the system. The system's representatives are the bosses. Every employer, such as the foreman of the truckers in scene 1, treats Adam in a heartless and exploitative manner.

Although the diction of the play uses the vocabulary of the uneducated worker, the dialogue is not very realistic. It is poetic in the brittle and economical Brechtian manner. For example, when Adam is fired, he claims that he can walk right across the street to get another job,

6. Claire Sifton and Paul Sifton, 1931–, p. xiii.

that a boss in any foundry, factory, woods, mine, or road will take one look at him and say, "Come to momma." (P. 8.)

The injustice of the conditions that defeat and destroy a man by preventing him from earning a living forms the body of the play. The title indicates, by means of its date and following dash, that the story had a beginning but is not ended. The dash indicates some change is to result, as does the silent march in the face of gunfire at the play's conclusion.

Harold Clurman noted that the play succeeded in moving the poorer masses to emotion and action. Although the critics blasted the play and it closed after only nine performances, the directors of the Group Theatre noticed an emotional fervor in the audience reaction each night—mainly in the balcony. And every night the balcony audience grew more vociferous. On the final night there was an actual demonstration inside the theatre, and later Clurman found out that some of the people who had come backstage had established discussion circles, clubs, and new amateur theatre groups.[7] The over-all emotional effect of the play is probably the most depressing of all the didactic plays of the thirties, and although the final march attempts a positive suggestion of action, the play ultimately arouses outrage only to answer with despair.

Among the didactic plays of the thirties, only a few contain many black characters or deal directly with the problems of racial prejudice: *Brass Ankle*, *Hymn to the Rising Sun*, *Stevedore*, *They Shall Not Die*, and *Mulatto*. *Mulatto* by Langston Hughes is noteworthy in its rhetorical presentation of the idea that "the way of the old South"—that aspect of the "way" by which white men take advantage of black women and produce bastard mulatto children—must end.[8]

The short, violent story follows in some respects the

7. Harold Clurman, *The Fervent Years: The Story of the Group Theatre and the Thirties*, pp. 70–72.
8. Langston Hughes, *Mulatto*, in *Five Plays*, ed. Webster Smalley.

form of a melodrama. Colonel Norwood, a plantation owner, has kept Cora Lewis for thirty years as housekeeper and mistress. They have begotten many mulattoes. Although the Colonel educated them and kept them from field work, he refuses to acknowledge them as true sons and daughters. One of the sons, Robert, returns from college in the North and begins to stir up rebellion. He refuses to kowtow to the Colonel or to any other white, and in an argument with the Colonel during which the old man threatens to shoot him, Robert strangles his father. All the vicious white men of the area join in hunting down Robert, and he finally shoots himself. He dies in the bedroom of his conception, just as the whites storm into the house.

The principles of melodrama the play employs include the emotional powers of fear and hate, fear for the blacks and hate of the whites. The threat to Robert is present at the opening, and it continues to grow during the action. The sympathetic black people, especially Cora and Robert, are ethically right throughout, with the exception of the crime of murder. The whites are the villains, and they are unremittingly vicious.

Two principles push this play into the realm of the overtly didactic. First, the protagonist is not Robert. Although he is the character who precipitates the action and is in a sense the hero, the central character is Cora, his mother. As an observer and commentator, she has the largest number of speeches in the play; the main character, then, is rhetorical in nature rather than active. Second, the play permits long rhetorical speeches that present most of its elements of thought. The extended speeches, in form and content, make up the play's major substance. Although some of the other didactic plays contain an occasional long speech, *Mulatto* has longer speeches and more of them than any other play of the whole group. The play as a whole, with its melodramatic story and with its rhetorical speeches, protests the outrageous injustice of white men and the indignities committed against all black people.

Each of the last three plays analyzed above illustrates that a didactic play may utilize principles from more than one type of traditional rhetorical construction. Each accuses in the manner of a forensic speech, and each exhorts in the manner of a deliberative speech. The economic system that permits widespread unemployment is accused in *1931–*, mainly in individual speeches; yet the play exhorts the audience, by means of its solidarity march at the end, to join the workers' revolution. Each extended rhetorical speech at the end of *We, the People* has for its object both justice and utility; it urges its audience to recognize which people are victims of social inequity and to protest the factors in society that permit such exploitation. Although *Mulatto* accuses a long-existing system and actions that occurred in the past, the play points to the future. These three plays look to justice as their goal, but their conclusions indicate the expedient actions that are necessary if justice for all is to be achieved in the future. Just as no persuasive speech is strictly limited to one set of rhetorical principles, no didactic play is bound to use only a simple combination of them. The plays that mix the rhetorical types, however, are less clear and less effective as persuasive pieces. Thus, *They Shall Not Die* is more persuasive than *We, the People*, but both are dynamic plays.

Aeschylus wrote the first great courtroom drama as the third play in his *Oresteia* trilogy, and in it he used the procedures of a trial to communicate ideas to his audience. Since Aeschylus, many writers have brought the courtroom onto the world's stages. To be sure, not all such plays are didactic, but the framework of a trial permits speeches of accusation and defense in the dialogue. Further, in the over-all action, the pattern of a trial is an appropriate form for conveying a persuasive message to an audience. Insofar as man is a social being, he must be concerned with justice and injustice. And that is precisely the concern of the six plays discussed in this chapter.

9

Arguments for Solidarity

For he who, himself imbued with public teachings, yet cares not to contribute aught to the public good, may be well assured that he has fallen far from duty; for he is not "a tree by the streams of waters, bearing his fruit in due season," but rather a devouring whirlpool, ever sucking in, and never pouring back what it has swallowed.

Dante, *De Monarchia*

The didactic dramatists of the thirties considered no man nor any institution sacred. They undertook to examine all men and institutions, as judges, as representatives of the assembly of the common man. These writers saw the will of the people as truly sacrosanct and transcendent, if and when it is provoked to expression. When they examined individuals or groups that worked against the interests of the sovereign people, they were ready to damn them, and they were equally quick to praise those who deserved their respect. These writers attempted in their polemic dramas to express universal thought as censure or praise of men, movements, and institutions.

When written thus, in the mode of an epideictic speech of praise or blame, the didactic drama was like a clap of Jovian thunder for those who were guilty of violating the interests of the people, or like the soft summer rustling of leaves for those who were innocent of oppressing the people. In order to help awaken the social awareness of the masses, the playwrights wrote plays to enlighten. Ten of the didactic plays of the Depression employ persuasive principles from the epideictic type of rhetoric rather than from the deliberative or the forensic.

Four plays form the first group within the epideictic

type to be discussed, and these might be termed dramas of awakening: *Paradise Lost* and *Awake and Sing!* by Clifford Odets, *Gentlewoman* and *The Pure in Heart* by John Howard Lawson. These plays center on moderate praise of the basically good but unenlightened central characters and on severe censure of the system responsible for the chaotic and unjust conditions of society. *Paradise Lost* best typifies this group because it is the most fully prelective and because its structural principles are both the clearest and the most efficient.

The purpose of this group of plays is not so easy to identify nor does the purpose appear so early in the scripts as in the more overtly persuasive plays. In each of the four plays, the central character arrives at a reflective perception at the end of the play. This perception indicates the organization of the play, although one must review the play backwards to identify the structure that renders the awakening at the end possible, credible, and effective. The general purpose of *Paradise Lost* is, of course, persuasion. More specifically, the final causes of the play are to place the responsibility for the world's dislocation upon the current economic system and to suggest that, if the members of the audience assume ethical attitudes, there is hope for an ordered future. The emotional conditions that produce the final persuasive effects of the play are confusion and wonder. From these, the characters and the audience move to awakening and enlightenment, for, the play warns, if they do not bring an enlightened vision to bear on the world's problems, we may all fall to decay and destruction.

The ideas in *Paradise Lost* activate the movement from confusion to enlightenment. Leo Gordon, the central character, expresses the play's key thought in a speech of awakening at the end; it is that "no man fights alone!"[1] Leo, an archetypal middle-class man, rejects the idea that he and his kind are finished because of the economic and social turmoil of the Depression. He believes

1. Clifford Odets, *Paradise Lost*, in *Six Plays of Clifford Odets*, p. 230.

in the future more strongly than in the past, and he declares that greatness does not exist in man but in men, because men are awakening everywhere to fight together for a new and better world (pp. 229–30). As a speech, the plays says: The middle-class man, if he is a good person, may lose his material possessions by joining the masses in their revolt, but by losing them he will gain a sense of vision and purpose. He will lose his economically based "paradise" and gain the world of freedom and brotherhood. The ending is an awakening with song, a beginning. According to the play's argument, every man must discover what is real in life by learning how to halt the economic and political breakdown of society.

The story of *Paradise Lost* is a working part of the play, and it contributes to the thought of the whole. Leo Gordon is focal in the play, and a number of story lines are woven around him. Leo is the head of a middle-class family and the co-owner of a business that manufactures purses and other such merchandise. The "profound dislocation" of the world overwhelms both his family and his business. One of his sons is killed during a robbery; another son has sleeping sickness; and his daughter withdraws into a world of her own. His business partner embezzles the firm's money, and the business collapses. Only Clara, Leo's wife, reacts vigorously and positively to each eventuality, and she provides him with strength and love. The ending points to the future, not by explaining how the Gordons will survive, but by proclaiming that those with the strength and insight of Clara and Leo, when joined with others, will prevail.

The line of argument in an epideictic speech is by degree, and the proof most characteristic of such a speech is amplification and diminution. *Paradise Lost* depends, in the main, upon arguments of degree and upon amplifications of thought for its progression. More thoughts are expressed as general or possible statements in this play than in any other play analyzed in this study. Of course, all its statements are general only in relation to the story. As they relate to the play's central thought and persuasive purpose, the statements are crucial as content and centric to the organization. For example, near the opening of the play Leo says that "the world has a profound dislocation." The statement does not advance the story, but it establishes a basis for many later persuasive speeches.

Thought exists principally in *Paradise Lost* as amplification and diminution. Leo's entire speech of awakening at the play's close contains amplification from the characters' specific situation to the situation of humanity, to symptoms and solutions for mankind (pp. 229–30). Near the end of Act II, Leo tells Clara that they will live to witness strange and marvelous events within fifty years. She replies that, before fifty years have passed, they will be gone and forgotten, to which Leo responds that social chaos cannot last forever. Humanity cannot stand still; it must go backwards or forwards; and even movement backwards means going ahead (p. 126).

Thought, typical of the epideictic speech, also materializes in this play as blame or praise of characters who represent sympathetic or antipathetic points of view. For instance, when a delegation of workers comes to ask for an improvement of salary and working conditions, they praise one co-owner, Leo, and blame the other, Sam Katz. Katz represents the businessman who exploits workers, and Leo represents employers who sympathize with their employees. During the meeting Leo declares that people who are trying to support a family on just five dollars each week have a right to rise and revolt. He promises to end any exploitation in his shop, with the effect that, as they are leaving the meeting, one of his workers calls Leo a "good man" (p. 187). Among those who receive blame in the play are: Kewpie the crook; Foley the politician; and May the arsonist. Each in his own way stands for one or more evils of the system. Among those who receive praise are Leo the awakening middle-class man; Clara his wife; and Pike the radical worker.

The discursive pattern in *Paradise Lost*, as in so

many epideictic speeches, is climactic rather than cumulative in its progressive order. Nor does the play proceed from incident to incident in a causal manner. Few of the antecedents to occurrences are within the play. For example, the family's eviction from their home results from the embezzlement that caused Leo's bankruptcy; Katz's crime preceded the time-span of the play. The persuasive and structural pattern at work in this play is nowadays called topical. The speaker, in this case the playwright, selects the order of the materials—both ideas and incidents—that will best hold the interest of the audience and best make provision for sequences of thought.

Although the principles of epideictic oratory function in *Paradise Lost* and in others of similar organization, those principles work more obviously in the next group of plays to be examined, the plays in which one "evil" capitalist is censured. Nevertheless, in *Paradise Lost* some of the epideictic principles, in addition to simple praise and blame, are operative.

Whereas in an epideictic *speech* the object is nobleness, in an epideictic *play* the object is meanness. Censure is far more dominant in such a play than is praise. *Paradise Lost* attacks the ignobleness of some men and the capitalistic system they perpetuate.

The play also deals with the present time. The past is worthless, like a dream. This image recurs often, as when Pike tells Pearl that not dreams but work is what counts, or when Ben expresses his unrealistic dream of material success (pp. 199, 173). The present is the time for awakening. The entire play demonstrates how a family lives in the present by attempting to find out what is to be done, by holding to their principles despite the social breakdown, and finally by joining others in the fight against the system for the sake of the future.

To be a man of worth joined with other men of worth is, according to *Paradise Lost*, the most honorable human condition. The materials of the play help to prove this major idea. As the various characters receive praise or blame, their effectiveness as persuaders grows. Some of the incidents both enhance the *ethos* of a character and put the audience in a certain frame of mind. For example, when Katz brings the arsonist to see Leo, Leo absolutely refuses to have anything to do with the man or his criminal proposal.

The diction furnishes the illusion of reality because it employs the vocabulary, syntax, and rhythms of ordinary speech. One of the chief virtues of this play—and of *Awake and Sing!*—is Odets' realistic dialogue. It imitates everyday conversation and yet rises above the commonplace by means of original idioms and metaphors. Examples abound, but one of the best is the speech of a bum who refuses Leo's charity. The man explains to Leo the situation the Gordons are in, and by extension, he reveals the situation of the entire middle class. He advises Leo not to be fooled by the notion that the good old days will return. They won't. Leo, he says, has been destroyed, and he should admit the fact (p. 229). The dialogue is clear in its presentation of ideas, and usually it avoids a pedagogical ring.

As for the characters, Odets subsumed them to the thought, but each achieves a balance between dramatic verisimilitude and rhetorical function. Many exhibit all levels of character traits, from physical to cognitive. Leo is the most fully portrayed. His traits are multiple and complex. He makes several revealing expedient choices, but his ethical decisions characterize him best.

Odets also gave each of the characters the function of representing a class or one aspect of a class. He gave each an idea to represent as well—an idea as a solution to the problem of society. Pike, for example, represents the working class; as such, he favors the idea of collective membership for the sake of the future. As with most didactic dramas, the characters in this play both express and symbolize the significant ideas that the author wanted to communicate.

Although the plot of *Paradise Lost* contains some vestiges of melodrama, all story principles are in it for the sake of the persuasive thought rather than for the action. Odets selected the incidents and arranged their sequence in order to communicate the thought, not merely to stimulate an aesthetic experience. Both suffering and discovery are important plot elements in the play, but there is no reversal of fortune or reversal of attitude; Leo's awakening is based upon discovery. In this play, minor discoveries by the characters permit the expression of minor ideas, and the major discovery permits the expression of the central idea.

Although some critics have rated *Paradise Lost* as less than successful, it was Odets' favorite among his plays. The Group Theatre first produced it in 1935; it received poor reviews and ran for only seventy-three performances. But such facts reveal little about the play's quality. With regard to its structure, it fulfills its purpose as well as any didactic play written during the Depression.

Awake and Sing! by Clifford Odets discloses its didacticism from its title onwards. The imperative of the title and of the entire drama extends from a central thought: Each individual must struggle to achieve a full life amidst the dire conditions brought on by the social dislocation of the time, and the struggle for betterment is hopeless unless individuals awaken to reality and join all other workers to arrange life so that dollar bills do not have such almighty importance.[2]

In this play, no character is so fully a protagonist as is Leo in *Paradise Lost*. Although Odets chose to people this play differently—a family from the New York working class rather than from the middle class—the structure of *Awake and Sing!* is similar to that of *Paradise Lost*; both plays proceed with a persuasive purpose. By means of the play, which has aesthetic values as well, the author attempted to enlighten an audience about conditions and their causes and to suggest the general solution for bringing individual happiness and for curing the woes of society.

The organization of the play depends upon its basic

2. Clifford Odets, *Awake and Sing!*, in *Six Plays*, p. 97.

recommendation of collective social action. In addition, *Awake and Sing!* has a topical structure that is imposed upon the material rather than a mimetic structure of melodrama or tragedy. It develops like a speech rather than like a conventional play. In brief, the story concerns the Berger family and their struggles, and it focuses on each member at some time in the play. The story of each character relates rhetorically rather than causally to that of the family unit. Bessie, the mother, assumed the leadership of the family when Myron, the father, became inactive because of disappointments in his career. Hennie, their daughter, who is pregnant, schemes with Bessie to marry an immigrant worker and thus legitimize her child. When the scheme fails, she runs away with Moe Axelrod, a wounded war veteran. Uncle Morty, a rich capitalist, lords it over the family, and his actions serve to illustrate the evil nature of such men. The two most sympathetic characters are Ralph, the son, and Jacob, the grandfather. Ralph is a young worker who is sensitive, intelligent, and eager to fulfill his own potential.

Social pressure from the family and financial pressure from the economic conditions of the time force Ralph away from his first love, a young orphan girl. Jacob, an old intellectual, observes the troubles of the others and comments on them, continually proposing Marxian solutions. Because of his disgust with society as represented by the family, and because of his hopes for Ralph, Jacob commits suicide by slipping from the roof of their apartment building. Jacob intended his insurance money to go to Ralph, but Ralph refuses it. What he inherits instead is to him more valuable—the old man's awareness of life, his thoughts about the ills of society, and his Marxian vision of the future. The play ends with the sort of awakening that also ends *Paradise Lost*. Ralph asserts his vision by contending that he is strong and will become even stronger by joining others in the cause of the workingman and by rejecting the crass materialism that seems to him to be at the heart of society and of the Berger household (pp. 95, 97).

The style of *Awake and Sing!* is quite similar to that of *Paradise Lost*. The dialogue heaps praise upon the sympathetic characters, such as Ralph and Jacob, and censure upon those who are weak or wrong, such as Myron and Bessie. But it is clear that Odets blamed the system more than those individuals who contribute to its perpetuation. The objectives of this play are to illuminate, first, the nobility of Jacob and the resurrected nobility later in Ralph, and second, the ignobility of the system that destroyed the old man, oppresses the family, and frustrates Ralph.

The play concentrates upon the present, upon the realization necessary for today's awakening in order that the future may be better than today. Amplification consistently acts as a proof, as when Jacob tells the capitalistic Uncle Morty that the established system shoves the myth of success down the throat of every youth in the country (p. 72). Ralph also uses amplification in the play's key speech near the end: "Get teams together all over. Spit on your hands and get to work. And with enough teams together maybe we'll get steam in the warehouse so our fingers don't freeze off. Maybe we'll fix it so life won't be printed on dollar bills" (p. 97).

Awake and Sing! differs most widely from *Paradise Lost* in its materials. The specific characters, incidents, and words are not identical, to be sure, but they are similar in type. Jacob makes choral comment as a Marxian, thereby corresponding to Pike in the other play. Ralph is the seeker in *Awake and Sing!* just as Leo is in *Paradise Lost*. Jacob commits suicide in one of the plays and Ben in the other. The list of parallels is long. Suffice it to say that the means of both plays match. *Awake and Sing!* offers more humorous material and *Paradise Lost* more bitter material. From Myron's constant references to Teddy Roosevelt to Moe's habitual wisecracks, humor constantly appears in *Awake and Sing!* to season the seriousness. For example, when Bessie breaks all of Jacob's Caruso records, the final act that shatters the old man's heart, Moe says: "Tough tit! Now I can sleep in the morning. Who the hell wants ta hear a wop air his tonsils all day long!" (P. 86.)

Upon first examination, both of these epideictic plays by Clifford Odets might appear to be mimetic dramas with loose structures. But ideas definitely control the progression of the scenes and the actions of the characters in both plays, and they are clearly didactic. The seriousness of tragedy, the threats of melodrama, and some of the ridicule of comedy are elements in these two plays. But those elements, like the qualitative parts of character and plot, are subsidiary to their central thoughts.

John Howard Lawson, the leading dramatic theorist of the leftist theatre, wrote two plays that were produced within two days of each other in March, 1934—*Gentlewoman* and *The Pure in Heart*. Neither pleased the critics of the commercial theatre nor those for the Communist press. The failure of the two was due in large measure to the fact that both treat basically mimetic materials in a quasi-didactic manner. Both sets of critics commented on the confusion in the scripts. The conventional critics objected to the lack of clarity in the action, and the leftist critics damned the uncertain handling of the Marxian message in each play. In *Gentlewoman* Lawson attempted to force the materials of a drawing-room comedy into the Marxian mold, and in *The Pure in Heart* he tried to do the same thing with what might have been a strong melodrama. These two plays, like the two by Odets just discussed, stand near the dividing line between the didactic and the mimetic, but when they are examined structurally, they are clearly didactic.

Gentlewoman asserts the idea that leftist social awareness in general and commitment to Communist militancy in particular can lend new balance and reason to empty lives. As with the two Odets plays, this play of awakening, by presenting the central characters as examples, urges the audience to come to a collective realization and commitment. Through its two major characters, the play says that individuals must give up their porno-graphic games in the corners of chaos and join the march toward the "red horizon" of the class struggle. Only through total commitment to the social revolution, ac-cording to the message of the play, can one achieve honor in life.

Each of *Gentlewoman*'s five scenes ends with a crisis that involves conflict, and in each a decision resolves the conflict. Gwyn Ballantine is the central character. She decides in turn not to go to bed with Rudy; to go away with him; to leave him; and to send him away. Each of her decisions illustrates a crisis in the class war, since Rudy represents the workers and Gwyn the managers. Since each decision points to the total argument of the play, the central thought dictates the organization and the supporting action. As an epideictic speech, the play illustrates and declares that one must be a certain type of person with a certain type of consciousness in order to attain a place of honor and to live a life of value in a time of chaos. Money, breeding, culture, love, and even intelligence do not really matter; commitment to the Marxian cause is man's only salvation, according to *Gentlewoman*.[3]

The Pure in Heart possesses many features of a skillful but contrived melodrama. The characters' actions are quite incredible and ill-motivated for a mimetic play, but when it is understood that the incidents and their sequence establish an environment and build to a cli-mactic scene in which the socioeconomic system can be blamed for the errors of individuals, then the structure of the whole becomes apparent. But the characters are unbelievable, even though they effectively communicate the requisite ideas. The central thought is that there is more to life than the rapacious clawing toward financial success. Love, money, crime, and their like will not pre-vent the system from crushing the individual. Only if all people work together to build a new world and to estab-

3. John Howard Lawson, *Gentlewoman*, in *With a Reckless Preface*, p. 220.

lish a new social and economic order will the individual be able to live rationally.[4]

The two plays by Odets and the two by Lawson, then, form a group in which one or more of the central characters comes to a realization, an awakening. Praise in some measure rewards those who awaken, but the plays deal more fully with censure of the system responsible for the total social dislocation. Since Marxian thought colors all four plays, capitalism is depicted as the motivating force in the evil system. Many critics have judged these four plays to be confused or loosely organized. As mimetic works they are indeed so, but as rhetorical pieces they are coherently persuasive.

Another set of didactic plays that employ rhetorical principles, especially those of epideictic speech, concentrates on censure of one individual. In each of the three plays of this set, the focal individual is a ruthless capitalist—Sol Ginsberg in *Success Story* by John Howard Lawson, Guy Button in *Gold Eagle Guy* by Melvin Levy, and McGafferty in *Panic* by Archibald MacLeish.

Lawson's *Success Story* stands not only as one of the most interesting and efficient of all the dramas of censure, but it also joins his *Marching Song* as an outstanding example of one subspecies of didactic drama. Unlike the other epideictic plays of this chapter, *Success Story* contains no awakening and little praise for anyone. It says that to be a capitalist is to ruin one's own life and the lives of those near you. It warns the audience to avoid success as a capitalist, and it recommends that people should join the movement to unseat such ruthless men from places of power in American society. This complex of ideas is at the heart of *Success Story*.

Sol Ginsberg, an ambitious young man from the Jewish ghetto of New York's East Side, works as a clerk in the Merritt advertising company. Sol got the job through the help of Sarah Glassman, his girl and Merritt's secretary. Early in the play, when a young executive

4. John Howard Lawson, *The Pure in Heart*, in *With a Reckless Preface*, p. 108.

fresh from Yale fails with an important assignment, Sol gets his job. Also in Act I, Sol reveals his desire for money as a source of power over things and people. Although he loves Sarah, he wants to own Merritt's beautiful mistress Agnes Carter. Act II takes place two years later, in 1930. Sol is now an important member of the firm, and he grows richer daily by selling short on the stock market, while Merritt and the others are rapidly losing money. Sol discovers that Merritt has been using the company's funds to pay off margin calls from his broker. By using this information and by suggesting to a backer a good plan for reorganization, Sol claws his way to a top executive post. Also, he alienates Sarah and talks the tinseled Agnes into marrying him. The action of Act III, two years later, shows Sol's final take-over of the company. His relationship to Agnes is that of owner to expensive toy. Sarah plans to leave the company, and Sol is pushing Merritt out entirely. But Sol realizes that his life is empty. His inner desire remains unsated, and he has betrayed the promise of his youth. When he attempts to force Sarah to love him, she shoots him. While Sol lies wounded and dying, Merritt and Agnes enter, and the four decide to call Sol's death a suicide.

The structure of the play, as represented in the events, depicts the three major movements in Sol's life: stage one, the youth with potential who capitulates to dreams of material success; stage two, the rising young man who rejects his radical and humane ideals for the sake of monetary gain; stage three, the business chief and speculator who destroys everything he touches, including himself. Sarah only shoots Sol; he has destroyed himself.

As these three stages evolve, the dialogue reveals the corresponding changes in Sol's thought. Early in the play, Sol declares his dual goal of money and social revolution. Sarah explains that the two are incompatible.[5] In the second movement, most of Sol's thoughts are of

5. John Howard Lawson, *Success Story*, pp. 38–40.

expedient ways to make money. He says that he fits life together like a picture puzzle; in matters of love or money, he wins because he waits and watches (p. 175). In Act III Sonnenberg, a rich banker who invests in Sol's firm, warns him that his egoism may ruin him. He accuses Sol of never being content, of always chasing a vision, of wanting to alter the world according to his own selfish interests (p. 183). And Sol comes to understand that the American materialistic dream follows a simple pattern: Americans work for money so they can buy enough goods to fill a house, then buy a larger house that will hold more goods. Everyone is on a materialistic treadmill (p. 186). He reflects that everyday life is like the stock market; both are games a person cannot win (p. 239). And Sol dies after this last speech: Once there was a Jewish carpenter named Jesus, robed in the colors of the rainbow; he revealed truth to mankind; and perhaps there will be others like him in the future. But Sol is not interested in saviors; he realizes that his major concern is himself. He asks to be buried in a solid silver coffin decorated with cupids in gold, the more expensive the better (p. 243). Sol's request for that particular kind of coffin is sardonic on his part and symbolic to the audience because Sol's brother, a small-time gangster shot down by the police, was buried in the same sort of coffin. Sol realizes that he has accomplished no more with his life than did his brother. Thus, Lawson hinted to the audience that capitalists are, after all, no better than common crooks. Sol remains to the end an unredeemed capitalist, the twentieth-century American Faust, the eternally damned organization man.

Success Story is realistic in style, especially when compared with such plays as *Bury the Dead*, *The Cradle Will Rock*, or *1931–*. Although Lawson chose an early attack on the story of Sol Ginsberg and passed over two years in each act break, he placed the action in one setting and involved only ten characters, most of whom participate in every act. The social milieu of the play—as represented by topics of conversation, modes of dress, the furnishings of the room, and even the motivating ideas—is evocative of the period in which it was written. From the idioms and dialects in the diction to the circumstances of the stock market, the play utilizes a realistic mode of communication. Nevertheless, its principal effect is idealistic—usually true of a didactic play, no matter how realistic its details may be. Because a dramatist is trying to communicate one or more ideal concepts to an audience rather than merely to present an action, every persuasive play, in the process of its formation and in its final form, must of necessity propound an ideal as its thought. Such works tend to stimulate an intellectual rather than an aesthetic response.

To consider *Success Story* as an epideictic speech is to see it as a drama of dishonor. Sol does nothing except for his own financial advancement or for his own sadistic delight. Sol has only one admirable quality, his capacity for hard work, but because he works for the wrong things, even that virtue is degraded. The ending sequence fulfills the epideictic pattern of the play. Neither Sarah, Merritt, Agnes, nor Sol himself express any sorrow when Sol is shot and is to die. Merritt and Agnes are startled, of course, but they—and Sol, too, surprisingly—are concerned that the police believe Sol's death to be suicide rather than murder by Sarah. As he dies, Sol speaks his own epitaph, and the play simultaneously speaks an epitaph for capitalism. He says he has been dead for a long time (p. 242).

The characterizations in *Success Story* are full, and they are important to the dramatic effects and the overall rhetorical goal. Each of the major characters—Sol, Sarah, Merritt, Agnes—shows facets that represent each of the six traditional categories of traits: biological, physical, dispositional, motivational, deliberative, and decisive. With regard to decision—the most highly characterizing element in any agent and the one that transforms character into action—*Success Story* best demonstrates a principle basic to many of the didactic plays. The major decision by the central character is made before the play, or early in the action. During Act I Sol decides to forsake his radical ideas for monetary success. In other didactic plays there are similar examples of early decision, or pre-decision. For example, in *Johnny Johnson*, Johnny has decided to be a pacifist before the play begins. Many characters in didactic drama, as in melodrama, are set before the play and change little or not at all during the play's action. The writer of a mimetic melodrama thus creates clearer conflict and better identifies the characters whom the audience should love or hate. In didactic drama, this preformation of characters works as part of the persuasive proof and creates an identifiable *ethos* to support the central complex of thought.

The plot of *Success Story* serves as material to the argument both by putting the audience in a sympathetic frame of mind—that is, arousing and holding interest and requisite emotions—and by operating as a dramatic allegory. To achieve both goals, Lawson arranged the story in a simple yet effective pattern. Sol, the volitional protagonist, decides early to pursue materialist goals; he encounters obstacles; scenes of conflict result; he overcomes one obstacle and moves on to the next. He finally attains his determined goal of wealth, but he finds his inner desires for reshaping the world still unsatisfied. In his last maneuver to grasp love, he destroys himself. In a limited sense, the play contains a plot of suffering and discovery. Sol discovers but rejects the fact that material success is worthless. Lawson did not organize the plot to fulfill the dramatic requirements of a mimetic form but rather to communicate the central idea in a dramatic and theatrical manner. The play accomplishes its author's intent effectively.

Gold Eagle Guy by Melvin Levy differs from *Success Story* only marginally, insofar as it is a persuasive piece. The purpose and effects, the structure and materials are strikingly similar in the two plays. In *Gold Eagle Guy*, the purpose is again to persuade an audience of the evil nature of capitalism, and the points are made in a negatively epideictic way. The principal character is a capitalist who is censured by his son and also by the play's action. In this instance, however, the subject character is not just any capitalist who scrambles to success but one of the original American robber-barons who helped establish the foundations of capitalistic commerce in North America.

In five carefully selected scenes separated by time-leaps of two to nineteen years, *Gold Eagle Guy* presents the crucial incidents in the life of Guy Button, shipping magnate and financial manipulator. In 1862, at age twenty-one, Guy jumps ship in San Francisco to pursue his goal of material fortune. He begins his climb by selling his sailing gear twice, to different men. In 1864 Guy takes over a shipping company because he is willing to transport masses of Chinese coolies to California. Parrot, a banker, gives Guy his true start as an exploitative capitalist. Fifteen years later during the financial panic of 1879, Guy is able to help Parrot save his bank, but in return he demands 60 per cent control and access to the financial records of all the other businessmen in the city. In 1898, after a lapse of nineteen years, Guy controls most of the economic machinations in California and is battling Japanese shipowners for control of the shipping in the entire Pacific. When he arrives at his shipping line's offices on April 18, 1906, he is one of the world's richest and most powerful men. He encounters there his son, who confronts him with accusations about his evil life. Guy refuses to be cowed by this confrontation. Instead, when his son is killed in the historic earthquake, he praises God. While he talks to the Lord, he compares himself to Samson and dances ecstatically; while he is dancing, the building collapses and destroys him.

Guy Button is even more ruthless, uncouth, and characterized by fewer human traits than Sol Ginsberg of *Success Story*. The only time Guy shows a sympathetic emotion occurs when he almost renounces his empire to go away with actress Adah Menken. Other than that, he is selfish, heartless, ambitious, and mean. But his self-righteousness outweighs even his egoism.

The thought of the play stands mainly in the examples of evil conduct in which Guy engages. The play maintains interest by means of the hypnotic effect of evil rather than by suspense about the outcome of a particular conflict. The over-all structure is episodic. So much time elapses between scenes that each scene becomes a one-act play in itself, with its own exposition, set of characters, conflict, and central incident.

By comparing the major characters of *Gold Eagle Guy* with those of *Success Story*, this particular kind of didactic play comes clear as a pattern. Sol and Guy, of course, represent the powerful and corrupt capitalist; Sarah and Guy's wife Jessie represent the lovingly human side of life, which the protagonist in each case rejects and crushes. Merritt and the banker Parrot represent the smaller fry of capitalism who lack the strength to retain control and who get trampled by more ruthless men. And Agnes in *Success Story* corresponds to Adah Menken in *Gold Eagle Guy* as a symbol of material success, the sort of woman men wish to own as a trophy.

The thought of *Gold Eagle Guy* emerges in words as well as in the dramatic working out of the incidents. But fewer dianoetic speeches occur in this play than in *Success Story*. The only praise for Guy comes from himself. In one of the most significant passages, he says that if it had not been for him there would be no great cities, no railroads, no great United States. He considers himself the instrument of the Lord and that he has directly shared in His power and glory.[6]

All the major characters except his lieutenant censure Guy. As a profiteer, they blame him for the financial woes of San Francisco and of the entire nation (p. 82). He is accused of fostering intersectionalism and internationalism, not as policies that help the country, but as devices to help only the men at the top (p. 90). And his

6. Melvin Levy, *Gold Eagle Guy*, p. 153.

son adds to these accusations blame for the destruction and murder of Guy's wife and of hundreds of other innocent people (pp. 180–81).

The play's most crucial and characterizing moment illustrates what it is really like to be a successful materialist. Adah Menken finally offers herself to Guy, not because he can buy her—she will not be bought—but because he mentions love. Guy could sell his Gold Eagle shipping line to the Japanese for a million dollars and use the money for an ample life with Adah. But he chooses to continue the fight for control of the Pacific. He sends Adah away by giving her a check for several thousand dollars. She starts to refuse because she does not want money, but she accepts his check when, in his one sympathetic moment, he says that money is all he has to give (p. 154).

Gold Eagle Guy joins *Success Story* as illustrative of drama that can be didactic through means other than direct exhortation of the audience. These two plays do not persuade by use of forensic structure and legal speeches that point to justice. Rather, they stand as polemic speeches of censure that arouse negative emotions, attitudes, and judgments in an audience. Their persuasive power controls their structure and pervades their action. But their dramatic effectiveness is undeniable, their interest level high.

The third among this set of epideictic plays that censure a single capitalist as representative of the entire system is *Panic* by Archibald MacLeish.[7] In a first reading this play's most immediately striking features are the emotive power of its diction, the thinness of its characterizations, the brevity of its story, and the principles of epideictic oratory that control its organization. Only to a minor degree does the play urge the audience to take action, but it is no less a rhetorical piece for that. To epitomize the play is to say that it works like an extended graveside epitaph. As a minister stands at a burial and

7. Archibald MacLeish, *Panic, a Play in Verse.*

praises or blames the man soon to be covered with earth, so MacLeish placed himself at the graveside of capitalism and ritually censured the giant he wished dead. Of all the plays in this set, *Panic* is the most truly ceremonial.

Although *Panic* is more catastrophic than the other two plays—it begins nearer the major incident of destruction—it nevertheless utilizes the same basic story. The details of the central thought complex are different, but the same general idea prevails as in the other two plays. Capitalism is a basically corrupt system, according to all three plays, and it is jerking in the throes of death brought on inevitably by historical change and paradoxically by its own leaders. More specifically, *Panic* concentrates on this idea: When panic strikes fear into a system's leaders, the system begins to totter; when confidence goes, the system falls; and when corrupt leaders hesitate, they fail because of their own destructive and cowardly natures and the unswerving march of oppressed people toward freedom.

Unless schooled in the arrangement of Greek tragedy, the principles of epideictic speech, the troubles of the thirties, the jargon of finance, and the techniques of verse, an audience might find this play nearly incomprehensible, or at least uncommunicative. The verse overpowers all elements of character and story, although it retains a material relationship to thought. And the choice of words is either suggestive or jargonal. *Panic* is, in short, ineffective dramatically and didactically, regardless of its potential for arousing the emotions and stimulating the imagination of a sophisticated reader.

Although the story assumes little importance when compared with the force of those in *Success Story* and *Gold Eagle Guy*, it does exist in *Panic*. The play advances quantitatively like a typical Greek tragedy. The focus onstage alternates between a street, in which a crowd stands below an electric news bulletin of the Times Square type, and the office of McGafferty, the leading industrialist of his time and the owner of the country's largest bank.

With a basic action similar to the other two plays,

MacLeish presented the fall of an archetypal capitalist. He did not trace the rise of McGafferty as the other stories traced the rise of Sol Ginsberg and Guy Button, but he used a similar situation of personal catastrophe to reflect the national crisis and self-destruction. *Panic* has a thought-controlled structure, however poetically articulated the dialogue may be.

Few, if any, commentators identified MacLeish as a Marxist during the thirties, but Marxian ideological influence is apparent in *Panic*. The play censures McGafferty, in his role of capitalist, for the conditions that produced the financial panic and also for his submission to the panic. A blind man blames McGafferty for the anguish of the poor and for the violence against the unemployed (pp. 28–33). A lawyer censures McGafferty for surrendering in the face of difficulties (p. 91). Not only individual speeches but also the whole play as a speech censure McGafferty both for creating the system and for not giving of himself in time of national need.

In the play, MacLeish revealed that in the making of the drama he was far more interested in the verse than in the supporting structure. The story is slight, the incidents lack intensity of conflict, the characters are unconcerned with decisions. The diction and thought, unaided by other dramatic elements, give structure and impact to the whole. The verse succeeds in being suggestive, emotive, and connotative, but it is far from clear as expression of ideas. The thoughts emerge with a careful reading, but it is unlikely they would be communicated intact from a stage.

It is justifiable to compose a play with the intent that it rise vertically to a climax of emotional intensity rather than to move horizontally to tell a story. Aeschylus wrote such plays, as has Samuel Beckett. But because MacLeish sacrificed dramatic structure to verse, thought takes over the play as the formal part, the Greek quantitative arrangement notwithstanding. Ironically, *Panic* is a play written in verse that is far more rhetorical than poetic. And, as Aristotle pointed out centuries ago, such a mixture makes either a weak play or an ineffectual speech.[8] So it is with *Panic*.

The next two plays are exceptional, not so much in their structure as in the object of their censure. *Till the Day I Die* by Clifford Odets and *Margin for Error* by Clare Boothe denounce those who supported the Nazis' Third Reich and praise those who opposed it. Although many plays written in the thirties condemned the Nazi and Fascist movements in dialogue, these two plays and *Judgment Day* by Elmer Rice are the major dramas in which anti-Nazi sentiments control the organization. The central thoughts each play propounds are that Nazis are evil and perpetrate every imaginable horror upon their opponents and that anyone who resists them is good. Each play reveals the depraved nature of the Nazi characters. These two plays, like the three about capitalists, do not harangue the audience so much as they present evil acts of Nazis.

Till the Day I Die, a short play first produced in 1935, contains an episodic narrative. While tracing the destructive incidents that occur during the last days of Ernst Tausig, a German Communist, each of the seven scenes takes the form of a minute melodrama that demonstrates the terror nazism imposes on the valuable people of the world. In the first scene, as three young Communists—Ernst, his brother Carl, and his lover Tilly —wait in an underground room for delivery of some leaflets, the secret police arrive to arrest Ernst. The sequence of scenes shows next, Captain Schlegel brutally interrogating him. A group of guards tortures five prisoners, Ernst among them, for sport. Major Duhring, as an old friend, advises Ernst to shoot himself. In scene 5, Ernst is temporarily free; he visits Tilly and they speak of the future. Then, a Communist cell condemns him. In the final scene, Ernst swears to Tilly and Carl that he is not an informer, but he realizes that he cannot bear much more torture and strain. After begging Carl unsuccess-

8. Aristotle, *Rhetoric*, trans. W. Rhys Roberts, Book III, Chapters 1 and 2.

fully to shoot him, he kills himself and thereby preserves his loyalty to the cause.

The incidents and involvements themselves stand as the play's strongest indictment of nazism. Insofar as praise for the good people is concerned, Ernst's resistance evokes the audience's respect. Several speeches rhetorically favor the Communist solution, especially Carl's speech before the cell, which ends when he says that the working class is more important to him than any brother, family, or mother. He hails the fight for true democracy.[9] Ernst articulates a Communist dream in his final speech. He looks to the time when the people's agony will be ended, when the great people of the future will live in joy, and when all men will live in brotherhood in soviets throughout the world (p. 154).

The play's message was startling in 1935. Then, the Nazi menace was a reality to be identified and faced for the first time. *Till the Day I Die*, with its simple characterizations and its straightforward story, constitutes an efficient speech of condemnation, a piece structured more for rhetorical than for aesthetic effect.

In form, *Margin for Error* by Clare Boothe relates as closely to the dianoetic melodramas of Chapter 6 as to the anti-Nazi play by Odets. It differs, however, from the melodramas in the directness of its censure of Nazis, and it differs from them, too, in that it resembles a special sort of melodrama, a murder mystery. Although the organizing purpose of the play is to derogate nazism, it also entertains by arousing fear for the good characters and hate for the Nazis. As with several other epideictic plays, it is near the border line that separates the didactic from the mimetic.

Margin for Error, first presented in November of 1939, was the first commercially successful anti-Nazi play produced in America. It was also the most financially successful of all the didactic plays of the thirties. It ran for 264 performances. This fact is perhaps extraneous

9. Clifford Odets, *Till the Day I Die*, in *Six Plays*, pp. 146–47.

to an examination of its structure, but it indicates that the degree to which it entertained enhanced its commercial success and perhaps hindered its propagandistic impact. The other distinction of this play among all the didactic pieces of the Depression, which it shares only with *The Cradle Will Rock*, is that it employs a great deal of humor.

The action of *Margin for Error* occurs before September, 1939, in the library of the German consul in an American city. The sequence of events is continuous, although arbitrarily interrupted once for an intermission. Act I establishes the relationships among the characters and gives each major character a motive for killing the German consul, Nazi Karl Baumer. He threatens Otto Horst, head of the American Nazi party, with liquidation. He blackmails his aide, Max von Alvenstor, with his knowledge that Max's grandmother was a Jew. Baumer's wife Sophie hates Baumer and would like to leave him for an American, news columnist Tom Denny, but Baumer restrains her with his threats against Sophie's father, who is still in Europe. Baumer has been taking money from a Dr. Jennings, with the promise to free the old man's daughter and her husband from a concentration camp in Germany, but Baumer finally admits that the young couple has been destroyed. The last major character to appear is a policeman, Moe Finklestein, a loquacious young American Jew, appointed by the mayor to guard the despised Nazi. The appointment of a Jewish policeman to such a post is a means of ironic harassment, but Moe takes his job seriously and tries to discharge it impersonally.

At the end of Act I Baumer sits at his library desk at the rear of the set, listening to a radio speech by Hitler, while Otto, Max, Sophie, Denny, and Dr. Jennings sit facing the audience. One by one they approach Baumer, but because a large upholstered chair obscures the view, only Dr. Jennings' action of shooting Baumer can be seen. Act II consists of the interrogation of suspects so typical of mystery plays. Young Moe Finklestein, as police officer, carries on the investigation. Moe wants to find the murderer so the shooting will not be blamed on him. Should he be accused of the crime, he knows that thousands of Jews will be massacred in Germany as reprisal. With convolutions of plot proper to the genre, Moe finally uncovers the truth. Dr. Jennings admits that he shot Baumer, but soon Sophie confesses that she stabbed him before the shooting. When the doctor examines the corpse, he discovers that Baumer died not from those two wounds but from poison; Baumer had poisoned a drink meant for his aide Max, but then drank the potion by mistake. Since it is not against the law to shoot or stab a corpse, all suspects go free. Moe arrests Otto, however, for carrying concealed weapons and for income-tax evasion.

The specific anti-Nazi thought in *Margin for Error* appears as criticism and censure of Hitler and his agent Baumer. When Baumer expresses Nazi doctrine, he arouses negative thought because the doctrine is so distasteful. Moe also states thought that expresses the ideals of American democracy. Although early in the play the characters seem powerless to harm Baumer, they all tell him what they think of him. His wife Sophie says that she deserves to die merely for having lived with such a swine.[10] The most extreme expression is Dr. Jennings' threat to kill Baumer (p. 113).

The ultimate deeds of censure that any of the characters enact against Baumer are Dr. Jennings' shooting and Sophie's stabbing. The fact that Baumer is dead when they do so does not diminish their judgment of him. Hitler is also a butt of censure and derision throughout the play. Sophie, speaking for the enlightened people of Europe, tells Max she does not want to hear Hitler's speech because they are all alike. She explains that the only novelty the speech could have for her would be if someone shot him during its delivery (p. 20). In an argument with Baumer, Moe reveals the attitude toward

10. Clare Boothe, *Margin for Error*, p. 62.

Hitler that the entire play advances. Moe explains that Baumer has made him realize the difference between living in a land of freedom and living in a land ruled by a half-crazy gangster. Baumer claims that Hitler is a genius, and Moe replies that he knows that Hitler is a genius, but a stupid one (p. 55).

Baumer often states thought generally as Nazi philosophy. At one point, he expresses to Max the hope that no other nations will understand the Fuehrer because peace is merely a static condition of misunderstanding, and when nations fully comprehend each others' motives war is unavoidable (p. 26). But even more often, Moe articulates democratic views. For example, Moe explains that America is the kind of nation in which a man defends another's life and freedom with his own life, even when the first man knows the second wishes him harm (p. 50).

Satire operates didactically in *Margin for Error* as derision of nazism. Ridicule is, in fact, one of the unique qualities of the play. Exposure of persons or ideas through ridicule has long been a feature of comedy. This play inculcates a derisive attitude toward Hitler. For example, Denny assures Sophie he will help her escape Baumer, and he explains how she can allay her fear by considering for a moment Hitler's real name—Schicklegruber. That name came from Hitler's mother, Denny says, and everyone intuitively realizes that Hitler's father never gave him a name. Finally, Denny asks Sophie to consider for a moment how history might have been altered if the dictator had not changed his name to Hitler. He asks her to imagine anyone saying, "Heil Schicklegruber!" (P. 140.) Also, the typically American gag line often serves the didactic purpose in *Margin for Error*. In the final act, after Max has learned about his Jewish blood, he begins to regret his persecution of the Jews in the past. He worries to Moe about what he has done to his own people, but Moe replies that both Jews and Christians are alike in their persecution of their own brothers. And when Max wonders what Hitler would say if he discovered his own mother was Jewish, Moe replies that Hitler would no doubt claim he was Jesus (p. 183).

Many of the humorous lines appear to exist in the play simply for their comic effect, but even these have some root in a thought or an attitude. The superbly funny curtain line that ends the play seems at first glance to work only for the laugh, but it actually expresses a negative attitude toward the murdered man and caps the principal thought of the play. At the very end, Mulrooney, captain of the Homicide Squad, bursts into the room and asks Moe what the hell has happened. Moe answers that Baumer was stabbed, shot, and poisoned. The last line of the play is Mulrooney's query, did it kill him? (P. 198).

In these two anti-Nazi plays—*Till the Day I Die* and *Margin for Error*—the thought inheres in the story probably more closely than in any of the other didactic dramas. And, although some rhetorical speeches appear in them, the plays function as affective exemplars. They repudiate the dishonor, vice, and evil of the Nazi party and its representatives. The Odets play argues with amplification as its main tool of deprecation; it amplifies the terror perpetrated by the Nazis. Clare Boothe's play sets forth its argument primarily by means of diminution through ridicule; it pokes fun at the grossness and stupidity of Nazi leaders. Both plays are saturated with international propaganda; the ideology of one country is held to be superior and preferable to that of another country.

Appropriately, *Black Pit* by Albert Maltz remains as the final didactic play to be examined. Not only is it one of the most effective of all the plays as a persuasive piece, but also it stands alone as the one most closely resembling a tragedy. Fear and pity arise in it as powers, but their effects in the play and upon an audience are for an instructive end.

The tragic story of Joe Kovarsky, a West Virginia coal miner, embodies the central thought of the play: Only by joining other workers in the common fight against those who exploit the masses can the individual hope to help himself to a better life. Personal compromise results in moral degeneration. This thought arises directly in the play through the speeches of one of the Polish-American coal miners, Tony. He explains to Joe, who sold out to the coal company for personal gain, that a "miner no can get by self . . . when cohmpany got everyt'ings you got go wit' odern miner, tak' cohmpany by t'roat, fight. . . ."[11] And, allegorically, the play urges all workers to eschew compliance with bosses and to enlist in the army of the masses for the betterment of life for the common man.

The play employs some principles of tragedy with its arousal of fear and pity for a good man and the eventual destruction of that man because of his error in judgment. It also utilizes some elements of melodrama, especially the singularly good or evil nature of each of the characters—the protagonist excepted—and the arousal of hate for the bosses. But the truth about *Black Pit*, as a structured whole, is that it arouses pity, fear, and hate not as ends but as means for communicating a lesson. The single-faceted characters represent one side or the other of the capitalist–collectivist conflict. The play shows that a thoroughly didactic drama can be dynamically interesting and emotionally stirring.

Most of the scenes take place in the "Patch" of the Henrietta Mine No. 4, McCulloh's Run, in northern West Virginia. The Prologue opens on the wedding of Joe Kovarsky and Iola Prescott. Immediately two detectives take Joe away to serve a sentence of three years in prison for participating in a strike against the coal company. While Joe is gone, Tony and Mary, his brother-in-law and sister, take his young bride into their home. As do all the miners, the family unit lives in abject poverty. When Act I opens, Joe returns from prison and learns he is on a blacklist and cannot get a job. His and Iola's worries deepen when they discover she is pregnant. The only

11. Albert Maltz, *Black Pit*, p. 105.

doctor available works for the company and will not attend Iola unless Joe is employed by the company. As a solution to their problem, Prescott, the mine superintendent, offers to take Joe off the blacklist, give him a job, slip him a bonus, and provide a doctor for Iola, provided Joe becomes an informer for the company. At first, Joe refuses Prescott's proposal, then he decides to accept the deal, hoping to avoid passing important information to Prescott. Subsequently, Prescott forces Joe to inform against a union organizer, and at that point the other miners discover Joe's betrayal. Painfully realizing his error, Joe agrees to exile himself to avoid damning his family by association. Although the strike is starting outside and although there is the hope that Joe's baby son will live in a better world, the play ends with the piteous and all but physical destruction of Joe, the worker who was unwilling to sacrifice his family for the common good.

The dialogue for each of Joe's decisions is carefully written. For example, throughout the first act, there is mention that anything is better than becoming an informer or siding with the coal company. By such preparatory technique, the incidents of decision gain credibility. The play teaches what is right and wrong under the circumstances before Joe faces his decisions. In this manner, not only Joe but also the audience feel that Joe chooses the expedient but unethical course when he accepts the job of informer at the end of Act I and when he betrays his fellow workers at the end of Act II. These two decisions establish the probability for the guilt, confession, and punishment of Joe in Act III. The instructive perception of what a worker must do, if he is to survive as an ethically clean person, thus emerges long before the ending.

Many speeches in *Black Pit* assert that the only hope for the individual resides in mass action. Such speeches communicate the play's basic thought. During Act I Joe expresses his despair at not finding work, and Tony explains the only solution open to the oppressed worker.

If a man tries to make his way alone, he will get nothing, but if he joins the brotherhood of workers, together they will be heard and get relief (p. 35).

Prescott, the mine superintendent, presents the opposing point of view each time he makes his Mephistophelian appearance. He explains that each man must help himself by betting on the right horse. He tells Joe that he cannot beat the company; the company is in the saddle, and the workingman is the horse (p. 41). One of Prescott's persuasive speeches reveals the true villain, the nationally powerful coal company. Ironically, as the speech persuades Joe that he cannot fight so strong a power, it simultaneously persuades the audience that only mass action can defeat such an enemy. Prescott later explains to an aide the ways to break a starving worker. This final part of the company philosophy prevails as hateful in the play and emerges as an idea the audience can oppose. He explains that a bite of pork chop and a bit of money in his pocket will sweeten Joe. He has seen it before, Prescott continues; one day a worker will fight, and the next day he will rub after a boss like a hound in heat (p. 50). Although only a minor functionary of the monstrous corporation, Prescott thus demonstrates the evil of the exploitive system. The play argues as much by negation as by positive statement.

The environmental circumstances in *Black Pit* operate as proof through elements of the physical spectacle. These details argue that people should not have to live wretchedly and that, under such conditions, they have reason to rebel by the only available means—striking. The most notable and operative circumstance of the characters is their extreme poverty. For instance, in Tony's small living room, the light source is an oil lamp; the wallpaper is rotting from the leaky walls. The furnishings are inadequate; boxes serve for dining chairs. People relax and sleep in their underwear. The women go about the house barefoot. The living room is clean, but its overall appearance is that of intense poverty (pp. 7–8).

Although thought appears in *Black Pit* in a manner

similar to its appearance in mimetic plays—as general statement, amplification, etc.—here it always contributes to the total thesis communicated by the play. Joe frequently voices thought to such ends, as expression of emotion in general and outrage in particular. He tells of quitting one job upon learning that he had been hired as a scab, but he explains that he does not want to starve. He is, after all, a man, and he needs to get a job, and a doctor for his wife (p. 36). Thus, Joe shows how poverty slowly corrupts a man's principles, and he also hints at the motivation that makes his later defection to the company believable.

The play is a rhetorically structured epideictic speech. Even though the play dramatizes the extenuating circumstances of Joe's decisions, as a whole it censures him. His fellow miners praise him for having fought in the previous strike, and they damn him for becoming a company lackey. Tony tells Joe that now he is no better than any other stool pigeon, that he is a rat. And Tony explains to Iola that now the other miners must hate Joe; they will spit at him (p. 105).

At the end, Tony represents honor among workingmen, and Joe represents dishonor. Tony's poverty is likely to become more extreme because of the strike, and yet he propounds the only honorable point of view. He would sleep on the ground, eat coal, and die of starvation before he would cheat on other miners. He refuses to stay in the same house with Joe (p. 103). After his emotional outburst and after Tony impels Joe to realize his error, Joe discovers the "truth." He expresses his inner pain and his feeling of shame, and he wishes for death (p. 104). He then asks two of the significant questions in the play: Why must a man make a living lie of himself in order to get a piece of bread? Why must he cut his heart out in order to have a woman? (P. 106.) His full awakening—so typical of the didactic plays in the epideictic group—is expressed in one of his final speeches. He realizes that life is no good if it means taking things from other people, and he despises himself for his betrayal of his fellow workers (p. 105).

The degree of Joe's dishonor gains consequence when one man dies because of Joe's lie that the mine is not "hot," by his receiving public and private censure, and by his expulsion from his home and the fellowship of his friends. Although Joe performed some commendable actions in the past and although some reference is made to the immediate future of the strike and the distant future of the baby's adulthood, the play concentrates on placing blame and praise in the present. In this respect, the epideictic mode of composition suits didactic drama.

As in the other polemic plays, the characters stand as rhetorical proof in *Black Pit*. When a character is sympathetic, then sympathy for his enacted or spoken thoughts arises. When a sympathetic character represents a larger entity, such as an institution or party, then what he represents elicits more sympathy. The converse is true with antipathetic characters. Hence, in the didactic play, and especially in *Black Pit*, characterization is less important as material to the story than it is as material to the thought propounded. Since the incidents are carefully selected to produce emotion in the audience rather than within the play, the story works dynamically as material to the thesis.

A final point about *Black Pit*, and one common to most didactic plays, is that the title is unusually meaningful. Most titles of the didactic plays indicate what the plays treat, and as epitomes they communicate the central thought of the play; each of them bears a particularly apt title. Some of the titles operate as symbols. *Peace on Earth* describes the subject of the play, *Awake and Sing!* recommends the central thought of its drama, and *Black Pit* symbolizes the coal mine, the pit of degradation into which Joe falls, and the evil in which anyone who supports the system of exploitation will inevitably be immersed.

The epideictically structured plays of the thirties

treat of the common man, the man who labors for his living. Without exception, even including the satiric *Margin for Error*, they concentrate upon the suffering of such men. The perceptions rendered through these stories evoke thought, and in some cases, if the author is successful with one or more individuals in the audience, precipitates action. The plays analyzed in this chapter, like most of the didactic plays of the thirties, present conditions and propound solutions that may apply to and stir a large number of audience members. They offer ideas that can affect, whether one agrees with them or not, the lives of everyone in the country. As their principal means of instruction, these epideictic plays present certain characters as exemplars who deserve praise or damnation.

10

For Pleasure or Learning?

The art of writing is not protected by immutable decrees of Providence; it is what men make it; they choose it in choosing themselves. . . . Of course all of this is not very important. The world can very well do without literature. But it can do without man still better.
Jean-Paul Sartre, *What Is Literature?*

The didactic dramas of the thirties point to the evolutionary social processes that generate new problems, conflicts, and questions to be faced and resolved if civilization is to advance. None of these dramatists were conservatives wishing for the decadent harmony of stasis. They believed strongly in social conflict and its result, mass cooperation among the workers. Although not nearly all the leftists admired the country's contemporary leaders, most agreed with the two central policies of the New Deal—economic intervention by the state and legislation for social reform. Few of these writers would admit the powerlessness of the individual; most thought of man as a social being with certain political potentialities and certain economic needs. They considered each man as a political entity. In their plays, man exists in a context whereby his membership in a group defines his individual role. Few of these plays end without some identification of man as member.

By means of such political emphasis, the polemic playwrights of the thirties restored a concern to the American theatre for the factor of origination, with the ways in which man is an unmoved mover. They saw man as a social force; as artists, they thought of themselves in that role, and they expressed this thought in their art objects. Whatever specific doctrines these playwrights espoused, they presented a vision of intellectual life that can loosely be called humanist. Social thought played an important part in their creative processes. They were obviously committed, passionate, curious, eager, and skeptical. They were ready to stand on the side of the oppressed against the traditions, institutions, and individuals that exercised economic power. Most were willing to fight not only the battle of creation but also, in critical journals or in the streets, the battles of both intellectual and physical conflict.

The problem of meaning persists as one of the urgent issues confronting civilization. Each individual of spirit understands in his own way the meaninglessness and hopelessness of most aspects of our world. Because man is threatened from all sides with technological accident, psychological disturbance, and institutional crisis, he must try to find some meaning in life. To grapple with the problems of existence, to avoid disconnection and despair, to oppose all dehumanizing neuroses, and to attack mass degeneracy, he must make meaning. Art, as one of man's most humanizing endeavors, can ill afford unintelligibility or mere sensory titillation. It is imperative that art should become more meaningful, not less, in our time.

Love, as one human being personally touching another; religion, as one human being intimately connecting himself with the nonhuman powers of the universe; and art, as one human being creating an object and thereby stirring numbers of his kind—these three human actions are possibly only as man uses meaning to provide himself with heightened sensibility, committed attitude, and dynamic imagination. A drama of ideas can help to lead men past despair; such works as the plays of Bertolt Brecht and Albert Camus, as James Clancy suggested, point the way.[1]

Art is not a dreamy abstraction. How could any drama live on a stage without the blood of thought? This

1. James Clancy, "Beyond Despair: A New Drama of Ideas," in *Essays in the Modern Drama*, ed. Morris Freedman, pp. 160–73.

is not to argue that every play should be didactic, although drama of high quality can indeed be written rhetorically as well as mimetically; rather, it is to argue against the denial of art's right to serve man and the interests of society. Art is debased when deprived of thought.

As an organic whole, a drama contains sensuous and conceptual knowledge, and the playwright concretizes that knowledge as he creates a full world of imagination on the analogy of nature. As the dramatist, like every other artist, struggles with the pressing human questions of his age, insight about the meaning of existence will help him to express them and to propose solutions. If he concentrates too much upon form or upon content, however, he is likely to ruin the ultimate unity and value of his work. For art to be valuable in itself and by extension in men's lives, it cannot reside only in the sensual pleasure of form or in the pure intellectuality of content. Although in a well-formulated play one cannot divorce form from meaning, every playwright must discover for himself and for each of his art objects the most appropriate balance of structure and idea, of beauty and truth.

As drama is one of the seven fine arts, so didactic drama is one of the two species of dramatic art; the other is mimetic drama. This study offers proof of the life and effectiveness of the didactic species of drama, and it identifies some of the formative principles of dramatic persuasion. The examination here of forty-one didactic plays begins a much-needed analysis of didactic drama as it has been created in every period and the necessary delineation of a poetics of didactic drama. The forty-one plays analyzed are not all the didactic plays, all the leftist plays, nor all the socially oriented plays of the thirties, but they are the chief works of their kind.

If one wishes to discover whether a play is didactic or not, an analysis of the inherent features of that drama is necessary. Insofar as a particular drama's meaning is rendered through implicit or explicit statement, it is mimetic or didactic. Any drama can arouse thought; one can identify a didactic drama with certainty only by distinguishing whether the thought in a drama is the formative part or merely a material part subsumed to character and plot. One may learn from any drama, but only didactic drama is meant primarily as an instrument of instruction or persuasion. The mimetic drama permits learning; the didactic drama compels it.

Bernard Weinberg has pointed out that, to write criticism of poetic works that have a rhetorical purpose, one must go through a long process of testing and rejection to discern the goals and devices of such works. He also declared that "criticism, analysis, evaluation, judgment, these must always remain indefinite and hypothetical; they must never be reducible to formula."[2] Because this study demonstrates that some of the traditional principles of rhetoric operate architecturally in the didactic plays does not mean that the classic principles of rhetoric can be taken as an arbitrary set of rules for the writing or for the criticizing of persuasive plays. Only by studying the individual work can one come to its just evaluation.

Unlike formal speeches or lyric poems, the subject plays were not intended primarily to be read. No one can fully comprehend a play as a work of dramatic art until it is performed; it is not a totally realized drama until then. As even Aristotle recognized in his famous definition of tragedy, a play requires reading, critical analysis, and production. Thus, dramatic criticism permits only partial understanding of a play. It is within these limitations that the following principles of didactic drama are discussed. They are neither rules nor total revelations but are the functional principles of some of the didactic dramas.

The final cause, or *purpose*, of a didactic drama is a function (persuasion) rather than a thing (of beauty with powers). Thus, function rather than powers gov-

2. Bernard Weinberg, "Formal Analysis in Poetry and Rhetoric," in *Papers in Rhetoric and Poetic*, ed. Donald C. Bryant, p. 44.

erns the construction of the whole. This fact tends to ally didactic drama with rhetoric perhaps more closely than with poetic. But since the function operates through a constructed action, there exist certain elements of poetic in the finished whole. A didactic play may tend toward tragedy, comedy, or melodrama (some more, some less). Any didactic drama is, therefore, complicated (1) by this combination of rhetoric and poetic, and (2) by the question of which is dominant in the construction of that specific play.

A playwright who chooses to write didactically is faced, first of all, with the problem of winning the audience, then of unifying and controlling its response, and finally of provoking it not only to understanding but also to excitement, commitment, and action. The didactic playwright must use art as analysis. He must use it also as a tool for setting the world in order and for translating chaos to intelligibility. According to Weinberg, a playwright who writes polemically creates a "work that seeks to achieve, in a particular audience, a particular effect of persuasion through the use of the various proofs proper to the art of rhetoric."[3]

Furthermore, a didactic playwright has the dual problem of organization and arrangement. Insofar as his play is rhetorical, he must arrange it logically as a pattern of thought, and insofar as it is dramatic, he must organize a sequence of incidents as a pattern of action that establishes a plot. Since the best kind of structure in a speech requires both a statement of a problem and the proof, a didactic dramatist can well use those elements in a polemical play. Structure, thus, relates to purpose by implementing the fulfillment of the persuasive goal.

However much an author stresses the didactic ends for which he makes his play, it remains nonetheless a play, and as such it must be entertaining. Well-written didactic plays nearly always divert as well as persuade. George Bernard Shaw declared that, even though a dra-

3. Weinberg, "Formal Analysis," p. 37.

matist writes a play with an ideological purpose, he has no claim to "any special indulgence for it from people who go to the theatre to be entertained."[4] Every didactic play must also be fascinating as a practicable stage piece that will hold the attention of its audience. The more firmly a didactic play sustains the interest of an audience, the more likely it is to drive home its point to the last word. The most persuasively successful of the rhetorical Depression plays demonstrate Shaw's point. *Bury the Dead, Stevedore,* and *They Shall Not Die,* to name only three, are not only effective as indoctrination but also as vigorous entertainment. "A play probably will not succeed in persuading," Oscar G. Brockett wrote, "unless it is reasonably successful aesthetically as well. We tend to label plays propagandistic or didactic only if the emotional and intellectual purposes have not been adequately assimilated into aesthetic powers."[5] Some of the didactic plays of the thirties, as well as those of other periods, have been produced with great emotional and aesthetic effectiveness. This fact attests to the dual purpose for which the best of the didactic plays are written. The two general goals, then, of each didactic play are persuasion and entertainment. If a given play does not accomplish both (*Awake and Sing!* is an example of this dual achievement), then it cannot be rated among the best of the didactic species.

None of the didactic plays examined in this book can be categorized as having only one of the three conventional purposes—emotional, intellectual, or aesthetic. All combine the intellectual, or didactic, with one or both of the other purposes. Thus, they are both complex and fascinating, especially to those people who are conditioned to enjoy only the emotionally aesthetic. What-

4. George Bernard Shaw and William Archer, "Widowers' Houses: A Collaboration," in *Playwrights on Playwriting,* ed. Toby Cole, p. 199.

5. Oscar G. Brockett, "Poetry as Instrument," in *Papers in Rhetoric and Poetic,* ed. Donald C. Bryant, p. 20.

ever the intended effects upon an audience, the purpose of a didactic play can be discerned in the play itself. It is not necessary to know the precise intent of the author as he might have stated it outside the script. Even with the didactic plays under discussion, if the powers or effects are not first in the play, they will never appear in the responses of an audience.

Each of the analyses in this book indicates the desired response as part of the final cause of each play. Most frequently, the desired response involves the arousal of sympathy and fear, sometimes pity and hate, and always outrage. These, then, are the deepest, if subsidiary, emotive powers of didactic drama as seen in the didactic plays of the Depression era.

Even the reader with only a superficial knowledge of the social conditions during the thirties and of Marxian theory should be able to identify the dianoetic purposes of these plays. The use to which they were or could be put, other than their professional production, would necessitate a long historical study. The important point here is that, even though the plays are didactic, their controlling purposes as well as their controlling ideas can be identified within the plays themselves.

As a group, the didactic dramas of the thirties were meant to be poetic instruments intended to serve certain purposes: (1) enlightening spectators about conditions, motivating forces, or responsibilities; (2) persuading them to accept social doctrines; and (3) provoking them to perform actions. Their collective purpose, stated actively, is to arouse emotion in order to persuade. These didactic plays also attempt to influence audience attitudes, action, or behavior. A didactic dramatist always teaches the truth (according to his beliefs) by instructing and converting. A didactic play results from analysis by the playwright; it is dramatization as discourse, by means of action. Thought determines and diction communicates the logic for the action in the play and for the activity recommended to the audience. The ultimate goal of the best of the didactic plays is instigation of action from the audience, rather than instilling knowledge in its members. Aristotle's tripartite arts of language meet in theatre art under the aegis of didactic drama. Persuasive plays exhibit dialectical conception, rhetorical order, and poetical rendering. A subject appears in the produced drama for an instrumental purpose. Since rhetoric involves practical activity, and since poetry involves a produced object, didactic drama is a practical object, a functional product.

The final cause of didactic drama is to lead the members of an audience to understanding of a central idea; to persuade them to accept it; to stimulate them to make it a part of their daily emotional life; and to impel them to take the recommended action, if any, in behalf of the idea advanced. The politically didactic play investigates causes and solutions of economic and social disturbances. It arouses sympathy for the "correct" characters and outrage against the "incorrect" ones, and it tries to persuade an audience, at least mentally, to espouse a certain cause. A didactic play attempts to move an audience into a desired pattern of life—realization, decision, and action.

The *formal* cause of any drama is the major unifying element. In mimetic drama, plot is the qualitative part that stands as form or organization to all the other parts: character, thought, diction, melody, and spectacle. The major features of plot—such as beginning, middle, and end; suffering, discovery, and reversal; story; unity; and probability—help to organize all the materials, from physical actions to moral decisions. In didactic drama, thought is the qualitative part that stands as form, or organization, to all the other parts. In the special sense that plot is organization, thought is plot in a didactic play.

In rhetorical dramas, thought organizes the action. An author selects and arranges a story and other plot elements so that they effectively advance a thought.

Thought also works in some respects in a didactic play as it does in a mimetic play—as material. Insofar as there is plot, action, and character, some of the thought of the play stands as material to them. As Aristotle recognized, thought has similar functions in both poetic and rhetoric.[6] In didactic and poetic drama, thought appears the same in some respects. In the more conventional mimetic drama, thought appears as argument (proof and disproof), arousal or expression of passion, amplification and diminution, and as language (statements of the appropriate or the possible). In each guise, thought arises in didactic drama as well. In the latter, however, thoughts as materials operate as proof; these materials furnish the argument for the central thought. In a didactic play, the central thought dominates the construction. Thus, in every didactic play, a central thought organizes, but some individual segments of thought also function as material to that chief thought and to both character and plot.

As one discerns whether thought or plot commands a play, then one identifies the play as didactic or mimetic. Here is the differentiation between rhetoric and poetic in a dramatic work. A didactic dramatist arouses emotion to move an audience to accept his thought or to act as he desires. He uses thought to transform the emotions aroused in the play into emotions and thoughts that operate in the spectators in their lives outside the theatre. Emotion provokes thought, which leads to decision, which impels action. Such is the affective pattern of didactic drama. But because in a didactic play the formulative principle is the central idea, it is never possible totally to separate, except perhaps for the sake of discussion, the form and the content.

In every play there is not only a qualitative hierarchy of parts, but also a quantitative arrangement. The quantitative arrangement of a mimetic play is not nearly so conventionally established as for a didactic play. An

6. Aristotle, *Poetics*, trans. Ingram Bywater, p. 248.

author usually arranges a mimetic play in acts, scenes, segments, and beats (paragraphs of dialogue). Although a didactic dramatist may use those terms, the disposition of most didactic plays more closely corresponds to the quantitative arrangement of a speech—exordium, argument, proof, and peroration. Incidentally, the introduction, body, and conclusion of a speech (and thus of a didactic play) matches the beginning, middle, and end of a mimetic play. Thus, the rhetorical quantitative pattern easily adapts itself to resemble the dramatic pattern.

The normal, logical arrangement of the quantitative parts of a speech exists in all didactic plays, no matter whether their authors organized them to be informative, as in *Power*; to resemble stories, as in *Success Story*; or to be lyric, as in *Panic*. The subject and basic thought in such plays emerge early; the proofs arise; and the conclusion, be it realization, revolt, or whatever, finally results. In a didactic play, beginning, middle, and end do not refer to a causal sequence of antecedents and consequences but to a dialectic sequence of effective disposition. Just as a scenario of action is basic to a mimetic drama, so a rhetorical pattern of arrangement, or line of argument, is basic to a didactic.

For the most efficient didacticism, a persuasive play cannot merely state a social problem. A problem play is not automatically a didactic play. For true didacticism, a solution or an attitude must be advanced. The best of the plays studied offer some sort of solution, however abstract or concrete. *Marching Song* proposes the workers' revolution; *Waiting for Lefty* proposes not just a taxi-drivers' strike but a generalized strike by all men against the prevailing conditions. Even *The Little Foxes* proposes that people recognize and work to control the evils of capitalism. These plays fulfill their authors' intentions better than *Mulatto* or *Precedent*, for example, both of which fail to propose clear solutions.

Didactic drama may be said to be drama of truth, for the dramatists are striving to influence their audiences toward the truth as they see it. The conceptual validity of the idea a play advances is not the point here. Indeed, the thought propounded may be reasonable or not, but it must be persuasively "true." The play must make the idea valid by means of its argument, its proofs. Even if a didactic playwright were to advance through his play a thought that he knows to be untrue, he would be doing so because he believed in the truth of the goal for the sake of which he persuades the audience of the lie. In these senses, truth, as the author knows it, is the organizing concept. An example of one complex of "truth" used by the didactic playwrights of the Depression era is Marxism. In plays such as *Black Pit, Marching Song,* and *Life and Death of an American,* not only does the Marxian ideology—with its class conflict, economic analysis of history, faith in revolution, etc.—furnish the truth in the play, but also the Marxian dialectical method affects the organization. The proof in *Marching Song,* both over all and in single speeches, moves from thesis to antithesis and finally to synthesis.

Universality in mimetic drama exists in the relation between character and action; the connections of character to action are causal and therefore universal. In didactic drama, universality is different. Universals appear as ideas in the dialogue, and they are meant to be communicated as such to the audience. This is seldom true in a mimetic play. The characters act in a didactic play for the purpose of communicating universals that exist in the author's mind. In mimetic drama, the causal relationship between a character and action is a pattern of organization that nature does not usually effectuate; thus, drama approaches philosophy through such universals. Universals are a means to an end in mimetic drama, and the end is unity of plot. Advancement of universals as conceptual thoughts is the most significant goal of didactic drama. A mimetic poet does not write plays to exemplify universals; he utilizes universals to organize the parts of drama. In the other species, a didactic poet writes plays to expound universals; he utilizes drama to express universals more persuasively. Hence, the characterizations of the agents in a didactic play tend to present them as universal types.

The form of any didactic play corresponds more closely to one or more forms of oratory than to any of the forms of mimetic drama. There are, however, some significant resemblances to the latter. The dianoetic dramas of Chapter 6 best show how a didactic play can closely resemble a form of mimetic play. Most of the forty-one plays studied tend somewhat toward melodrama. Only one, *Black Pit*, resembles tragedy more nearly than melodrama, and only one, *The Cradle Will Rock*, resembles comedy. The principles of melodrama that are most appropriate in a didactic play are: (1) the action is temporarily serious, and the conflict is resolved; (2) the sympathetic characters deserve and get rewards, and the antipathetic ones suffer damnation and punishment; (3) fear and hate arise; (4) the protagonist is often a victim, and the antagonist is often the oppressor. Thought sometimes unifies the episodic incidents of melodrama, though melodrama does employ antecedents and consequences. At the beginning of a melodrama the villain sets about attaining a goal; he usually initiates the action. Each of his successive actions becomes probable in terms of his originally chosen goal. Thus, thought ties together the loose incidents that make up the plot. Melodrama can thus be an excellent instrument of propaganda. But when a playwright uses thought as the sole control of plot and character, and when he omits necessary elements of the form, a play can no longer be classified as a true melodrama. Although it still may resemble a melodrama, as do *The Gentle People* and *The Little Foxes*, it becomes a didactic play.

The principles of organization common to various types of speeches correspond to the principles employed in the foregoing analyses and operative in didactic dramas. Political oratory exhorts the audience to act or not to act in a certain way; it deliberatively argues that one course of action is more expedient than another. Legal oratory attacks or defends a person or an act on the evidence of past events or conditions in order to establish the justice or injustice of some action or circumstance. Ceremonial oratory, with concern for the present, praises or censures in order to prove a man, an institution, or a system deserving of honor or dishonor. One can reasonably group the didactic plays of the Depression according to these rhetorical types. Such grouping is possible, not because the three are facile categories, but because the individual plays possess inherent principles that correspond to a rhetorical type and relate them to other plays.

The most frequently used ideas in the didactic drama of the thirties and the verbs that indicate the associated persuasive actions can be grouped in relation to the specific type of play. In the dianoetic melodramas the operative ideas are to reveal that the capitalistic system crushes the good people and the good in people, that the system produces criminals of violence and exploitation, that man cannot live peacefully by means of simple personal isolation, and that the system creates sweeping socioeconomic problems that must be solved. Some of the ideas common to exhortative plays are to urge that man must oppose war and refuse to fight, that workers must strike and oppose the system, and that the socioeconomic problems must be defined and solved. The chief ideas in the forensic plays are to accuse the unjust individuals in the legal system and to fix responsibility for the chaotic and oppressive social conditions. The epideictic plays use as ideas censure of the capitalistic system, of the financial bosses, of the men who sacrifice themselves and others for material wealth, of fascism and its representatives, and of workers who fail their class.

Many of the polemic writers of the thirties used their plays as guns to shoot ideas as bullets. They constructed their dramas to be practical weapons. The best of their plays reveal that thought can effectively organize a certain type of drama, one of stature and fascination. The poorest of them demonstrate that a crystallized doctrine is as deadening in a play as it is in life.

Lionel Trilling wrote that only when we "think of ideas as living things, inescapably connected with our wills and desires, as susceptible of growth and their tendency to change," only then can we understand how ideas can structure great drama.[7] And only then will our playwrights begin to write great dramas again, be they didactic or mimetic.

As with any drama, the efficient cause of a didactic play is the playwright and the manner in which he constructs the whole. The manner relates in general to the over-all *style* of the play and in particular to the preconceived patterns, or body of technique, the author imposes on the material. To some degree, a didactic playwright alters the manner of his composition in accordance with the institutions or movements to which he belongs. Any didactic playwright may compose autonomously, but he must inspect the doctrinal limitations he has imposed upon himself by his very commitment. A playwright may or may not be affected by journalists, critics, or party bosses. In every period, arbiters of culture pontificate about what poetry can and cannot be. The truth is that poetry can be whatever the individual poet, as effectuator, wishes. A poet is always a maker, be he a writer of works nonfunctional and mimetic or of works functional and didactic. The didactic playwright, as illustrated by the leftists of the thirties, looks upon drama as both an art form and a medium for expressing ideas, a social force.

Ideas—about ethics, morality, politics, or whatever —must first exist as well-shaped concepts in the mind of a playwright before he undertakes to communicate them in a play. The quality of those ideas—their proximity to truth, logic, and moral value—will depend upon the profundity of the writer's mind and upon his hierarchy of values and will affect the ultimate values evinced in the play. No matter that *Everyman* is written well; it communicates, according to most Christians, worthy thought. The same might be said of *They Shall Not Die*. Whether

7. Lionel Trilling, *The Liberal Imagination: Essays on Literature and Society*, p. 287.

or not the pro-Nazi propaganda plays were written skillfully, their ideas are odious to most moral and intelligent
persons, just as Lawson's Marxian *Marching Song* is
repugnant to some. Value cannot be assigned to didactic
drama purely on the basis of beauty of form, as with
mimetic drama. Nor can a didactic drama be judged solely
as being more or less effective as persuasion. The worth
of any didactic drama depends upon both the value of its
ideas and the beauty of its composition.

During the thirties, the playwrights who wrote didactically committed themselves to multiform social concern, to political parties or movements, and to theatre
groups associated with a definite philosophy of production or politics. Their primary points of view, as elements
in the efficient cause of the plays, can be labeled as individual protest, social protest, collective protest, or
revolutionary protest. They wrote didactic plays to propound a doctrine or to create an emotional attitude toward a doctrine. They wanted to perfect a style that
would express and promote social change. As persuaders,
they put criticism and suggestion side by side, and they
wrote disparagement and protest into dramas of instruc-
tional optimism.

The style of didactic drama, when most effective, displays attributes of clarity and appropriateness—especially in the diction, the characterizations, and the story. The
dialogue must be clear. The ideas to be expressed must
be simple enough for mass understanding, and each
element must be appropriate to the expression of those
ideas. The characterizations must be simple, in the manner of melodrama. And the story must not be so compelling that the audience concentrates on it and misses
the ideas. The style of didactic drama must be much more
audience-oriented than that of mimetic drama. The best
of the mimetic dramatists wish their plays to be fully
experienced by an audience. The best of the didactic
dramatists also wish their plays to move the audience to
action. The didactic dramatist fires the same weapon as
his less skillful polemicist brother; both must first com-

municate ideas to an audience convincingly. And, of course, every dramatist has the obligation to entertain. To achieve appropriate ends, the didactic writer usually employs realism, at least in diction. It is certainly the common style of diction in these didactic plays. Unobtrusive, ordinary, but not mean—these qualities of speech are necessary for best communicating the ideas in rhetorical drama.

Three important considerations are necessary for summarizing the *means*, the material cause, of didactic drama: rhetorical proofs, the qualitative parts of drama as they are subsumed to thought, and subject matter as appropriate factual material. The three classic rhetorical types of artistic proof are (1) *ethos*, or ethical proof, furnished by the character of the speaker; (2) *pathos*, pathetic or emotional proof, the power to stir the audience's emotions; and (3) *logos*, or logical proof, the presentation of truths or apparent truths in the speech. These three types of proof appear in didactic drama, and they can be identified as the argumentative materials of the species. The *ethos* of oratory corresponds to characterization in didactic drama; the audience comes to sympathize and identify with and to believe in the positive characters, and to hate, oppose, and doubt the negative. Thus, character is material to thought. The *pathos* of didactic drama results from the incidents and their arrangement. Plot is therefore material to thought. The diction of a persuasive play furnishes the *logos*; the individual ideas, which make up the complex of thought of the entire play, are logically expressed in words. Clearly, both ideas and diction are material to thought.

Melody and spectacle, the other two of the six qualitative parts of mimetic drama, also serve as material parts subsumed to thought in didactic drama. Melody, as in mimetic drama, is materially represented as the specific sounds that make up the words; it also involves the vocal presentation of the diction. Melody, therefore, operates materially in didactic drama just as it does in mimetic drama. Spectacle, the physical representation of the other parts of drama, works similarly in mimetic and didactic plays. In didactic drama it can contribute to ethical proof, as a sympathetic character's wearing ragged clothes to show that he is poor and piteous. Spectacle may also aid pathetic proof; to further the plot of a didactic play the writer may provide a setting of poverty for the sympathetic characters and one of riches for the antipathetic ones. The spectacle of striking physical action on the stage, as Adam in *1931*— joining the marching throngs of jobless men, can in itself furnish the materials of thought. Spectacle in didactic drama is strongly supportive to the other parts and especially to the thought.

To consider the subject matter of a didactic drama is to examine its informational materials, which contribute to one or more of the qualitative parts. The illustrative matter of a given didactic play will vary from that of another according to the circumstances of the particular time in which the play was written. The primary subject areas of the didactic plays of the American Depression were social, political, economic, legal, and international issues. The specific subjects that furnished materials most frequently were the decay of the middle class; injustice in the courts; persecution of minorities; importance of unions and strikes; the horror of fascism in general and the Nazi party in particular; the problems facing the government of the United States, such as housing and farm finance; poverty and unemployment; the exploitative nature of capitalism; and the development of class consciousness. For most of the leftist playwrights, Marxism provided a basic theory and Russian communism a practical example for the selection of subject matter and for the conception of the central thoughts of the plays. Broadly stated, the subject matter for the didactic plays of the thirties emerged from economic problems and social conflicts.

Although diction in didactic drama functions similarly as it does in mimetic drama, a few important differences must be noted. In didactic drama, the action of the plot moves toward a practical end. The author translates the discourse of the play into action and elaborates it with verbal expression for the provocation of social enactment. Since linguistic meaning cannot be separated from psychological meaning, a thought becomes one with the language that expresses it. Perhaps the most significant difference in the employment of diction between mimetic and didactic drama is how "possible" diction functions. "Possible" diction does not exist in didactic drama as it does in mimetic drama. In mimetic plays a sequence of words, perhaps stating a kernel of philosophy, frequently makes a statement not directly contributory to the story. Such statements are not scrupulously essential to the over-all action, the organizing part. In didactic drama, however, such "possible" statements are usually crucial to the over-all thought, the organizing part. In the plays examined, most such expressions are essential to the thought propounded by the play.

Some didactic works become dated rapidly because they are so well adapted to their particular audience and time, some because they speak only to a specific audience whose attitudes are products of a given period, and some because they are overly dependent on slang and idiomatic language for their effects. A few didactic works apply to more than one period because of the philosophic universality of their ideas. The drama of the thirties comprised all these types. *We, the People* was specially adapted to its audience and, hence, is dated. *Marching Song* appealed only to a small audience sympathetic to strict Marxian doctrine. *1931–* is overly dependent on current slang and idiomatic speech. The magnitude and universality of the thought in some of the plays—*The Gentle People, Johnny Johnson, They Shall Not Die, Judgment Day, Success Story,* and *Black Pit*—keep them vital and worthy of production today.

* * * * *

The forty-one didactic plays examined in this study illustrate the marvelous variety of the didactic species of drama. It would be difficult to find a wider variation among the mimetic dramas of the same period than exists between *Triple-A Plowed Under*, *Black Pit*, and *Margin for Error*. Each didactic play has its own singular structure, style, materials, and purpose. Imitation in mimetic drama is of specific actions of men; imitation in didactic drama is of an idea in the mind of an artist as illustrated in actions, in characters, and in words.

The principles of didactic drama set it apart from other species of dramatic art. It stands in the theoretic tradition of both rhetoric and poetic, but primarily in the tradition of rhetoric. Although practical and productive knowledge is necessary for the writing of such a play, the practical is the more important. In a didactic drama, the formative part is a thought, an idea, an attitude, or a doctrine. The chief material for it is language. A playwright as effectuator speaks through his characters as portrayed by actors. The over-all purpose is the persuasion of an audience to adopt his attitudes and to act on them.

The rhetorical playwrights of the thirties insisted that artists need not avoid metaphysics or morality, politics or ethics. They built their plays upon the concept that ideas are necessary for man's everyday survival and for his constant resistance to dehumanizing forces that press upon him from all sides. The didactic plays of the Depression demonstrate that such drama can attain greatness proportionately to the stature of the ideas propounded and the expressiveness of the form in which they are presented. At its best, didactic drama succeeds in emphasizing—perhaps at the expense of the beautiful and perhaps not—the good and the true. The didactic can range from the religious to the political, from moralistic bias to doctrinal position, from the analytic to the dogmatic. Didactic plays comprise the drama of attack.

Bibliography

PLAYS

Ardrey, Robert. *Thunder Rock*. New York: Dramatists Play
    Service, Inc., 1939.
Arent, Arthur, ed. *One-Third of a Nation*. In *Federal Theatre
    Plays: Prologue to Glory, One-Third of a Nation, Haiti*,
    edited by Pierre de Rohan. New York: Random House,
    Inc., 1938.
————. *Power*. In *Federal Theatre Plays: Triple-A Plowed
    Under, Power, Spirochete*, edited by Pierre de Rohan.
    New York: Random House, Inc., 1938.
————, and the Editorial Staff of the Living Newspaper, eds.
    Triple-A Plowed Under. In *Federal Theatre Plays: Triple-
    A Plowed Under, Power, Spirochete*, edited by Pierre de
    Rohan. New York: Random House, Inc., 1938.
Atlas, Leopold. *But for the Grace of God*. New York: Samuel
    French, Inc., 1937.
Bein, Albert. *Little Ol' Boy*. New York: Samuel French, Inc.,
    1935.
Blitzstein, Marc. *The Cradle Will Rock*. In *The Best Short
    Plays of the Social Theatre*, edited by William Kozlenko,
    pp. 119–72. New York: Random House, Inc., 1939.
Boothe, Clare. *Margin for Error*. New York: Random House,
    Inc., 1940.
Golden, I. J. *Precedent*. New York: Farrar & Rinehart, Inc.,
    1931.
Green, Paul. *Hymn to the Rising Sun*. In *Five Plays of the
    South*, pp. 179–204. New York: Hill & Wang, Inc., 1963.
————. *Johnny Johnson*. In *Five Plays of the South*, pp. 1–104.
    New York: Hill & Wang, Inc., 1963.
Hellman, Lillian. *The Children's Hour*. In *Four Plays*, pp. 1–86.
    New York: Random House, Inc., 1942.
————. *Days to Come*. In *Four Plays*, pp. 89–166. New York:
    Random House, Inc., 1942.
————. *The Little Foxes*. In *Four Plays*, pp. 167–252. New
    York: Random House, Inc., 1942.
Heyward, DuBose. *Brass Ankle*. New York: Farrar & Rine-
    hart, Inc., 1931.
Holmes, John Haynes, and Reginald Lawrence. *If This Be
    Treason*. New York: The Macmillan Company, 1935.

Hughes, Langston. *Mulatto.* In *Five Plays,* edited by Webster Smalley, pp. 1–36. Bloomington: Indiana University Press, 1963.

Kingsley, Sidney. *Dead End.* In *Twenty Best Plays of the Modern American Theatre,* edited by John Gassner, pp. 681–738. New York: Crown Publishers, Inc., 1939.

———. *Men in White.* In *Three Plays about Doctors,* edited by Joseph Mersand, pp. 101–85. New York: Washington Square Press, 1961.

Lawson, John Howard. *Gentlewoman.* In *With a Reckless Preface,* pp. 112–221. New York: Farrar & Rinehart, Inc., 1934.

———. *Marching Song.* New York: Dramatists Play Service, Inc., 1937.

———. *The Pure in Heart.* In *With a Reckless Preface,* pp. 1–111. New York: Farrar & Rinehart, Inc., 1934.

———. *Success Story.* New York: Farrar & Rinehart, Inc., 1932.

Levy, Melvin. *Gold Eagle Guy.* New York: Random House, Inc., 1935.

MacLeish, Archibald. *Panic, a Play in Verse.* Boston: Houghton Mifflin Company, 1935.

Maltz, Albert. *Black Pit.* New York: G.P. Putnam's Sons, 1935.

Odets, Clifford, *Awake and Sing!* In *Six Plays of Clifford Odets,* pp. 33–102. New York: Random House, Inc., 1939.

———. *Golden Boy.* In *Six Plays of Clifford Odets,* pp. 231–322. New York: Random House, Inc., 1939.

———. *Paradise Lost.* In *Six Plays of Clifford Odets,* pp. 155–230. New York: Random House, Inc., 1939.

———. *Rocket to the Moon.* In *Six Plays of Clifford Odets,* pp. 323–418. New York: Random House, Inc., 1939.

———. *Till the Day I Die.* In *Six Plays of Clifford Odets,* pp. 103–54. New York: Random House, Inc., 1939.

———. *Waiting for Lefty.* In *Six Plays of Clifford Odets,* pp. 1–32. New York: Random House, Inc., 1939.

———. *Waiting for Lefty.* In *Three Plays.* New York: Random House, Inc., 1935.

Peters, Paul, and George Sklar. *Stevedore.* New York: Covici, Friede, Inc., 1934.

Rice, Elmer. *Judgment Day.* In *Seven Plays,* pp. 293–374. New York: The Viking Press, Inc., 1950.

———. *We, the People.* New York: Coward-McCann, Inc., 1933.

Shaw, Irwin. *Bury the Dead*. In *The Best Short Plays of the Social Theatre*, edited by William Kozlenko, pp. 39–86. New York: Random House, Inc., 1939.

————. *The Gentle People*. New York: Dramatists Play Service, Inc., 1939.

Sifton, Claire, and Paul Sifton. *1931–*. New York: Farrar & Rinehart, Inc., 1931.

Sklar, George. *Life and Death of an American*. New York: The John Day Company, Inc., 1942.

————, and Albert Maltz. *Peace on Earth*. New York: Samuel French, Inc., 1934.

Wexley, John. *They Shall Not Die*. New York: Alfred A. Knopf, Inc., 1934.

BOOKS AND ARTICLES

Aaron, Daniel. *Writers on the Left*: Episodes in American Literary Communism. New York: Harcourt, Brace & World, Inc., 1961.

Arent, Arthur, "Technique of the Living Newspaper." *Theatre Arts Monthly*, 22 (November 1938), 820–25.

Aristotle. *The Basic Works of Aristotle*, edited by Richard McKeon. New York: Random House, Inc., 1941.

————. *Poetics*, trans. by Ingram Bywater. New York: Random House, Inc., 1954.

————. *Rhetoric*, trans. by W. Rhys Roberts. New York: Random House, Inc., 1954.

Baldwin, Charles Sears. *Ancient Rhetoric and Poetic, Interpreted from Representative Works*. Gloucester, Mass.: Peter Smith, 1959.

————. *Medieval Rhetoric and Poetic to 1400, Interpreted from Representative Works*. Gloucester, Mass.: Peter Smith, 1959.

Bentley, Eric. *The Life of the Drama*. New York: Atheneum Publishers, 1965.

————. *The Playwright as Thinker*. New York: Meridian Books, 1955.

————. *The Theatre of Commitment*: And Other Essays on Drama in Our Society. New York: Atheneum Publishers, 1967.

Blake, Ben. *The Awakening of the American Theatre*. New York: Tomorrow Publishers, 1935.

Blankfort, Michael, and Nathaniel Buchwald. "Social Trends in the Modern Drama." In *American Writers' Congress*, edited by Henry Hart, pp. 128–34. New York: International Publishers Co., Inc., 1935.

Blau, Herbert. *The Impossible Theatre.* New York: The Macmillan Company, 1964.

Block, Anita. *The Changing World in Plays and Theatre.* Boston: Little, Brown and Company, 1939.

Brecht, Bertolt. "A Little Organum for the Theatre," trans. by Beatrice Gottlieb. *Accent,* 11:1 (Winter 1951), 13–40.

———. "Theatre for Pleasure or Theatre for Learning?" *Mainstream,* 11 (June 1958), 1–9.

Brockett, Oscar G. "Poetry as Instrument." In *Papers in Rhetoric and Poetic,* edited by Donald C. Bryant, pp. 15–25. Iowa City: University of Iowa Press, 1965.

———. *The Theatre: An Introduction.* New York: Holt, Rinehart and Winston, Inc., 1964.

Brooks, Cleanth. "Metaphysical Poetry and Propaganda Art." In *Modern Poetry and the Tradition,* pp. 39–53. Chapel Hill: University of North Carolina Press, 1939.

Bryant, Donald C., ed. *Papers in Rhetoric and Poetic.* Iowa City: University of Iowa Press, 1965.

Camus, Albert. *The Rebel: An Essay on Man in Revolt,* trans. by Anthony Bower. New York: Alfred A. Knopf, Inc., 1956.

Clancy, James H. "Beyond Despair: A New Drama of Ideas." In *Essays in the Modern Drama,* edited by Morris Freedman, pp. 160–73. Boston: D.C. Heath and Company, 1964.

Clark, Barrett H., ed. *European Theories of the Drama.* Rev. ed. New York: Crown Publishers, Inc., 1947.

Clark, Donald Lemen. *Rhetoric and Poetry in the Renaissance: A Study of Rhetorical Terms in English Renaissance Literary Criticism.* New York: Russell & Russell Publishers, 1963.

Clurman, Harold. "Groups, Projects, Collectives. . . ," *Theatre Arts,* 44 (September 1960), 15–18.

———. *The Fervent Years: The Story of the Group Theatre and the Thirties.* New York: Alfred A. Knopf, Inc., 1945.

Cole, Toby, ed. *Playwrights on Playwriting: The Meaning and Making of Modern Drama from Ibsen to Ionesco.* New York: Hill & Wang, Inc., 1960.

Crane, Ronald S. Introduction to *Critics and Criticism: Ancient and Modern,* by Ronald S. Crane and others, pp. 1–24. Chicago: The University of Chicago Press, 1952.

———. *The Languages of Criticism and the Structure of Poetry.* Toronto: University of Toronto Press, 1953.

———. "The Varieties of Dramatic Criticism." In *The Context and Craft of Drama: Critical Essays on the Nature of Drama and Theatre*, edited by Robert W. Corrigan and James L. Rosenberg, pp. 189–213. San Francisco: Chandler Publishing Co., 1964.

———, and others. *Critics and Criticism: Ancient and Modern*. Chicago: The University of Chicago Press, 1952.

Eliot, T.S. " 'Rhetoric' and Poetic Drama." In *Selected Essays*, pp. 25–30. New York: Harcourt, Brace and Co., 1932.

Else, Gerald F. *Aristotle's Poetics: The Argument*. Cambridge, Mass.: Harvard University Press, 1963.

Fergusson, Francis. *The Idea of a Theatre: A Study of Ten Plays, the Art of Drama in Changing Perspective*. New York: Doubleday & Company, Inc., 1953.

———. *The Human Image in Dramatic Literature*. New York: Doubleday & Company, Inc., 1957.

Flanagan, Hallie. *Arena: The History of the Federal Theatre*. New York: Duell, Sloan & Pearce, Inc., 1940.

———. Introduction to *Federal Theatre Plays: Triple-A Plowed Under, Power, Spirochete*, edited by Pierre de Rohan, pp. vii–xiii. New York: Random House, Inc., 1938.

———. "A Theatre Is Born." *Theatre Arts Monthly*, 15 (November 1931), 908–15.

Flexner, Eleanor. *American Playwrights 1918–1938: The Theatre Retreats from Reality*. New York: Simon and Schuster, Inc., 1938.

Gagey, Edmond M. *Revolution in American Drama*. New York: Columbia University Press, 1947.

Gassner, John. "Social Realism and Imaginative Theatre." In *Theatre and Drama in the Making*, edited by John Gassner and Ralph G. Allen, Vol. II, pp. 992–1007. Boston: Houghton Mifflin Company, 1964.

Gorelik, Mordecai. "Theatre Is a Weapon." *Theatre Arts Monthly*, 18 (June 1934), 420–33.

Green, Paul. *The Hawthorn Tree*. Chapel Hill: University of North Carolina Press, 1943.

Hart, Henry, ed. *American Writers' Congress*. New York: International Publishers Co., Inc., 1935.

———. *The Writer in a Changing World*. New York: Equinox Cooperative Press, 1937.

Heffner, Hubert. Introduction to *The Nature of Drama*, edited by Hubert Heffner, pp. 339–51. Boston: Houghton Mifflin Company, 1959.

———, Samuel Selden, and Hunton D. Sellman. *Modern Theatre Practice*. 4th ed. New York: Appleton-Century-Crofts, 1959.

Hellman, Lillian. Introduction to *Four Plays*, pp. vii–xiv. New York: Random House, Inc., 1942.

Herrick, Marvin T. "The Place of Rhetoric in Poetic Theory." *Quarterly Journal of Speech*, 34 (February 1948), 1–22.

Hicks, Granville. *The Great Tradition: An Interpretation of American Literature Since the Civil War*. 2d ed. New York: The Macmillan Company, 1935.

———, Michael Gold, Isidor Schneider, Joseph North, Paul Peters, Alan Calmer, eds. *Proletarian Literature in the United States: An Anthology*. New York: International Publishers Co., Inc., 1935.

Himelstein, Morgan Y. *Drama Was a Weapon: The Left-Wing Theatre in New York, 1929–1941*. New Brunswick, N.J.: Rutgers University Press, 1963.

Howe, Irving. *A World More Attractive*. New York: Horizon Press, 1963.

Hudson, Hoyt H. "Rhetoric and Poetry." In *Historical Studies of Rhetoric and Rhetoricians*, edited by Raymond F. Howes, pp. 367–79. Ithaca: Cornell University Press, 1961.

Hummel, William G., and Keith G. Huntress. *The Analysis of Propaganda*. New York: Henry Holt & Co., 1949.

Huxley, Aldous. "The Art of Selling." In *Readings in Speech*, edited by Haig A. Bosmajian, pp. 73–81. New York: Harper & Row, Publishers, 1965.

Kitto, H.D.F. *Greek Tragedy: A Literary Study*. New York: Doubleday & Company, Inc., 1955.

———. *Poiesis: Structure and Thought*. Berkeley: University of California Press, 1966.

Krutch, Joseph Wood. *The American Drama Since 1918*. New York: George Braziller, Inc., 1957.

Lawson, John Howard. "Technique and the Drama." In *American Writers' Congress*, edited by Henry Hart, pp. 123–27. New York: International Publishers Co., Inc., 1935.

———. *Theory and Technique of Playwriting*. New York: G.P. Putnam's Sons, 1936.

Levin, Harry. *Contexts of Criticism*. Cambridge, Mass.: Harvard University Press, 1958.

McCarthy, Mary. *Mary McCarthy's Theatre Chronicles 1937–1962*. New York: Farrar, Straus & Giroux, Inc., 1963.

McKeon, Richard. "Aristotle's Conception of Language and the Arts of Language." In *Critics and Criticism: Ancient and Modern*, by Ronald S. Crane and others, pp. 176–231. Chicago: The University of Chicago Press, 1952.

————. "The Concept of Imitation in Antiquity." In *Critics and Criticism: Ancient and Modern,* by Ronald S. Crane and others, pp. 147–75. Chicago: The University of Chicago Press, 1952.

Mantle, Burns. *Contemporary American Playwrights.* New York: Dodd, Mead & Company, 1938.

————, ed. *The Best Plays of 1929–30* through *The Best Plays of 1939–40.* New York: Dodd, Mead & Company, 1930 through 1940. 11 vols.

Martin, L. John. *International Propaganda.* Minneapolis: University of Minnesota Press, 1958.

Marx, Karl. *Capital, The Communist Manifesto, and Other Writings,* edited by Max Eastman. New York: Random House, Inc., 1932.

————, and Friedrich Engels. *Literature and Art: Selections from Their Writings.* New York: International Publishers Co., Inc., 1947.

Mathews, Jane De Hart. *The Federal Theatre, 1935–1939: Plays, Relief, and Politics.* Princeton, N.J.: Princeton University Press, 1967.

Matlaw, Ralph E., ed. *Belinsky, Chernyshevsky, and Dobrolyubov: Selected Criticism.* New York: E.P. Dutton & Co., Inc., 1962.

Mersand, Joseph. *The American Drama Since 1930: Essays on Playwrights and Plays.* New York: The Modern Chapbooks, 1949.

Nannes, Caspar H. *Politics in the American Drama.* Washington, D.C.: The Catholic University of America Press, 1960.

Olson, Elder. "The Argument of Longinus on the Sublime." In *Critics and Criticism: Ancient and Modern,* by Ronald S. Crane and others, pp. 232–59. Chicago: The University of Chicago Press, 1952.

————. "A Dialogue on Symbolism." In *Critics and Criticism: Ancient and Modern,* by Ronald S. Crane and others, pp. 567–94. Chicago: The University of Chicago Press, 1952.

————. "An Outline of Poetic Theory." In *Critics and Criticism: Ancient and Modern,* by Ronald S. Crane and others, pp. 546–66. Chicago: The University of Chicago Press, 1952.

————. "The Poetic Method of Aristotle: Its Powers and Limitations." In *Aristotle's "Poetics" and English Literature: A Collection of Critical Essays,* edited by Elder Olson, pp. 175–91. Chicago: The University of Chicago Press, 1965.

———. "A Symbolic Reading of the Ancient Mariner." In *Critics and Criticism: Ancient and Modern*, by Ronald S. Crane and others, pp. 138–44. Chicago: The University of Chicago Press, 1952.

———. *Tragedy and the Theory of Drama*. Detroit: Wayne State University Press, 1961.

———. "William Empson, Contemporary Criticism, and Poetic Diction." In *Critics and Criticism: Ancient and Modern*, by Ronald S. Crane and others, pp. 45–82. Chicago: The University of Chicago Press, 1952.

———, ed. *Aristotle's "Poetics" and English Literature: A Collection of Critical Essays*. Chicago: The University of Chicago Press, 1965.

Ong, Walter J. "The Province of Rhetoric and Poetic." In *The Province of Rhetoric*, edited by Joseph Schwartz and John A. Rycenga, pp. 48–56. New York: The Ronald Press Company, 1965.

Peters, Paul (presumably). Preface to the section on Drama. In *Proletarian Literature in the United States: An Anthology*, edited by Granville Hicks, Michael Gold, Isidor Schneider, Joseph North, Paul Peters, and Alan Calmer, pp. 261–64. New York: International Publishers Co., Inc., 1935.

Plato. *The Dialogues*, trans. by B. Jowett. Oxford: Clarendon Press, 1953. 4 vols.

Rabkin, Gerald. *Drama and Commitment: Politics in the American Theatre of the Thirties*. Bloomington: Indiana University Press, 1964.

Rice, Elmer. Preface to *Six Soviet Plays*, edited by Eugene Lyons, pp. v–vi. Boston: Houghton Mifflin Company, 1934.

Rideout, Walter. *The Radical Novel in the United States, 1900–1954*. Cambridge, Mass.: Harvard University Press, 1956.

Roosevelt, Franklin D. "Second Inaugural Address." In *The Public Papers and Addresses of Franklin D. Roosevelt*, edited by Samuel I. Rosenman, 1937 vol., pp. 1–6. New York: The Macmillan Company, 1941.

Santayana, George. *Interpretations of Poetry and Religion*. New York: Charles Scribner's Sons, 1900.

Sartre, Jean-Paul. *Being and Nothingness*, trans. by Hazel E. Barnes. New York: Philosophical Library, Inc., 1956.

———. *Literary and Philosophical Essays*, trans. by Annette Michelson. New York: Collier Books, 1962.

———. *What Is Literature?* trans. by Bernard Frechtman. New York: Philosophical Library, Inc., 1949.

Shaw, George Bernard, and William Archer. "Widowers' Houses: A Collaboration." In *Playwrights on Playwriting: The Meaning and Making of Modern Drama from Ibsen to Ionesco*, edited by Toby Cole, pp. 193–200. New York: Hill & Wang, Inc., 1961.

Simmons, Ernest J., ed. *Continuity and Change in Russian and Soviet Thought*. Cambridge, Mass.: Harvard University Press, 1955.

Sinclair, Upton, ed. *The Cry for Justice: An Anthology of the Literature of Social Protest*. Rev. ed. New York: Lyle Stuart, Inc., 1963.

Skriletz, Dorothy. "The *Rhetoric*: An Aid in the Study of Drama." *Southern Speech Journal*, 25 (1960), 217–22.

Smiley, Sam. "Friends of the Party: American Writers' Congresses." *Southwest Review*, 54 (Summer 1969), 290–99.

———. "Peace on Earth: Four Anti-War Dramas of the Thirties." *Central States Speech Journal*, 21 (Spring 1970), 30–39.

———. *Playwriting: The Structure of Action*. Englewood Cliffs, N.J.: Prentice-Hall, Inc., 1971.

———. "Rhetorical Principles in Didactic Drama." *Quarterly Journal of Speech*, 57 (April 1971), 147–52.

———. "Rhetoric on Stage in Living Newspapers." *Quarterly Journal of Speech*, 54 (February 1968), 29–36.

Spender, Stephen. *The Creative Element: A Study of Vision, Despair and Orthodoxy Among Some Modern Writers*. New York: British Book Center, Inc., 1954.

Strachey, John. *Literature and Dialectical Materialism*. New York: Covici, Friede, Inc., 1934.

Swados, Harvey, ed. *The American Writer and the Great Depression*. Indianapolis: The Bobbs-Merrill Company, Inc., 1966.

Taine, H.A. *History of English Literature*, trans. by H. Van Laun. New York: Henry Holt & Co., 1886.

Trilling, Lionel. *The Liberal Imagination: Essays on Literature and Society*. New York: Doubleday & Company, Inc., 1953.

Trotsky, Leon. *Literature and Revolution*, trans. by Rose Strunsky. Ann Arbor: University of Michigan Press, 1960.

Tynan, Kenneth. "Art for Our Sake." In *Curtains*, pp. 116–18. New York: Atheneum Publishers, 1961.

Wecter, Dixon. *The Age of the Great Depression 1929–1941*. New York: The Macmillan Company, 1952.

Weinberg, Bernard. "Formal Analysis in Poetry and Rhetoric." In *Papers in Rhetoric and Poetic*, edited by Donald C.

Bryant, pp. 36–45. Iowa City: University of Iowa Press, 1965.

———. *A History of Literary Criticism in the Italian Renaissance.* Chicago: The University of Chicago Press, 1961. 2 vols.

Weiss, Peter. "The Material and the Models." *Theatre Quarterly,* 1:1 (January–March 1971), 41–43.

Wellek, René. "Social and Aesthetic Values in Russian Nineteenth-Century Literary Criticism (Belinskii, Chernyshevskii, Dobroliubov, Pisarev)." In *Continuity and Change in Russian and Soviet Thought,* edited by Ernest J. Simmons, pp. 381–97. Cambridge, Mass.: Harvard University Press, 1955.

Whitman, Willson. *Bread and Circuses: A Study of Federal Theatre.* New York: Oxford University Press, 1937.

Whittler, Clarence J. *Some Social Trends in WPA Drama.* Washington, D.C.: The Catholic University of America Press, 1939.

Zola, Émile. "Naturalism on the Stage." In *Playwrights on Playwriting: The Meaning and Making of Modern Drama from Ibsen to Ionesco,* edited by Toby Cole, pp. 5–14. New York: Hill & Wang, Inc., 1961.

Index